Praise for *The War Against Boys*

"One may agree with Ms. Sommers or one may disagree, but it is hard not to credit her with a moral urgency that comes both from the head and from the heart."

—Richard Bernstein, *The New York Times*

"A stinging indictment of an anti-male movement that has had a pervasive influence on the nation's schools. . . . Sommers, an expert at debunking shoddy (and trendy) research, exposes the ballyhooed 'crisis of young girls' as the creation of feminists armed with dubious studies and savvy PR skills. . . . an indispensable book."

—Richard Lowry, *National Review*

"Provocative . . ."

—Richard Morin, *The Washington Post*

"Perhaps the most informed study yet in this area, this engrossing book sheds light on a controversial subject. It deserves close reading by parents, educators, and anyone interested in raising healthy, successful children of both sexes."

—*Publishers Weekly*

"A brazen attack against leading child researchers. . . . Sommers's book has sparked a furious debate."

—Claudia Kalb, *Newsweek*

"Like a number of other social scientists who have called attention to alarming trends only to be ridiculed and dismissed, and then eventually proved right, Christina Hoff Sommers appears to be well ahead of her time."

—Chester E. Finn, Jr., *Commentary*

"[An] important new book."

—John Leo, *U.S. News & World Report*

"Christina Hoff Sommers, in her refreshing, alarming, convincing book . . . exposes the fallacies behind the campaign for so-called 'gender neutrality.'"

—Frank Wooten, *The Charleston Post and Courier*

"[Sommers] has a keen intellect, a sense of fairness, and a deep respect for facts. . . . Ms. Sommers is at her best in calling liberal genderists to account for their lack of authenticated research."

—Robert Holland, *The Richmond Times-Dispatch*

"Parents nationwide owe a debt of gratitude to Christina Hoff Sommers for her new, hotly debated book."

—*The Indianapolis Star*

"Like the clear-eyed child of the fairy tale, Sommers . . . makes a compelling case that schools today are primarily failing boys."

—Clyde Frazier, *The Raleigh News and Observer*

"Sommers makes a powerful case for treating boys with more concern and compassion, while calling for a moratorium on the depiction of girls (and boys) as psychologically crippled victims of an oppressive society. . . . Sommers ably and convincingly rebuts the claims of a 'girl crisis.'"

—Cathy Young, *Salon.com*

"Superb . . . Sommers makes mincemeat of educators and academics who insist that girls are suffering in school because of sexism and discrimination."

—Danielle Crittenden, *Slate*

"Sommers skewers the widely-accepted belief that young girls are American society's foremost victims and offers concrete proof that our culture is actually biased against boys."

—*Monterey County Post*

"Sommers's argument is a welcome ally to any parent of an active boy who cringes when a well-meaning teacher hints 'medication' might calm him down, or who tries in vain to stop her son from fashioning a gun from a finger or a stick."

—Peggy O'Crowley, *The Star-Ledger*

"Sommers produces convincing, even devastating evidence of the academic dishonesty practiced by those who support the opposite thesis—the so-called 'girl-crisis' writers. . . . A sharp study that raises troubling questions."

—*Kirkus Reviews*, starred

"An interesting and thought-provoking book."

—*Library Journal*

"A brilliant exposé of the falsehoods used to justify pro-feminist education. . . . a necessary piece of corrective research."

—Mark Cochrane, *The Vancouver Sun*

"Girls are well-adjusted, happy, and thriving. Can we say the same about boys? Not according to Christina Hoff Sommers, author of a new book in which she answers the question in profound and certain terms."

—Kathleen Parker, *Carribbean Watch*

Also by Christina Hoff Sommers
Who Stole Feminism?: How Women Have Betrayed Women

Christina Hoff Sommers

How Misguided Feminism

THE WAR AGAINST BOYS

Is Harming Our Young Men

A TOUCHSTONE BOOK
PUBLISHED BY SIMON & SCHUSTER
New York   London   Toronto   Sydney   Singapore

TOUCHSTONE
Rockefeller Center
1230 Avenue of the Americas
New York, NY 10020

10 9 8 7 6 5 4 3 2 1

The Library of Congress has cataloged the Simon & Schuster edition
as follows:

Sommers, Christina Hoff.
    The war against boys : how misguided feminism is
harming our young men / Christina Hoff Sommers.
        p.   cm.
    Includes bibliographical references and index.
    1. Teenage boys—United States.   2. Teenage boys—
United States—Psychology.   3. Feminism—United States.
I. Title.
HQ797 .S6 2000
305.235—dc21   00-028517
ISBN 0-684-84956-9
        0-684-84957-7 (Pbk)

ACKNOWLEDGMENTS

THIS BOOK could not have been written without the support of the W. H. Brady Foundation. As a Brady Fellow at the American Enterprise Institute, I was able to devote all my time and efforts to this project. Elizabeth Lurie, Brady Foundation president, helped me with commonsense advice. She suggested, for example, that I avoid the overused and infelicitous word 'gender.' " 'Sex,' she correctly pointed out, is better than 'gender.' "

The American Enterprise Institute (AEI) is an ideal scholarly environment. There are all the stimulating colleagues. There is the exemplary support staff. And there is its president, Christopher DeMuth, the best dean I ever had. He graciously read through the entire manuscript and made many acute comments.

I am greatly indebted to Elizabeth Bowen, my brilliant research assistant at AEI. I have relied heavily on her counsel. She was indispensable in getting at the facts. Elizabeth made a lot of awkward phone calls to ferret out information I could never have obtained. On one occasion, she traveled through a blinding snowstorm to attend a seminar on boys. She designed several of the charts and graphs. Her judiciousness, her tireless efforts, and her uncanny ability to find almost anything on the Internet markedly enhanced the book.

Several interns at AEI contributed substantively to the research: Christina Bishop, David Houston, and Hugh Liebert. Hugh continued to help me when he returned to Harvard. He, too, carefully read drafts of the manuscript, offering insightful commentary on every chapter.

Bob Bender, my editor at Simon & Schuster, kept an eagle eye on my argument, always monitoring its cogency and constantly insisting that I adequately document its more controversial claims. His tactful, responsible oversight has made this a much stronger book than it would otherwise have been. Johanna Li, Toni Rachiele, George Turianski, and Edith Fowler ably shepherded the book through the production process.

My friends, old and newly made, were not spared. In one way or another, they were subjected to the ideas and themes of the book and forced into the roles of sounding board and critic. Chief among these are Evelyn Rich, Suzanne Cadisch, Diana Furchtgott-Roth, Claudia Winkler, and Erika Kors. I discussed the manuscript at length with Cathy Young. She often disagrees with me, but she is unfailingly helpful, full of apt and reliable information that she generously shares.

Several scholars strongly influenced me: Diane Ravitch, research fellow at the Brookings Institution; William Damon, director of the Stanford Center on Adolescence; Michael Gurian, author of *The Wonder of Boys*; and E. D. Hirsch, the famed English professor at the University of Virginia. I owe special thanks to American University professor Leon Clark and to his former graduate student Chris Garran for alerting me to the plight of the nation's boys in the early nineties.

When the fashion of male-bashing reached a new high in the early nineties, Camille Paglia alone had the courage to remind the male-averse feminists that masculinity is the "the most creative cultural force in history." I benefit as much from her dazzling example as a brave, incisive, funny, and outspoken intellectual as from her scintillating ideas.

My life has changed a lot since 1997 when I left Clark University and moved from Massachusetts to Washington, D.C., and not least because Sally Satel and Barbara Ledeen have become such dear friends. Sally and I share a passion for clear thinking and tough-mindedness and an aversion to pseudo-science and advocacy research. With good humor Sally has traveled with me to conferences where we were both unwelcome. Her perspective as a psychiatrist helped shape and strengthen my argument. Barbara Ledeen inspired me with her energy, her courage, and her integrity. I thank her for believing in this book and for organizing a number of forums for me to try out my ideas.

There is no adequate way to thank my husband, Fred Sommers, for all he has done helping me with this project. He is more interested in formal logic and metaphysics, but he patiently discussed every page with me. If he is tired of hearing about the plight of American boys, he has yet to let on.

My sons, David and Tamler, were always on the forefront of my consciousness, throughout the writing of *The War Against Boys*. They are the paradigmatic boys whose cause the book defends.

To my mother and father

CONTENTS

PREFACE

It's a bad time to be a boy in America. As the new millennium begins, the triumphant victory of our women's soccer team has come to symbolize the spirit of American girls. The defining event for boys is the shooting at Columbine High.

"The carnage committed by two boys in Littleton, Colorado," declares the *Congressional Quarterly Researcher*, "has forced the nation to reexamine the nature of boyhood in America."[1] William Pollack, director of the Center for Men at McLean Hospital and author of the best-selling *Real Boys: Rescuing Our Sons from the Myths of Boyhood*, tells audiences around the country, "The boys in Littleton are the tip of the iceberg. And the iceberg is *all* boys."[2]

Hundreds of boys attend Littleton's Columbine High. Some of them behaved heroically during the shooting there. Seth Houy threw his body over a terrified girl to shield her from the bullets; fifteen-year-old Daniel Rohrbough paid with his life when, at mortal risk to himself, he held a door open so others could escape. Later, heartbroken boys attended the memorial services. At one service, two brothers performed a song they had written for their lost friends. Other young men read poems. To take two morbid killers as being representative of "the nature of boyhood" is profoundly misguided and deeply disrespectful of boys in general.

This book tells the story of how it has become fashionable to attribute pathology to millions of healthy male children. It is a story of how we are turning against boys and forgetting a simple truth: that the energy, competitiveness, and corporal daring of normal, decent males is responsible for much of what is right in the world. No one denies that boys' aggressive tendencies must be checked and channeled in constructive ways. Boys need discipline, respect, and moral guidance. Boys need love and tolerant understanding. They do not need to be pathologized.

That boys are in disrepute is not accidental. That did not happen all at once. For many years women's groups have been complaining that boys are benefiting from a school system that favors boys and is biased against girls. "Schools shortchange girls," declared the American Association of University Women.[3] "Teachers . . . pay more attention to boys—their learning styles, needs and futures, than to girls in all grades and all subjects," complains the Ms. Foundation for Women.[4] A stream of girl-partisan books and pamphlets cites research showing that boys are classroom favorites given to schoolyard violence and sexual harassment.

The research commonly cited to support the claims of male privilege and sinfulness is riddled with errors. Almost none of it has been published in professional peer-reviewed journals. Some of the data are mysteriously missing. Yet the false picture remains and is dutifully passed along in schools of education, in "gender-equity" workshops, and increasingly to children themselves.

In this book I try to correct the misinformation and to give an accurate picture of "where the boys are." A review of the facts shows boys, not girls, on the weak side of an educational gender gap. Boys, on average, are a year and a half behind girls in reading and writing; they are less committed to school and less likely to go to college.[5] In 1997, college full-time enrollments were 45 percent male and 55 percent female. The U.S. Department of Education predicts that the ratio of boys' entry into college will continue to worsen. But none of this has affected the "official" view that our schools are "failing at fairness" to girls. Diane Ravitch, a fellow at the Brookings Institution and former assistant secretary of education, has aptly remarked, "When will it be fair? When women are 60 percent or 75 percent of college enrollments? Perhaps it will be fair when there are no men at all."

In the mid-nineties, the new and equally corrosive fiction that boys as a group are disturbed was already accompanying the myth of short-changed girls. How our culture binds boys in a "straitjacket of masculinity" had suddenly became a fashionable topic. Prominent intellectuals, wielding great influence in education circles, gave respectability and power to the burgeoning save-the-males movement. There are now conferences, workshops, and institutes dedicated to transforming boys. Carol Gilligan, professor of gender studies at Harvard Graduate School of Education, writes of the problem of "boys' masculinity . . . in a patriarchal social order."[6] Barney Brawer, director of the Boys' Project at Tufts University, told *Education Week:* "We've deconstructed the old version of manhood, but we've not [yet] constructed a new version."[7] In the spring of 2000, the Boys' Project at Tufts offered five workshops on "Reinventing Boyhood." The planners promised emotionally exciting sessions: "We'll laugh and cry, argue and agree, reclaim and sustain the best parts of the culture of boys and men, while figuring out how to change the terrible parts."[8]

Questions abound. What sort of credentials do the critics of masculinity bring to their project of reconstructing the nation's schoolboys? How well do they understand and like boys? Who has authorized their mission?

American boys face genuine problems that cannot be addressed by constructing new versions of manhood. They do not need to be "rescued" from their masculinity. On the other hand, too many of our sons are languishing academically and socially. The widening education gap threatens the futures of millions of American boys. We should be looking not to "gender experts" and activists for guidance but to the example of other countries that are focusing on boys' problems and dealing with them constructively.

Like American boys, boys in Great Britain and Australia are markedly behind girls academically, notably in reading and writing. They, too, get most of the failing grades and are more likely to be alienated from school. The big difference is that British educators and politicians are ten years ahead of Americans in confronting and specifically addressing the problem of male underachievement. The British government has introduced a highly successful back-to-basics program into primary schools called the Literacy Hour. Its explicit purpose is to help boys catch up with the girls. The British are also experimenting with all-male classes in coed public schools. They are again allowing "gender stereotypes" in their educational materials. They have found that boys enjoy and will read adventure stories with male heroes. War poetry is back. So is classroom competition.[9]

The plight of Britain's schoolboys was an issue in the 1997 election. Estelle Morris, a Labour MP who is now the British Education Minister, said, "If we do not start to address the problem young men and boys are facing we have no hope."[10] So who in the United States is working to improve boys' achievements? No one. No national organizations alert the public to boys' academic shortcomings, no politically powerful groups lobby Congress to help boys. The climate for American boys is unfriendly. The mood in Great Britain is constructive and informed by plain common sense. The mood in the United States is contentious and ideological, and shaped by the girl advocates.

In the war against boys, as in all wars, the first casualty is truth. In the United States, the truth about boys has been both distorted and buried. I begin by showing how the plight of boys came to be buried and by whom. I then report on actual condition of boys, giving readers documented accounts of how boys are faring and suggesting what we can do to brighten their prospects. Boys badly need our attention. It is late, but not too late.

CHAPTER ONE

WHERE THE BOYS ARE

THE MYTH OF THE FRAGILE GIRL

IN 1990, CAROL GILLIGAN announced to the world that America's adolescent girls were in crisis. In her words, "As the river of a girl's life flows into the sea of Western culture, she is in danger of drowning or disappearing."[1] Gilligan offered little in the way of conventional evidence to support this alarming finding. Indeed, it is hard to imagine what sort of empirical research could establish so large a claim. But Gilligan quickly attracted powerful allies. Within a very short time the allegedly fragile and demoralized state of American adolescent girls achieved the status of a national emergency.

I will be subjecting Gilligan's research on girls and boys to extensive analysis in later chapters. She is the matron saint of the girl crisis movement. Gilligan, more than anyone else, is cited as the academic and scientific authority conferring respectability on the claims that American girls are being psychologically depleted, socially "silenced," and academically "shortchanged."

Popular writers, electrified by Gilligan's discovery, began to see evidence of a girl crisis everywhere. Former *New York Times* columnist

Anna Quindlen recounted how Gilligan's research cast an ominous shadow on the celebration of her daughter's second birthday: "My daughter is ready to leap into the world, as though life were chicken soup and she a delighted noodle. The work of Professor Carol Gilligan of Harvard suggests that some time after the age of 11 this will change, that even this lively little girl will pull back [and] shrink." [2]

Soon there materialized a spate of popular books with titles such as *Failing at Fairness: How America's Schools Cheat Girls; Reviving Ophelia: Saving the Selves of Adolescent Girls; Schoolgirls: Self-Esteem and the Confidence Gap. Time* writer Elizabeth Gleick remarked on the new trend in literary victimology: "Dozens of troubled teenage girls troop across [the] pages: composite sketches of Charlottes, Whitneys and Danielles who were raped, who have bulimia, who have pierced bodies or shaved heads, who are coping with strict religious families or are felled by their parents' bitter divorce." [3]

The country's adolescent girls were both exalted and pitied. Novelist Carolyn See wrote in *The Washington Post*, "The most heroic, fearless, graceful, tortured human beings in this land must be girls from the ages of 12 to 15." [4] In the same vein, Myra and David Sadker, in *Failing at Fairness*, predicted the fate of a lively six-year-old girl on top of a playground slide: "There she stood on her sturdy legs, with her head thrown back, and her arms flung wide. As ruler of the playground she was at the very zenith of her world." But all would soon change: "If the camera had photographed the girl . . . at twelve instead of six . . . she would have been looking at the ground instead of the sky; her sense of self-worth would have been an accelerating downward spiral." [5]

The picture of confused and forlorn girls struggling to survive would be drawn again and again with added details and increasing urgency. In Mary Pipher's *Reviving Ophelia*, by far the most successful of the girl-crisis books, girls undergo a fiery demise: "Something dramatic happens to girls in early adolescence. Just as planes and ships disappear mysteriously into the Bermuda Triangle, so do the selves of girls go down in droves. They crash and burn." [6]

The description of America's teenage girls as silenced, tortured, voiceless, and otherwise personally diminished is indeed dismaying. But there is surprisingly little evidence to support it. If the nation's girls are in the kind of crisis that Gilligan and her acolytes are describing, it has escaped the notice of conventional psychiatry. There is, for example, no mention of this epidemic in the *Diagnostic and Statistical Manual of Mental Disorders (DSM-IV)*, the official desk reference of the American Psychiatric Association.[7] The malaise that comes closest to matching the symptoms mentioned by the crisis writers is a mood disorder called dysthymia. Dysthymia is characterized by low self-esteem, feelings of inadequacy, depression, difficulty in making decisions, and social withdrawal. According to *DSM-IV*, it occurs equally in both sexes among children, and while it is more common in adult women than men, it is still relatively rare. No more than 3 or 4 percent of the population suffers from it.

Scholars who abide by the conventional protocols of social science research describe adolescent girls in far more optimistic terms. Dr. Anne Petersen, a former professor of adolescent development and pediatrics at the University of Minnesota and now senior vice president for programs at the W. K. Kellogg Foundation, reports the consensus of researchers working in adolescent psychology: "It is now known that the majority of adolescents of both genders successfully negotiate this developmental period without any major psychological or emotional disorder, develop a positive sense of personal identity, and manage to forge adaptive peer relationships at the same time they maintain close relationships with their families."[8] Daniel Offer, professor of psychiatry at Northwestern University, concurs with Petersen. He refers to a "new generation of studies" that find a majority of adolescents (80 percent) normal and well adjusted.[9]

At the same time Gilligan was declaring a girl crisis, a University of Michigan/U.S Department of Health and Human Services study asked a scientifically selected sample of three thousand high school seniors the question "Taking all things together, how would you say things are these days—would you say you're very happy, pretty happy, or not too happy these days?" Nearly 86 percent of girls and 88 percent of boys responded that they were "pretty happy" or "very happy."[10] If the girls who were polled were "caught in an accelerated downward spiral," they were unaware of it.

Clinical psychologist Mary Pipher calls American society a "girl-poisoning" and "girl-destroying culture." What is her evidence? In *Reviving Ophelia*, she informs readers that her clinic is filled with girls "who have tried to kill themselves." And she cites statistics suggesting that the condition of America's girls is worsening: "The Centers for Disease Control in Atlanta reports that the suicide rate among children age ten to fourteen rose 75 percent between 1979 and 1988. Something dramatic is happening to adolescent girls in America." [11]

But Pipher's numbers are misleading.[12] Insofar as anything "dramatic" is happening to America's children with respect to suicide, it is happening to boys. A look at the sex breakdown of the CDC's suicide statistics reveals that for males aged ten to fourteen, the suicide rate increased 71 percent between 1979 and 1988; for girls the increase was 27 percent. Furthermore, the actual number of children aged ten to fourteen who kill themselves is small. A grand total of 48 girls in that age group committed suicide in 1979, and 61 in 1988. Among boys, the number rose from 103 to 176. All of these deaths are tragic, but in a population of 9 million ten- to fourteen-year-old girls, an increase in female child suicide by 13 is hardly evidence of a girl-destroying culture.

Contrary to the story told by Gilligan and her followers, by the early 1990s American girls were flourishing in unprecedented ways. To be sure, some—among them those who found themselves in the offices of clinical psychologists—felt they were drowning in the sea of Western culture. But the vast majority of girls were occupied in more constructive ways, moving ahead of boys academically in the primary and secondary grades, applying to colleges in record numbers, filling the more challenging academic classes, joining sports teams, and generally enjoying more freedoms and opportunities than any young women in human history.

AN AMERICAN TRAGEDY

GILLIGAN'S IDEAS had special resonance in women's groups already committed to the proposition that our society is unsympathetic to women. Such organizations were naturally receptive to bad news about girls. The interest of the venerable and politically influential American Association of University Women (AAUW), in particular, was piqued. Officers at the AAUW were reported to be "intrigued and alarmed" by Gilligan's findings.[13] "Wanting to know more," they commissioned a polling firm to study whether American schoolgirls were being drained of their self-confidence.

In 1991, the AAUW announced the disturbing results: "Most [girls] emerge from adolescence with a poor self-image." Anne Bryant, then executive director of the AAUW and an expert in public relations, organized a media campaign to spread the word that "an unacknowledged American tragedy" had been uncovered. Newspapers and magazines around the country carried the bleak tidings that girls were being adversely affected by gender bias that eroded their self-esteem. Susan Schuster, at the time president of the AAUW, candidly explained to *The New York Times* why the AAUW had undertaken the research in the first place: "We wanted to put some factual data behind our belief that girls are getting shortchanged in the classroom." [14]

At the time the AAUW's self-esteem results were making headlines, a little-known journal called *Science News*, which has been supplying information on scientific and technical developments to interested newspapers since 1922, quoted leading adolescent psychologists who questioned the validity of the self-esteem poll. [15] But somehow the doubts of the experts were not reported in the hundreds of news stories the AAUW study generated. [16]

The AAUW quickly commissioned a second study, *How Schools Shortchange Girls*. This new study, carried out by the Wellesley College Center for Research on Women and released in 1992, asserted a direct causal relationship between girls' (alleged) second-class status in the nation's schools and deficiencies in their level of self-esteem. Carol Gilligan's psychological girl crisis was thus transformed into a pressing civil rights issue: girls were victims of widespread sexist discrimination in our nation's schools. "The implications are clear," said the AAUW; "the system must change." [17]

Education Week reported that the AAUW spent $100,000 for the second study and $150,000 promoting it. [18] With great fanfare, *How Schools Shortchange Girls* was released to uncritical, even enthusiastic, media. The promotion proved to be spectacularly successful, generating more than 1,400 news reports and a flurry of TV discussions of the "tragedy" that had struck the nation's girls.

Susan Chira's 1992 article for *The New York Times* was typical of media coverage throughout the country. The headline read "Bias Against Girls Is Found Rife in Schools, with Lasting Damage." [19] The piece could have been written by the AAUW's publicity department. Indeed, the entire *Times* article was later reproduced by the AAUW and sent out as part of its fund-raising package. Chira had not interviewed a single critic.

In March 1999, I called Ms. Chira and asked her about the way she had handled the AAUW report on diminished girls. There was a long silence. "I don't want to talk about this," she finally said. I tried delicately to broach the question of why she had not sought out critics. "I see where this is going. . . . I wish you the best of luck. Goodbye," she said, taking the journalistic equivalent of the Fifth Amendment.

But she called back a few hours later, saying she was prepared to answer my questions. Would you write it the same way today? I asked. No, she said, pointing out that we have since learned so much more about boys' deficits. Why had she not canvassed dissenting opinions? She explained that when the AAUW study had come out, she had been traveling and was on a short deadline. Yes, perhaps she had relied too much on the AAUW's report. She had tried to reach Diane Ravitch, the former assistant secretary of education and a known critic of women's advocacy "findings," but had not been able to.

Had Chira been able to reach Ravitch, or any number of other experts on sex differences in education, she would quickly have learned that the report was at the very least unbalanced: it highlighted studies in support of the "shortchanged girl" thesis and downplayed studies that contradicted it.

Six years after the release of *How Schools Shortchange Girls, The New York Times* ran a story that, for the first time, questioned the validity of the report. By then, of course, most of the damage to the truth about boys and girls was irreparable. This time the reporter, Tamar Lewin, did reach Diane Ravitch, who told her, "The AAUW report was just completely wrong. What was so bizarre is that it came out right at the time that girls had just overtaken boys in almost every area. It might have been the right story 20 years earlier, but coming out when it did it was like calling a wedding a funeral. . . . There were all these special programs put in place for girls, and no one paid any attention to boys." [20]

One of the many things the report was wrong about was the "call-out" gap. According to the AAUW, "In a study conducted by Myra and David Sadker, boys in elementary and middle school called out answers eight times more often than girls. When boys called out, teachers listened. But when girls called out, they were told to 'raise your hand if you want to speak.' " [21]

One reporter who belatedly decided to check on some of the AAUW's data was Amy Saltzman, then of *U.S. News & World Report*. She asked David Sadker for a copy of the research backing up the celebrated eight-to-one call-out claim. Sadker explained that he had presented the finding in an unpublished paper at a symposium sponsored by the American Educational Research Association (AERA); neither he nor the AERA had a copy. Sadker conceded that the eight-to-one ratio he had announced might have been inaccurate. Saltzman cited an independent study done by Gail Jones, an associate professor of education at the University of North Carolina, who found that boys called out answers twice as often as girls.[22] Whatever the accurate number may be, no one has even shown that permitting a student to call out answers in the classroom confers any kind of academic advantage. What does confer advantage is a student's *attentiveness*. Boys are less attentive[23]—which could explain why some teachers might call on them more or be more tolerant of call-outs.

Despite its anti-boy bias and factual errors, the campaign to persuade the public that girls are being diminished personally and academically was a spectacular success. As the AAUW's exultant director, Anne Bryant, told her friends, "I remember going to bed the night our report was issued, totally exhilarated. When I woke up the next morning, the first thought in my mind was 'Oh my God, what do we do next?' "[24] Political action came next, and here, too, the girl advocates were successful.

In 1994, the allegedly low state of America's girls moved the U.S. Congress to pass the Gender Equity in Education Act, which categorized girls as an "under-served population" on a par with other discriminated-against minorities. Millions of dollars in grants were awarded to study the plight of girls and learn how to cope with the insidious bias against them. At the UN Fourth World Conference on Women in Beijing in 1995, members of the American delegation presented the educational and psychological deficits of American girls as a pressing human rights issue.[25]

WHERE DO BOYS FIT IN?

HOW DO BOYS fit into the "tragedy" of America's "shortchanged" girls? Inevitably, boys are resented, being seen both as the unfairly privileged gender and as obstacles on the path to gender justice for girls. There is an understandable dialectic: the more girls are portrayed as diminished, the more boys are regarded as needing to be taken down a notch and reduced in importance. This perspective on boys and girls is promoted in schools of education, and many a teacher now feels that girls need and deserve special indemnifying consideration. "It is really clear that boys are no. 1 in this society and in most of the world," says Dr. Patricia O'Reilly, professor of education and director of the Gender Equity Center at the University of Cincinnati.[26]

It may be "clear," but it isn't true. If we disregard the girl advocates and look objectively at the relative condition of boys and girls in *this* country, we find that it is boys, not girls, who are languishing academically. Data from the U.S. Department of Education and from several recent university studies show that far from being shy and demoralized, today's girls outshine boys.[27] Girls get better grades.[28] They have higher educational aspirations.[29] They follow a more rigorous academic program and participate more in the prestigious Advanced Placement (AP) program. This demanding program gives top students the opportunity of taking college-level courses in high school. In 1984, an equal proportion of males and females participated. But according to the United States Department of Education, "Between 1984 and 1996, the number of females who took the examinations rose at a faster rate . . . In 1996, 144 females compared to 117 males per 1000 12th graders took AP examinations" (see Table 1).

TABLE 1

Number of Students Who Took AP Examinations
(per 1,000 Twelfth-Graders), by Sex

	1984	1985	1986	1987	1988	1989	1990	1991	1992	1993	1994	1995	1996
Total	50	59	64	66	81	88	100	103	109	117	115	125	131
Male	50	61	65	68	76	86	101	96	102	108	101	111	117
Female	50	58	63	65	85	90	98	111	117	127	129	140	144

Source: U.S. Department of Education, National Center for Education Statistics, The Condition of Education 1998, *p. 90.*

According to the National Center for Education Statistics, slightly more female than male students enroll in high-level math and science courses (see Table 2).

The representation of American girls as apprehensive and academically diminished is not true to the facts. Girls, allegedly so timorous and lacking in confidence, now outnumber boys in student government, in honor societies, on school newspapers, and even in debating clubs.[30] Only in sports are the boys still ahead, and women's groups are targeting the sports gap with a vengeance.

At the very time the AAUW was advertising its discovery that girls were subordinates in the schools, the Department of Education published the results of a massive survey showing just the opposite (see Figure 1).

Girls read more books.[31] They outperform males on tests of artistic and musical ability.[32] More girls than boys study abroad.[33] More join the Peace Corps.[34] Conversely, more boys than girls are suspended from school. More are held back and more drop out.[35] Boys are three times as likely as girls to be enrolled in special education programs and four times as likely to be diagnosed with attention deficit/hyperactivity disorder

TABLE 2

Percentage of 1994 High School Graduates
Taking Selected Math and Science Courses, by Sex

	Males	Females
MATHEMATICS		
Algebra I	64.7	68.1
Geometry	68.3	72.4
Algebra II	55.4	61.6
Trigonometry	16.6	17.8
Analysis—Pre-calculus	16.3	18.2
Statistics/Probability	2.0	2.1
Calculus	9.4	9.1
AP Calculus	7.2	6.8
SCIENCE		
Biology	92.3	94.7
AP/Honors Biology	4.0	5.1
Chemistry	53.2	58.7
AP/Honors Chemistry	4.1	3.7
Physics	26.9	22.0
AP/Honors Physics	3.0	1.8
Engineering	0.4	0.2
Astronomy	2.0	1.5
Geology/Earth Science	22.8	23.2

Source: U.S. Department of Education Statistics, National Center for Education Statistics, Digest of Education Statistics 1998, May 1999, p. 152, table 138.

FIGURE 1

Percentage of High School Seniors Participating in
Extracurricular Activities in 1992, by Sex

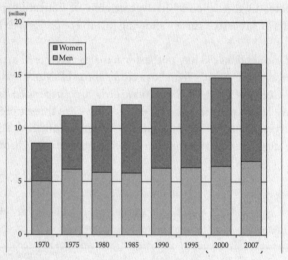

Source: U.S. Department of Education, National Center for Education Statistics, Digest of
Education Statistics 1998, *May 1999, p. 155, table 144.*

(ADHD).[36] More boys than girls are involved in crime, alcohol, and
drugs.[37] Girls attempt suicide more than boys, but it is boys who actually
kill themselves more often. In a typical year (1997), there were 4,493 sui-
cides of young people between the ages of five and twenty-four: 701 females, 3,792 males.[38]

BOYS ARE TRAILING

QUIETLY, some educators will tell you that it is boys, not girls, who are on
the fragile side of the gender gap. In 1997, I met the president of the
Board of Education of Atlanta, Georgia. Who is faring better in Atlanta's
schools, boys or girls? I asked. "Girls," he replied without hesitating. In
what areas? I asked. "Just about any area you can mention."[39] A high

school principal from Pennsylvania tells of the condition of boys in his school: "Students who dominate the drop-out list, the suspension list, the failure list and other negative indices of non-achievement in school are males at a wide ratio."[40]

Three years ago, Scarsdale High School in New York State held a gender-equity workshop for its faculty. It was the standard girls-are-being-shortchanged fare, with one notable difference: a male student gave a presentation in which he pointed to evidence suggesting that girls at Scarsdale High were well ahead of boys. David Greene, a social studies teacher, thought the student must be mistaken. But when he and some colleagues analyzed department grading patterns, they saw that the student was right. They found that in Advanced Placement social studies classes, there was little or no difference in grades between boys and girls. But in standard classes, the girls were doing a lot better. Greene also learned from the school's athletic director that its girls' sports teams were far more successful in competition with other schools than the boys' teams were. Of the twelve athletes from Scarsdale High named as All-American in the past ten years, for example, three had been boys, nine girls. Greene came away with a picture flatly at odds with the administrators' preconception: one of ambitious girls and relatively disaffected boys who were willing to settle for mediocrity.

Like schools everywhere, Scarsdale High has been strongly influenced by the girl-crisis climate. The belief that girls are systematically deprived prevails on the school's Gender Equity Committee; it is the rationale for the school's offering a special senior elective class on gender equity. Greene has tried gingerly to broach the subject of male underperformance with his colleagues. Many of them concede that in the classes they teach, the girls seem to be doing better than the boys, but they do not see this as part of a larger pattern. After so many years of hearing about the silenced, diminished girls, the suggestion that boys are not doing as well as girls is not taken seriously even by teachers who see it with their own eyes in their own classrooms.

SCHOOL "ENGAGEMENT"

A 1999 *Congressional Quarterly Researcher* article about male and female academic achievement takes note of a common parental experience:

FIGURE 2

Percentage of High School Sophomores
Who Arrive at School Unprepared, by Sex

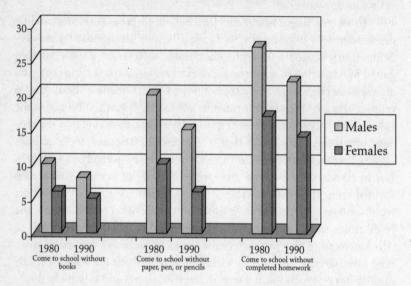

Source: NCES, National Longitudinal Study of 1988, First Follow-up Student Survey, 1990, U.S. Department of Education, National Center for Education Statistics, The Condition of Education 1994, p. 126.

"Daughters want to please their teachers by spending extra time on projects, doing extra credit, making homework as neat as possible. Sons rush through homework assignments and run outside to play, unconcerned about how the teacher will regard the sloppy work."[41] In the technical language of education experts, girls are academically more "engaged." School engagement is a critical measure of student success. The U.S. Department of Education gauges student commitment by the following criteria:

- How much time do students devote to homework each night?
- Do students come to class prepared and ready to learn? (Do they bring books and pencils? Have they completed their homework?)

That boys are less committed to school than girls was already well documented by the Department of Education in the eighties and nineties. Higher percentages of boys than of girls reported they "usually" or "often" come to school without supplies or without having done their homework (see Figure 2). Surveys of fourth, eighth, and twelfth grades show girls consistently reporting that they do more homework than boys. By twelfth grade, males are four times as likely as females not-to do homework (see Table 3).

Here we have a genuinely worrisome gender gap, with boys well behind girls. It is this gap that should concern educators, parents, school boards, and legislators. Engagement with school is perhaps the single most important predictor of academic success.[42] But boys' weaker commitment is not addressed at the equity seminars and workshops around the country. Instead, the fashionable but spurious self-esteem gap continues to be the prevailing concern—the gap that the AAUW, in its zeal to "know more" about Carol Gilligan's findings, claims to have exposed.

There are some well-tested ways of reengaging boys, improving their study habits, and interesting them in learning and achievement. (I'll discuss what works with boys in later chapters.) But until boys' problems are acknowledged, they cannot be addressed. And until they are addressed, another educational disparity is likely to persist: far more girls than boys go on to college.

TABLE 3

Percentage of Time Spent on Homework in 1996, by Sex

	Grade 4		Grade 8		Grade 12	
	Males	Females	Males	Females	Males	Females
Don't have	11.8	10.2	7.2	6.0	15.7	11.9
Don't do	4.4	1.6	9.6	4.9	13.2	3.1
½ hour or less	40.0	40.7	28.0	19.7	25.2	19.5
1 hour	27.7	30.9	34.0	38.7	25.4	30.0
1 hour or more	16.1	16.6	21.1	30.8	20.5	35.5
Total	100	100	100	100	100	100

Source: U.S. Department of Education, National Center for Education Statistics, The Condition of Education 1998, *p. 262.*

FIGURE 3

Enrollment in Institutions of Higher Education, by Sex

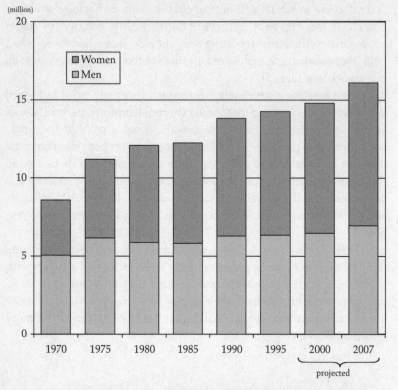

Source: U.S. Department of Education, National Center for Education Statistics, Digest of Education Statistics 1998, 1999, p. 196, and Projections of Education Statistics to 2007, 1997, p. 26.

THE COLLEGE GAP

THE U.S. DEPARTMENT OF EDUCATION reports that in 1996 there were 8.4 million women but only 6.7 million men enrolled in college. It also shows women holding on to and improving this advantage well into the next decade. According to one Department prediction, by 2007 there will be 9.2 million women in college and 6.9 million men (see Figure 3).[43]

Girl partisans offer ingenious, self-serving arguments for why the higher enrollment of women in college should not count as an advantage for women. According to feminist essayist Barbara Ehrenreich, "One of the reasons why fewer men are going to college may be because they suspect that they can make a living just as well without a college education; in other words they still have such an advantage over women in the non-professional workforce that they don't require an education."[44]

Ehrenreich is suggesting that a seventeen- or eighteen-year-old boy about to graduate from high school, with no plans for college, may still be better off than the college-bound girl sitting next to him. There may be a handful of enterprising high school students for whom this is true, but for the vast majority of boys a college education allows entrance into the middle class—to say nothing of the personal benefits of a liberal arts education.

In recent years, the economic value of a college education has increased dramatically. An economist at the American Enterprise Institute, Marvin Kosters, has quantified the trend: "The average wage of a mature adult college graduate was about 25 percent higher in 1978 than the wage of a high school graduate. By 1995, the difference had more than doubled to an average wage of more than 50 percent higher for the college-educated worker."[45]

Someone should have noticed that the boys were lagging behind. The college gap was a genuine and dangerous trend. But at just the time the girls were surpassing the boys in this critical way, the gender activists in the Department of Education, the AAUW, the Wellesley Center, and the Ms. Foundation chose to announce the "shortchanged-girl" crisis. For the next several years, the gender gap in college enrollment continued to widen, but the attention of the American public and government was focused on the nation's "underserved girls."

WHY DO BOYS TEST BETTER?

THE GIRL ADVOCATES cannot plausibly deny that girls get better grades, that they are more engaged academically, or that they are now the majority sex in higher education. So they point to psychological and sociological differences: self-esteem gaps, "call-out" gaps, confidence gaps. But these, we have seen, do not withstand scrutiny. There is a better argument advanced by the girl-crisis crowd that is based on correct data: boys do score better on almost every significant standardized test, especially high-stakes tests such as the Scholastic Aptitude Assessment Test (SAT) and law school, medical school, and graduate school admission tests.

In 1996, I wrote an article for *Education Week* reporting on the many ways in which female students were moving ahead of males. Seizing on the test data that suggest that boys were doing better than girls, David Sadker, in a critical response, wrote, "If females are soaring in school, as Christina Hoff Sommers writes, then these tests are blind to their flight." [46] Boys do, indeed, tend to test better than girls. On the 1998 Scholastic Assessment Test, boys were 35 points (out of 800) ahead of girls in math, 7 points ahead in English. [47] Is Sadker right in suggesting that the boys' superior scores are a manifestation of their privileged status?

The answer is no. A careful look at the pool of students who take the SAT and other such tests shows that the girls' lower scores have little or nothing to do with bias or unfairness. Indeed, the scores do not even signify lower achievement by girls. First of all, a greater percentage of girls than boys take the SAT (54 percent to 46 percent). Furthermore, according to the College Board's *Profile of SAT and Achievement Test Takers*, many more girls from "at-risk" categories take the test than do "at-risk" boys. Specifically, more girls from lower-income homes or with parents who never graduated from high school or never attended college attempt the SAT than boys from the same background. "These characteristics," says the College Board *Profile*, "are associated with lower than average SAT scores." [48]

In other words, because boys at risk tend not to take the test while girls at risk tend to do so, the girls' average score is lower. Instead of wrongly using SAT scores as evidence of bias against girls, scholars should be concerned about the boys who never show up for the tests they need if they are to move on to higher education.

Yet another extraneous factor skews test results so they appear to favor boys. Nancy Cole, president of the Educational Testing Service, terms it the "spread" phenomenon. [49] : On almost any intelligence or achievement test, male scores are more spread out than female scores at the extremes of ability and disability: there are more male prodigies at the high end and more males of marginal ability at the low end. Or, as the political scientist James Q. Wilson once put it, "There are more male geniuses and more male idiots."

We should also take into account that males dominate the dropout lists, the failure lists, and the learning disability lists. Such students rarely take high-stakes tests. On the other hand, the exceptional boys who take school seriously show up in disproportionately high numbers for the standardized tests. Gender-equity activists such as Sadker ought to apply their logic consistently: if the shortage of girls at the high end of the ability distribution is evidence of "unfairness" to girls, the excess of boys at the low end must be deemed evidence of "unfairness" to boys.

Suppose we were to turn our attention away from the highly motivated self-selected two fifths of high school students who take the SAT and instead consider a truly representative sample of American schoolchildren. How would girls and boys then compare? The National Assessment of Educational Progress (NAEP), started in 1969 and mandated by the U.S. Congress, offers the best and most comprehensive measure of achievement for students of all levels of ability. Under the NAEP program, a large scientific sample of 70,000 to 100,000 students drawn from forty-four states is tested in reading, writing, math, and science at ages nine, thirteen, and seventeen. (The NAEP scale scores range from 0 to 500.) In 1996, seventeen-year-old boys outperformed girls by 5 points in math and 8 points in science, while the girls outperformed boys by 14 points in reading and 17 points in writing.[50] Throughout the past two decades, girls have been catching up in math and science, while boys continue to lag far behind in reading and writing, a gap that is not narrowing.[51]

NEW RESEARCH FINDINGS

IN THE JULY 7, 1995 ISSUE of *Science,* Larry Hedges and Amy Nowell, researchers at the University of Chicago, observed that girls' deficits in math were small but not insignificant. These deficits, they noted, could adversely affect the number of women who "excel in scientific and technical occupations." Of boys' writing skills, they wrote, "The large sex differences in writing . . . are alarming. The data imply that males are, on average, at a rather profound disadvantage in the performance of this basic skill."[52] Hedges and Nowell go on to warn, "The generally larger numbers of males who perform near the bottom of the distribution in reading comprehension and writing also have policy implications. It seems likely that individuals with such poor literacy skills will have difficulty finding employment in an increasingly information-driven economy. Thus, some intervention may be required to enable them to participate constructively."[53]

Hedges and Nowell are describing a serious problem of national scope, but because the focus has been exclusively on girls' deficits, it is not a problem Americans know much about or even suspect exists. It is very hard to look at the school data on adolescents or the most recent data on college students without coming to the conclusion that girls and young women are thriving, while boys and young men are languishing.

In 1995, perhaps in reaction to criticism—from an increasing number of unpersuaded scholars—the AAUW commissioned a more serious scientific study of gender and academic achievement. That study, *The Influence of School Climate on Gender Differences in the Achievement and Engagement of Young Adolescents,* by University of Michigan professor Valerie E. Lee and her associates, was released without the fanfare the AAUW usually lavishes on such publications. This is not surprising. Lee's study strongly suggests that earlier reports of a tragic demoralization and shortchanging of America's schoolgirls have been greatly exaggerated.

Lee and her associates analyzed data on the educational achievement and engagement of more than nine thousand eighth-grade boys and girls and found that the differences between boys and girls were "small to moderate."[54] Moreover, the pattern of gender differences is "inconsistent in direction." In some areas, females are favored; in others, males are favored.[55] The study showed that the girls were more engaged academically than the boys: they were better prepared for class, had better attendance records, and evinced more positive academic behavior overall.[56]

Lee's temperate conclusions, in research sponsored by the AAUW, were based on U.S. Department of Education data and were fully consistent with the findings of Hedges and Nowell. But they are at odds with the disturbing picture that the AAUW earlier so successfully sold to the American public and Congress. Lee concluded, "The public discourse around issues of gender in school needs some change . . . Inequity can (and does) work in both directions."[57] As far as I have been able to ascertain, Valerie Lee's responsible and objective study was not mentioned in a single newspaper.

The AAUW did not spend $150,000 promoting Lee's study, nor did it tone down its own partisan rhetoric. On the contrary, dissenting views provoked the organization to anger and abuse. In the spring of 1997, the AAUW newsletter *AAUW Outlook* attacked the "gender bias revisionists" who "like John Leo, Christina Hoff Sommers, or your local columnist" had questioned the myth of the fragile girl: "We have all heard of revisionist history. There will always be some individuals who will insist that the Holocaust did not happen. . . . The revisionists often distort the facts so thoroughly that their take on history loses all semblance of reality." [58]

In the summer of 1997, the AAUW followed this attack on its critics with a four-day "leadership conference" at which the AAUW's "media staff" trained thirty teachers and other equity leaders in strategies for coping with "revisionists" in the media and elsewhere. I attended one of the sessions at the AAUW's Washington, D.C., headquarters. (I was not a welcome guest and was eventually politely asked to leave.) Outside the conference room, there were tables filled with shortchanged-girl souvenirs. The teachers could buy "equity teddy bears," coffee mugs, and T-shirts bearing the slogan "When We Shortchange Girls, We Shortchange America." There were "I am a star" buttons intended for hapless girls with lagging self-esteem.

The AAUW staff coached the teachers in coping with questions about boys. In a special training workshop entitled "Why Focus on Girls?," teachers rehearsed their answers to queries about boys and AAUW personnel critiqued their performance. One AAUW equity trainer advised the teachers to use "key AAUW words and phrases" as often as possible in their answers—especially the AAUW all-time favorite, "shortchanged girls." Trainers advised the teachers to practice using "confident language," such as "research shows that."

Although the AAUW headquarters where this conference took place was the epicenter of the girl-crisis movement, some of the teacher-fellows had the temerity to speak up for boys. A young teacher from Baltimore volunteered that in her school the boys were just as vulnerable as the girls—"if not more." And in a discussion of how to defend the "girls-only" character of Take Our Daughters to Work Day, four teachers protested that boys should be included. In both instances, the AAUW equity experts gently guided the discussion back to girls.

MORE DISSONANT NOTES

THE GIRL PARTISANS love to gather in groups to tell stories abut how girls are being victimized. In November 1997, the Public Education Network (PEN), a council of organizations that support the public schools, sponsored a conference entitled "Gender, Race and Student Achievement." The conference's honored celebrities were Carol Gilligan and Cornel West, a professor of Afro-American studies and philosophy of religion at Harvard University. Gilligan talked about how girls and women "lose their voice," how they "go underground" in adolescence, and how women teachers are "absent," having been "silenced" within the "patriarchal structure" that governs our schools. Cornel West spoke of having had to overcome his own feelings of "male supremacy."

Even at this most politically correct of gatherings, the serious deficits of boys kept surfacing. On the first day of the conference, during a special three-hour session, the PEN staff announced the results of a new teacher/student survey entitled *The American Teacher 1997: Examining Gender Issues in Public Schools*. The survey was funded by Metropolitan Life Insurance Company as part of its American Teacher series and conducted by Louis Harris and Associates.[59]

During a three-month period in 1997, 1,306 students and 1,035 teachers in grades seven through twelve were asked a variety of questions about gender equity. The MetLife study was not produced by a feminist advocacy organization; it had no doctrinal ax to grind. What it found contradicted most of the pet "findings" of the AAUW, the Sadkers, and the Wellesley Center for Research on Women. It politely said as much: "Contrary to the commonly held view that boys are at an advantage over girls in school, girls appear to have an advantage over boys in terms of their future plans, teachers' expectations, everyday experiences at school and interactions in the classroom."[60]

Here are some other conclusions from the MetLife study:

- Girls are more likely than boys to see themselves as college bound.
- Girls are more likely than boys to want a good education.
- More boys than girls (31 percent versus 19 percent) feel teachers do not listen to what they have to say.

The MetLife report informed a conference busily lionizing Carol Gilligan that the nation's boys needed attention more than its girls. The participants were hearing—many for the first time—that the conventional talk about studies that show "girls losing self-confidence . . . and as a result perform[ing] less well" in school was simply untrue. This should have been big news for media long inundated with findings on the tragic fate of our nation's girls. But where girls are concerned, good news is no news.

There were other dissonant notes at the conference. During a panel discussion on race and gender issues in schools, one high school panelist said that at her school, a selective Washington, D.C., public high school, it is so rare for a boy to do well that "it's a big occasion when a guy gets into an honor society or wins an award." [61] No one commented.

At another session, "How Do the Academic Experiences of Boys and Girls Differ?," Nancy Leffert, a child psychologist at the Search Institute in Minneapolis, reported the results of a massive survey she and her colleagues had recently completed of more than 99,000 sixth- through twelfth-graders.[62] The children were asked about their "developmental assets." The Search Institute has identified forty critical assets ("building blocks for healthy development"). Half of these are external—for example, a supportive family, adult role models—and half internal—motivation to achieve, sense of purpose in life, interpersonal confidence. Leffert explained to the PEN audience, somewhat apologetically, that girls were ahead of boys in thirty-four of the forty assets! On almost every significant measure of well-being, girls had the better of boys: they felt closer to their families, they had higher aspirations and a stronger connection to school—even superior assertiveness skills. Leffert concluded her talk by saying that in the past, she had referred to girls as fragile or vulnerable, "but if you look at [our survey], it tells me that girls have very powerful assets."

The original AAUW study, so successfully promoted by the AAUW, had been based on a survey of three thousand children. The Search Institute research that Leffert summarized was incomparably more reliable—it was based on a survey of nearly a hundred thousand students. This massive study definitively showed that the shortchanged-girls premise—on which the PEN conference was based—was false.

Yet no one called this to the attention of the conferees. The allegedly tragic fate of girls in "our sexist society" remained the dominant motif.

Leslie Wolfe, president of the Center for Women Policy Studies in Washington, D.C., duly denounced the "hidden curriculum of sexism" in the schools. "We must teach boys that male supremacy is unacceptable," said Wolfe. Workshop speakers held forth on subjects like "girl empowerment" and "proven classroom strategies to boost achievement and engagement of females." David Sadker led a session in which he described "the ocean of gender bias [against girls] that exists all around us."

The "official" view, uncompromisingly articulated by the then AAUW president Jackie DeFazio in 1994, has yet to be challenged by the education establishment: "Girls still receive an unequal education in the nation's schools. Whatever the measure—test scores, textbooks, or teaching methods—study after study showed that girls are not living up to their potential *as boys are*" (emphasis is added).[63]

BRITISH CONCERN, AMERICAN NEGLECT

BRITAIN HAS no Carol Gilligan, no Mary Pipher, no AAUW. It is therefore unsurprising that in Britain the plain truth about male underperformance has been reaching an informed and concerned public. For almost a decade, British newspapers and journals have been reporting on the distressing scholastic deficits of British schoolboys. The *Times* of London warned the prospect of "an underclass of permanently unemployed, unskilled men."[64] "What's Wrong with Boys?" asked the Glasgow *Herald*.[65] *The Economist* referred to boys as "tomorrow's second sex."[66] In Britain, the public, the government, and the education establishment are well aware of the increasing numbers of underachieving young males and they are looking for ways to help them. They have a name for them—the "sink group"—and they call what ails them "laddism."

The difference between Britain and the United States is perhaps most striking in government policy. At a time when the British government is confronting and constructively dealing with boys' underachievement as a serious national problem, American government agencies are behaving like resource-rich chapters of the AAUW, dutifully pursuing policies of girl advocacy, including initiatives to raise girls' self-esteem and help them find their "voices." The U.S. Department of Education disseminates more than 300 pamphlets, books, and working papers on gender equity, none of these aimed at helping boys achieve parity with girls in the nation's schools.[67] As the plight of boys grows, with no relief in sight, programs for girls multiply. One recent initiative is Girl Power! In 1997, U.S. Health and Human Services Secretary Donna Shalala launched Girl Power! to raise public awareness about the needs of America's demoralized girls.[68] The National Science Foundation spends millions each year to offer remedial programs to help girls with their science and math skills. The idea of special reading and writing classes for boys rarely surfaces. In schools, boys are the gender at risk. But no one is asking for money to cope with their academic shortfalls.

In this climate, so inhospitable to boys, American educators who wish to help boys face formidable obstacles. Prince George's County, Maryland, just outside Washington, D.C., includes several poor, mostly black public schools. According to one school board member, many of the boys "are at the bottom in every respect, in every academic indicator, every social development indicator."[69] To help such boys, the county organized a "Black Male Achievement Initiative." Beginning in the early nineties, approximately forty young men met two weekends a month with a group of professional men for tutoring and mentoring. The program was popular and effective. But in 1996, it was radically restructured by order of the U.S. Department of Education Office of Civil Rights, which found that it discriminated against girls. The woman who chaired the Prince George's County School Board was pleased: "The point here is that we were shortchanging female students, and we're not going to do that anymore."[70]

In the United States, a proposal to do something special for boys usually gets plowed under before it has a chance to take root.[71] In 1996, New York City public schools established the Young Women's Leadership School, an all-girls public school in East Harlem. The school is a great success and many, including *The New York Times*, urged then Schools Chancellor Rudy Crew to establish a "similar island of excellence for boys."[72] Crew rejected the idea of a comparable all-boys school. He regarded the girls' school as reparatory for past educational practices that neglected girls. That made it permissible. As he told the *Times*, "This is a case where the existence of the all-girls school makes an important statement about the viable education of girls. I want to continue to make that statement."[73] Presumably the statement would lose its force and point if an all-boys school were allowed to exist alongside.

What do such statements say to the boys in East Harlem? For the record, African-American women *vastly* outnumber African-American men in higher education. According to the *Journal of Blacks in Higher Education*, "Black women in the United States account for nearly all of the gains in black enrollment in higher education over the past 15 years." In 1994, for example, African-American women earned 63 percent of bachelor's degrees and 66 percent of master's degrees awarded to African Americans. At historically black colleges women comprise 60 percent of enrollments, and make up 80 percent of the honor roll.[74] The disparities are worsening.

One wonders what happened to black males between the early eighties and the late nineties. It would be an apt question for another PEN conference to explore. It would have been an apt question for Chancellor Crew to consider. But in gender-equity circles, that question is of little interest, if not altogether taboo.

THE TRUTH ABOUT BOYS

DESPITE THE anti-boy climate generated by the girl partisans, concern over boys was growing, and in the late 1990s the myth of the fragile girl was showing some signs of unraveling. Articles about boys' educational deficits began to appear in American newspapers with headlines much like those in the British press: "U.S. Colleges Begin to Ask, Where Have the Men Gone?,"[75] "How Boys Lost Out to Girl Power,"[76] "Survey Shows Girls Setting the Pace in School,"[77] and "Girls Overtake Boys in School Performance."[78] Studies showing the existence of a serious educational gender gap adverse to boys began to surface. This time, the media took notice.

The Horatio Alger Association, a fifty-year-old organization devoted to promoting and affirming individual initiative and "the American dream," released its annual back-to-school survey in 1998.[79] It contrasted two groups of students: the highly "successful" (approximately 18 percent of American students) and the "disillusioned" (approximately 15 percent of students). The students in the successful group work hard, choose challenging classes, make schoolwork a top priority, get good grades, participate in extracurricular activities, and feel that their teachers and administrators care about them and listen to them. According to the report, the successful group is 63 percent female and 37 percent male. At the other extreme, the disillusioned students are pessimistic about their own futures, get low grades, have minimal contact with their teachers, and believe that "there is no one . . . they can turn to for help." The disillusioned group could accurately be characterized as demoralized. According to the report, "Nearly seven out of ten are male." [80]

In the spring of 1998, Judith Kleinfeld, a psychologist at the University of Alaska, published a thorough critique of the schoolgirl research entitled *The Myth That Schools Shortchange Girls: Social Science in the Service of Deception.*[81] Kleinfeld exposed a number of errors and concluded that the AAUW/Wellesley Center research on girls was "politics dressed up as science." Kleinfeld's report prompted several newspapers, including *The New York Times* and *Education Week,* to take a second look at the earlier claims that girls were in a tragic state.

The AAUW did not adequately respond to any of Kleinfeld's substantive objections; instead, its president, Maggie Ford, complained in *The New York Times* letters column that Kleinfeld was "reducing the problems of our children to this petty 'who is worse off, boys or girls?' [which] gets us nowhere." [82] From the leader of an organization that spent nearly a decade promoting the proposition that America's girls are being "shortchanged," this comment is rather remarkable.

The association's executive director, Janice Weinman, added a more candid explanation for the persistent neglect of boys' problems: "We're the American Association of University Women," she said, "and our mission is to look at education for girls and women." [83] That would be fair enough had the girl partisans not relentlessly promoted the idea that boys were unfairly advantaged while girls were neglected. The AAUW had not merely *ignored* boys' problems, it had *dismissed* them, coaching teachers at its 1997 Leadership Conference on how to deflect questions about boys' deficits and comparing those who questioned bias against girls to "Holocaust revisionists" in its newsletter.

In this connection, it should be pointed out that while Gilligan and the AAUW had devised and successfully promoted the myth of the silenced girl, that myth had never taken hold among the students themselves. The AAUW was aware that the way students think of themselves and their teachers is at odds with the official picture it was presenting to the public. Surveying the perceptions of schoolboys and schoolgirls, the AAUW had learned that it is boys who feel neglected and girls who feel favored by their teachers. But evidently the AAUW leaders did not consider it part of the association's mission to publish these findings in the brochures that announced the tragedy of the shortchanged girl (see Table 4).

Did anything of value come out of the manufactured crisis of di-

TABLE 4

Unpublished AAUW Data from the 1990 Self-Esteem Survey

Responses by Sex (%)

	Total	Girls' perception	Boys' perception
1. Who do teachers think are smarter?			
Boys	16	13	26
Girls	79	81	69
Other response	5	5	5
2. Who do teachers punish more often?			
Boys	91	92	90
Girls	6	5	8
Other response	3	3	2
3. Who do teachers compliment more often?			
Boys	8	7	15
Girls	87	89	81
Other response	4	5	4
4. Who do teachers like to be around?			
Boys	14	12	21
Girls	78	80	73
Other response	8	8	6
5. Who do teachers pay more attention to?			
Boys	32	33	29
Girls	59	57	64
Other response	9	10	7
6. Who do teachers call on more often?			
Boys	35	35	36
Girls	57	57	59
Other response	7	8	5

Source: AAUW/Greenberg-Lake Full Data Report: Expectations and Aspirations: Gender Roles and Self-Esteem (Washington, D.C.: American Association of University Women, 1990), p. 18.

minished girls? There were some positive developments. Parents, teachers, and administrators now pay more attention to girls' deficits in math and science, and they offer more support for girls' participation in sports. But these benefits could and should have been achieved without promulgating the myth of the incredible shrinking girl or presenting boys as the unfairly favored sex.

A boy today, through no fault of his own, finds himself implicated in the social crime of "shortchanging" girls. Yet the allegedly silenced and neglected girl sitting next to him is likely to be a better student. She is not only more articulate, she is probably a more mature, engaged, and well-balanced human being. He may be uneasily aware that girls are more likely to go on to college. He may believe that teachers prefer to be around girls and pay more attention to them.[84] At the same time, he is uncomfortably aware that he is considered to be a member of the unfairly favored "dominant gender."

American schoolboys are lagging behind girls academically. The first step in helping them is to repudiate the partisanship that has distorted the issues surrounding sex differences in the schools. The next step is to make every effort to bring balance, fairness, and objective information into an urgently needed analysis of the nature and causes of those differences. But neither step can be taken while the divisive pro-girl campaign is allowed to go on unchecked and unchallenged.

The media and the education establishment can help by publicizing the studies by the U.S. Department of Education, MetLife, the Search Institute, and the Horatio Alger Association, as well as the academic research of Larry Hedges and Amy Nowell, Judith Kleinfeld, and Valerie Lee and her associates. All such studies expose the falsehoods disseminated by the girl partisans, and all show that the very term "shortchanged girls" is a travesty of the truth.

It is time the American public learned about the findings that supersede and contradict the accepted view that girls are academically weaker than boys. Because the British public is well informed about its boys, British schools have a significant head start in programs designed to lift boys out of the "disillusioned" category and to deal with their chronic underachievement. We have much to learn from their initiatives and even more from their healthy, commonsense approach to what they rightly see as a serious national emergency. For the time being, however, the academic problems of American boys are invisible.

WHAT NEXT?

THE GENDER THEORISTS and activists who in the past had little to say about boys have recently begun to tell us that boys too need attention—not because schools are neglecting their academic needs but because "under patriarchy," males are socialized to destructive masculine ideals. Gender experts at Harvard, Wellesley, and Tufts, and in the major women's organizations, believe that boys and men in our society will remain sexist (and potentially dangerous) unless socialized away from conventional maleness. It may be too late to change adult men: boys, on the other hand, are still salvageable—provided one gets to them at an early age. Such thinking presents a challenge that many an egalitarian educator is eager to embrace. As one keynote speaker at a convention of gender-equity experts pointed out to her audience, "We have an incredible opportunity. Kids are so malleable."[85]

The belief that boys are being wrongly "masculinized" is inspiring a movement to "construct boyhood" in ways that will render boys less competitive, more emotionally expressive, more nurturing—more, in short, like girls. Gloria Steinem summarizes the views of many in the boys-should-be-changed camp when she says, "We badly need to raise boys more like we raise girls."[86]

This novel agenda is no utopian fantasy. Indeed, as I will show, the movement to overhaul boys is already well under way. And like many other well-intentioned but ill-conceived reforms, this one has enormous potential to make a lot of people—in this case, millions of schoolboys—very miserable indeed.

CHAPTER TWO

REEDUCATING THE NATION'S BOYS

This general evil they maintain:
All men are bad and in their badness reign.

SHAKESPEARE, *Sonnet 121*

TAKE OUR DAUGHTERS TO WORK DAY, the school holiday for girls introduced by the Ms. Foundation for Women, is now in its ninth year.[1] For the first few years, it was a girls-only event. But as the holiday grew more successful, protests multiplied. Increasingly, parents and teachers asked, Why not include boys? Indeed, in recent years many participating companies have changed the name to Take Our Children to Work Day. For their part, the Ms. organizers remain adamantly opposed to including boys. They have been constantly trying to find ways to preserve the feminist purity of the day.

In 1996, Marie Wilson, president of the Ms. Foundation, began working with some feminist men's groups to design a separate holiday for boys. If boys had their own day, the pressure would be off. Ms.'s idea of what boys should have in the way of a holiday speaks volumes about how girl advocates think and feel about boys. The first "Son's Day" was planned for Sunday, October 20, 1996. October was especially desirable because, as the Ms. planners pointed out, "October is Domestic Violence Awareness Month, so there will be lots of activities scheduled."[2] Here are some of the ways "Son's Day" was to be celebrated:

- "Take your son—or 'son for a day'—to an event that focuses on . . . ending men's violence against women. Call the Family Violence Prevention Fund at 800 END-ABUSE for information."
- "Plan a game or sport in which the contest specifically does not keep score or declare a winner. Invite the community to watch and celebrate boys playing on teams for the sheer joy of playing."
- "Since Son's Day is on SUNDAY, make sure your son is involved in preparing the family for the work and school week ahead. This means: helping lay out clothes for siblings [and] making lunches."

For boys not exhausted by all the fun and excitement of the day's activities, the Ms. planners had a suggestion for the evening:

- "Take your son grocery shopping then help him plan and prepare the family's evening meal on Son's Day."

As the Ms. staff had planned it, Son's Day would not even give the boys a day off from school. One friend of mine aptly dubbed it "a holiday in hell for Junior." It is not easy to understand how the Ms. Foundation could imagine that a special Sunday when boys are encouraged to focus on male violence to women, to lay out clothes for siblings, and so on could constitute a boys' "holiday."

In the end, Son's Day was canceled and Ms. aborted the project. Nevertheless, Ms.'s attempt to initiate a boys' holiday is illuminating. It shows the kind of thinking girl advocates do when they reflect on what would be good for boys. Clearly they believe boys need to be reeducated. But why?

SCHOOLYARD TERRORISTS

BOYS HAVE BEEN affectionately described as "human machines that operate on the principle of perpetual commotion." Girl partisans look on these perpetual motion machines as inherently dangerous, especially to girls.

As they see it, violence is "gendered" and its gender is male.[3] They regard male aggression as the root of most social evils. Many activists in the Ms. Foundation, the AAUW, the National Education Association, and the U.S. Department of Education are persuaded that boys, as unwitting carriers of a pernicious sexism, need special remedial attention.

Leaders in the equity movement take a very dim view of errant boys, speaking with straight faces about schoolyard harassers as tomorrow's batterers, rapists, and murderers. Sue Sattel, an "equity specialist" with the Minnesota Department of Education and coauthor of an anti-harassment guide for children aged five to seven, says, "Serial killers say they started harassing at age 10 . . . they got away with it and went on from there."[4] Nan Stein, a director at the Wellesley College Center for Research on Women and a major figure in the movement to get anti-harassment programs into the nation's elementary schools, has referred to little boys who chase girls in the playground and flip their skirts as "perpetrators" committing acts of "gendered terrorism."[5] What motivates the girl partisans to sow their bitter seeds? The views of a prominent equity specialist shed some light on this question.

THE HEART AND MIND OF A GENDER-FAIRNESS LEADER

KATHERINE HANSON is director of the Women's Educational Equity Act (WEEA) Publishing Center. The WEEA Center serves as a national clearinghouse for and publisher of "gender-fair materials." It is also the "primary vehicle" by which the U.S. Department of Education promotes gender equity. As director, Hanson works with schools and community organizations to "infuse equity" into all education policies, practices, and materials.[6]

In February 1998, an exultant Hanson announced that the WEEA center had just been awarded a new five-year contract with the Department of Education that offered "exciting new opportunities to become a more comprehensive national resource center for gender equity."[7] She also told WEEA subscribers that her center had been commissioned by the Department of Education to write a report for Congress on the status of women and girls in schools. Hanson wrote:

> The approach of the 21st Century is a good time to examine our past and present. As part of our WEEA contract, we are de-

veloping a national report on the status of education for women and girls for the U.S. Department of Education. This is an exciting opportunity for the education field, the Department, Congress and the nation to explore the successes, challenges, and complexity of gender equitable education.[8]

Who is Katherine Hanson, and what are her credentials for educating "Congress and the nation" on gender equity? Judging from Hanson's writings, she seems to share the view of Nan Stein, Sue Sattel, and the Ms. Foundation's would-be creators of "Son's Day" that early intervention in the male "socialization process" is critical if we are to stem the tide of male violence.[9] Underscoring the need for radical changes in how we raise young males, Hanson offers some horrifying statistics concerning violence in the United States.

- Every year nearly four million women are beaten to death.[10]
- Violence is the leading cause of death among women.[11]
- The leading cause of injury among women is being beaten by a man at home.[12]
- There was a 59 percent increase in rapes between 1990 and 1991.[13]

This "culture of violence," says Hanson, "stem[s] from cultural norms that socialize males to be aggressive, powerful, unemotional, and controlling."[14] She urges us to "honestly and lovingly" reexamine what it means to be a male or a female in our society. "And just as honestly and lovingly, we must help our young people develop new and more healthful models."[15] One old and unhealthful model of maleness that needs to be "reexamined" is found in Little League baseball. Writes Hanson, "One of the most overlooked arenas of violence training within schools may be the environment that surrounds athletics and sports. Beginning with little league games where parents and friends sit on the sidelines and encourage aggressive, violent behavior. . . ."[16]

History is one long lesson in the dangers of combining moral fervor with misinformation. So the first question we should ask is: Does Hanson have her facts right? Her organization, under the auspices of the U.S. Department of Education, sends out more than 350 publications on gender equity and distributes materials to more than 200 education conferences each year. I have written a book about feminist "Ms/information"; Katherine Hanson's "facts" are the most outrageously distorted I have yet come across.

If Hanson were right, the United States would be the site of an atrocity unparalleled in the twentieth century. *Four million women beaten to death by men! Every year!* In fact, the total number of annual female deaths in the entire country *from all causes combined* is approximately *one* million. Only a minuscule fraction of these deaths is caused by violence, and an even tinier fraction is caused by battery. According to the FBI, the total number of women who died by murder in 1996 was 3,631. But according to Director Hanson, 11,000 American women are beaten to death *every day.*

I spoke to Hanson in June 1999 to ask about her sources. Where did she get the statistic about 4 million American women being fatally beaten each year? Or the information that violence is the leading cause of death for women? She explained that "those were pulled from the research." What research? I asked. "They are from the Justice Department." I inquired about her academic background. She told me she had been "trained as a journalist" and had done many things in the past, including "studies in theology." She has been with the WEEA program since 1984.

Hanson, Stein, and other "gender-fair" activists regularly whip themselves into an anti-male frenzy with their false statistics.[17] They use their lurid "facts" to devise and justify programs and curricula spreading the gospel of gender equity. "The leading cause of injury among women is being beaten by a man at home. . . . Violence is the leading cause of death for women." Shockers like these are used by some advocates to make the case for radically resocializing boys.

For the record, the leading cause of death among women is heart disease (c. 370,000 deaths per year), followed by cancer (c. 250,000). Female deaths from homicide (c. 3,600) are far down the list *after* suicide (c. 6,000).

Male violence is also far down the list of causes of injury to women. Two studies of emergency room admissions, one by the U.S. Bureau of Justice Statistics and one by the Centers for Disease Control and Prevention, suggest that approximately 1 percent of women's injuries are caused by male partners.[18] Hanson's other factoids are no more reliable: between 1990 and 1991 rapes increased by 4 percent, not 59 percent, and the number has gone down steadily since.[19]

Hanson, who clearly believes her own propaganda, is convinced that "our educational system is a primary carrier of the dominant culture's assumptions," [20] and that "dominant culture" (Western, patriarchal, sexist, and violent) is sick. Since the best cure is prevention, reeducating boys is a moral imperative. She gratefully quotes the words of male feminist Haki Madhubuti: "The liberation of the male psyche from preoccupation with domination, power hunger, control, and absolute rightness requires . . . a willingness for painful, uncomfortable and often shocking change." [21]

The gender-fairness activists are eager to be in the forefront of effecting that "shocking change" by overhauling the way boys are raised to manhood. To that end, Hanson and her taxpayer-funded organization are working to make classrooms a place for radically changing boys. Should we be permitting Hanson and her fellow equity professionals to subject boys to their liberating ministrations without being reasonably sure that their program has at least a minimal grounding in fact and common sense? By all indications, the would-be reformers of boys lack both.

A small percentage of boys are destined to become batterers and rapists; boys with severe conduct disorders are at high risk of becoming criminal predators. Such boys do need strong intervention, the earlier the better. But this small number of boys cannot justify a gender-bias industry that looks upon millions of normal male children as pathologically dangerous.

What Is at Stake?

How MUCH does it matter that equity experts in the Department of Education, the WEEA, and the Wellesley Center disseminate so much false information about males in our "patriarchal culture"? Does it matter that they assume that men must be violent, that some think of little boys as protobatterers in need of intervention programs and a new kind of socialization that avoids masculine stereotypes?

None of these things would be of much moment if the zealous women promoting these views were not a major force in American education. Schools have to listen to Hanson, Stein, Sattel, and their colleagues to avoid running afoul of complicated federal laws concerning sex equity. Title IX of the Education Amendments of 1972 prohibits sex discrimination in any educational institution that receives public funds. The WEEA Center's mission is to "provide assistance to enable educational agencies to meet the requirement of Title IX."[22] Eager to avoid charges of discrimination that trigger the punitive provisions of Title IX, many schools and school districts have hired trained "equity" coordinators.

Since 1980, the Women's Educational Equity Program (which funds the Equity Center) has received approximately $75 million in federal funds. This and several other federal equity programs have created a cottage industry of gender-bias specialists. Researchers at the Wellesley Center received WEEA grants, as did Myra and David Sadker and staff at the NOW Legal Defense and Education Fund. In turn, these activists did studies and disseminated information that have led to ever more expansive and aggressive interpretations of Title IX.

Data from the Wellesley Center, WEEA, or the Sadkers are offered to give "scientific" weight to the contention that schools are failing at fairness to girls. By 1993, the Ms. Foundation would get the uncritical cooperation and tacit approval of thousands of school administrators in running a girls-only holiday involving millions of children. Everyone "knew" that girls were "shortchanged." School officials, always under pressure to show they are acting in the spirit of Title IX, have given the gender-equity protagonists a free hand to promote their perception of girls as victims of bias and boys as the unfairly favored gender.

The promoters of "gender fairness" have a great deal of power in our schools, but they are far too reckless with the truth, far too removed from the precincts of common sense, and far too negative about boys to be properly playing any role in the education of our children. Yet their influence is growing. In 1998, the WEEA Center received a new five-year government contract. At the same time, the Wellesley College Center for Research on Women was chosen by the Centers for Disease Control and Prevention to codirect its new national center on Prevention of Violence Against Women. Nan Stein, who is co-directing the research, explains, "My focus will be to strengthen collaboration between school personnel and sexual assault and domestic violence staff working in schools."[23]

Supportive officials in the Department of Education and at the CDC do not appear to mind that Hanson and Stein and company are committed gender warriors. All the same, it is not easy to understand how statistically challenged, anti-male organizations such as the WEEA Center and the Wellesley Center keep being awarded federal government funds to promote their anti-male brand of "gender equity."

A CIRCLE OF FRIENDS

CONVINCED THAT we are living in a girl-destroying, male-dominated society, and empowered by schools that reasonably fear running afoul of Title IX, the gender-bias researchers and coordinators are engaged in reforming the nation's "sexist" boys. Most parents have no idea what their children are facing in the gender-charged atmosphere of the public schools.

Quit It!—a 1998 K-3 antiharassment and antiviolence teacher guide and curriculum—is the joint effort of several groups, including WEEA, the Wellesley Center, and the National Education Association. Its authors explain why children as young as five need this kind of special training: "We view teasing and bullying as the precursors to adolescent sexual harassment, and believe that the roots of this behavior are to be found in early childhood socialization practices." [24]

Quit It! includes many activities designed to render little boys less volatile, less competitive, and less aggressive. It is not that "boys are bad," the authors assure us, "but rather that we must all do a much better job of addressing aggressive behavior of young boys to counteract the prevailing messages they receive from the media and society in general." [25]

The curriculum promises to develop children's cooperative skills though "wonderful noncompetitive activities." [26] The game of tag, for example, which may seem an innocent playground pastime, has features the authors consider socially undesirable. *Quit It!* shows teachers how to counteract the subtle influences of tag that encourage aggressiveness: "Before going outside to play, talk about how students feel when playing a game of tag. Do they like to be chased? Do they like to do the chasing? How does it feel to be tagged out? Get their ideas about other ways the game might be played."

After students share their fears and apprehensions about tag, the teacher is advised to announce that there is a new, nonthreatening version of the game called "Circle of Friends"—"where nobody is ever 'out.' " Here is how to play Circle of Friends: "If a [tagged] student calls for help, two students hold hands and form a circle around her/him. This circle of friends unfreezes the student so he or she can continue playing. Students can't be tagged while making a circle."

Should students become overexcited by Circle of Friends, the guide suggests that once back in the classroom the teacher use "stress relief [exercises] to help the transition from active play to focused work." [27] Some of the students might experience anger during playtime, in which case the guide provides the teacher with the tools for organizing an in-class anger management workshop: "Outlets for angry feelings can be expressed through puppets, role-plays, dramatizations, drawing, dictating or writing." [28]

In reading through *Quit It!*, you have to remind yourself that its suggestions are intended not for disturbed children but for normal five- to seven-year-olds in our nation's schools. These are mainstream materials. *Quit It!* was funded by the Department of Education, and according to the National Education Association's (NEA) Web site it is a "best-seller" among teachers.

A similar curriculum guide, *Girls and Boys Getting Along: Teaching Sexual Harassment Prevention in the Elementary Classroom*,[29] was also funded by the Department of Education. This 144-page curriculum includes special antiharassment/self-esteem-building pledge for second- and third-graders:

> *I pledge to do my best to stop sexual harassment,*
> *I will show RESPECT, by caring for myself and others;*
> *I have dignity and will give it to others;*
> *I am special, you are special, and we are all equal.*[30]

Children, including kindergartners, learn to say "Stop it. That's sexual harassment, and sexual harassment is against the law."

The curriculum guide is right that peer harassment is against the law. For the past ten years, girl-advocacy groups such as the American Association of University Women, the Ms. Foundation for Women, and the NOW Legal Defense and Education Fund have been successfully lobbying the federal government to impose strict harassment codes on the schools. In August 1996, the U.S. Department of Education's Office of Civil Rights issued a 26-page guideline on the subject of "peer harassment." No age limits were specified. Rooting out schoolyard harassers is now a prime objective of the Department of Education. Local schools are sensitive to this policy and know that the Education Department's national policies have rendered them vulnerable to litigation.

The National School Board Association has complained that the Education Department's guidelines "appear to be more involved with trying to help plaintiffs' attorneys win cases against school districts." [31] That does not perturb the harassment activists. On the contrary, it heartens them. Nan Stein, the Wellesley Center schoolyard harassment expert (and contributor to *Quit It!*), appears in an antiharassment video produced by the National Education Association. When she was asked how school administrators are reacting to government policies on sexual harassment, she smiled and replied, "I'd say they are in a panic. . . . There have been so many lawsuits with so many monetary damages. . . . They are panicked." [32]

PANICKY SCHOOLS

THE FEAR of ruinous lawsuits is forcing schools to treat normal boys as sexist culprits. Young boys in schools throughout the country are punished when they show signs of incipient misogyny. The climate of anxiety helps explain why in 1996 six-year-old Jonathan Prevette, who kissed a female classmate, was punished as a harasser. In another unpublicized case, a mother in Worcester, Massachusetts, who came to pick up her son was told he had been reprimanded and made to sit in the "time-out chair" for having hugged another child. "He's a toucher," she was told. "We are not going to put up with it." That little boy was three years old.

Older children face more punitive consequences. In 1997, at the Glebe Elementary School in Arlington, Virginia, a nine-year-old boy already had a reputation as a potential harasser: he had been caught drawing a picture of a naked woman in art class (following a school trip to the National Gallery of Art). When he was accused of deliberately rubbing up against a girl in the cafeteria line, school officials notified the police. The boy was charged with aggravated sexual battery, and was handcuffed and fingerprinted. The family's lawyer, Kenneth Rosenau, said, "This is really a case of political correctness run amok. A 9-year-old bumps into a girl in the lunch line while reaching for an apple and all of a sudden you've got World War III declared against a fourth grader." [33] Eventually the charges were dropped.

Sharon Lamb, a committed feminist and a professor of psychology, was shocked to hear that her ten-year-old son and a friend had been charged with sexual harassment. A girl had overheard them comment that her dangling belt looked like a penis. "It's against the law," the teacher informed the mother. This moved the mother to ask, "If the message, the only message, to boys is that their sex and sexuality is potentially harmful to girls, how will we ever raise them to be full partners in healthy relationships?" [34]

In early October 1998, Jerry, a seventeen-year-old at a progressive private school in Washington, D.C., received the customary greeting card from the school director on his birthday. It was affectionately inscribed, "To Jerry—You are a wonderful person—a gift to all of us." Two weeks later, this same director would expel him after Jerry was accused of harassing a classmate, and school officials would urgently advise his parents to "get him professional attention. . . ." [35]

A female classmate accused Jerry of verbally harassing her. On one occasion, the girl claims, he said to her, "Why don't you give so-and-so a blow job." She also alleged that he licked his lips in a suggestive way. He denied these allegations. Finally (and this may have been the last straw), someone overheard him ask another boy on the bus, referring to the other boy's girlfriend, "Did you get into her pants yet?"

When these three alleged transgressions came to the notice of the school administration, Jerry was ordered off school property. Following a hasty investigation, he was thrown out of the school. All this happened in little more than twenty-four hours.

His parents are appalled. They don't defend Jerry's behavior. "He's a great kid with a big mouth," says his mother. "If he really said those things, he should be punished." His mother explains that she would have understood and fully accepted it had the school reprimanded him, even suspended him: "It was a teachable moment." But what was he to learn from being expelled without a single warning, in October of his junior year, from the school he had attended since ninth grade?

Why did the school react with so draconian a punishment? Schools rightly fear lawsuits, and many feel they cannot afford to tolerate the antics of teenage boys, however natural or understandable. "He's being punished for being an adolescent boy," says his mother. And she is right. What she may not know is that no school today can afford to take the risk of being charged with tolerating behavior that offends a female student. The prudent school policy is to act the moment a girl accuses a boy of having made her sexually uncomfortable.

Parents of boys like Jerry and the other boys mentioned in this chapter are always surprised at the punishments meted out for their sons' behavior. They have been rudely made aware that schools today are under pressure to act quickly to eliminate any trace of a "hostile environment" for girls. As for the girl advocates, they apparently believe that the misery or ruin of a few boys who, in their judgment, disregard the feelings of girls is more than justified by the gains achieved. Anything that weakens the sex-gender system is worth the cost, for that system fosters male violence and misogyny.

More Harassment Curricula

In the meantime, the equity experts continue to crusade against boy culprits. *Quit It!* was published in 1998; the following year, Nan Stein and her colleagues at the Wellesley Center brought out *Gender Violence/Gender Justice*, an antiharassment guide for students in grades seven to twelve.[36] They recommend it for use in core courses such as English and social studies. The opening sentence of the preface announces the urgent need for such a curriculum: "Schools may well be the training grounds for domestic violence through the practice and permission given to the public performance of sexual harassment."[37]

The Department of Education supported the writing of *Gender Violence/Gender Justice*, and it supports its promotion in the schools. The project is an example of the kind of "gender-think" that counselors and facilitators force-feed schoolchildren in the name of equity. *Gender Violence* provides lessons designed to render boys aware of the ways males systematically inflict suffering on females; at the same time, it aims to make girls aware of what they are facing in our misogynist male-dominated society. Some of the consciousness-raising exercises designed for the boys seem better suited for convicted sex criminals than for seventh-graders. This one, for example: "Ask the students to close their eyes. . . . Once they've closed their eyes, say 'Imagine that the woman you care about the most (your mother, sister, daughter, girlfriend) is being raped, battered or sexually abused. . . . Give them at least 30 seconds to think about the scenario before asking them to open their eyes."[38]

Students are asked to write down their feelings. The guide also suggests that teachers explain to students that "We need to understand how boys and men are learning to equate violent behavior with 'manhood' in order to de-link the concepts."[39] *Gender Violence* provides students with a ten-page state-by-state list of domestic violence and sexual assault organizations. This is followed by information on "Temporary Restraining Orders for Non-Cohabiting Minors."[40]

Besides wasting precious classroom time, what effect do these "sensitivity" exercises have on the students? Girls cannot fail to be provoked to anger against the male sex, which, they are told, "learns violent behavior with manhood." Boys, on the other hand, must feel branded as the violent, callous sex. Can these effects be what the authors of the guide want to achieve?

Without impugning the motives of those who write such guides, one can predict that the lessons they impart will have other undesirable effects as well. Teachers who use them will be conveying to girls the message that boys are protoharassers, potential batterers, stalkers, and rapists who learn to be violent as they are socialized to manhood. As for the boys in the class, they can only feel confused, hurt, or helplessly defiant.

WHAT ARE BOYS FEELING?

MORE AND MORE SCHOOLBOYS inhabit a milieu of disapproval. Routinely regarded as protosexists, potential harassers, and perpetuators of gender inequity, boys live under a cloud of censure, in a permanent state of culpability. Martin Spafford, a high school teacher in London, has made observations about British boys that apply to American boys as well. Spafford favored the pro-girl, antisexist measures of the eighties. But now he observes that boys are under siege: "Boys feel continually attacked for who they are. We have created a sense in school that masculinity is something bad. Boys feel blamed for history, and a school culture has grown up which is suspicious and frightened of boys."[41]

In my own experience, I often find boys expecting to be "attacked for who they are." In 1997, I delivered a commencement address at the Hun Academy, a private high school in Princeton, New Jersey. Following the graduation, a group of young men told me they were gratefully surprised that I had not said anything against them: "When we heard you were going to talk on feminism we figured we were going to be attacked at our own graduation." When I spoke at another prep school, the Westminster School in Connecticut, the feminist dean who invited me told me that she did not agree with my position on gender and education, but if she invited one more speaker with a strong feminist message the boys would rebel. The message of male sinfulness is broadcast constantly. Boys at University High School in Pacific Heights, California, are obliged to sit quietly through an annual "Women's Assembly" in which women are celebrated and men are blamed. One student who endured it told me that three boys had slipped out. The miscreants were caught walking back to class and duly punished.

Even some sexual harassment instructors feel uneasy about the message being conveyed to boys. In 1997, Nan Stein did a national survey of domestic violence/sexual assault experts who present programs in public schools. She asked them what they liked least about the educational materials they had to work with (guides, handouts, videos, and so on). Stein reported that among the most common complaints were that "males are never positively portrayed" and "males are never shown in a positive light." However, she did not see this as a reason to change the message: when boys object, it only shows the "need for materials to defuse male resistance." [42] She seemed not to notice that the instructors, not the boys, were the ones objecting to the materials.

All around them, boys find their sex regularly condemned, while girls receive official sympathy as a "historically under-served population." At the same time, many boys are unhappily aware that girls are outpacing them. Boys believe that teachers prefer girls, are more interested in girls, and think they are smarter.[43] Yet boys are told that we live in a patriarchy in which men are unfairly "in control of our country, our businesses, our schools and . . . the family." [44]

A SEX-EQUITY CONFERENCE

ANYONE WHO WANTS a firsthand experience of male-averse attitudes and anti-boy rhetoric can get it anywhere the girl partisans gather. It is at their conferences that they are most uninhibitedly themselves.

In July 1998, I attended the 19th Annual Conference of the National Coalition for Sex Equity in Education (NCSEE, pronounced "Nice-ee") in Kansas City. NCSEE is the professional organization of some six hundred "sex-equity experts" who work in the federal government, state departments of education, local schools, and activist agencies such as the Wellesley College Center for Research on Women and the AAUW. These experts formulate and implement "gender-fair" educational policies and programs and offer guidance to school administrators and teachers on combating sexism and complying with Title IX.

The conference met just a few days after the release of the startling news story that 59 percent of would-be teachers in Massachusetts had failed an elementary competency test that average tenth-graders would be expected to pass. The report generated hundreds of news articles and dismayed editorials. But none of this intense public concern penetrated the halls of a gathering dedicated to the mission of dismantling our schools' systematic unfairness to girls.

I attended the NCSEE conference with a friend, psychiatrist Sally Satel. We were not exactly welcome guests. At the first evening's barbecue/balloon toss, the chair of NCSEE, Darcy Lees (an equity coordinator for the state of Washington, who is also a WEEA associate), startled the two hundred conferees by announcing my presence over the loudspeaker. A distraught woman approached me in the dessert line. "Your attendance here has stirred up a lot of controversy," she said. "We are wondering why you came since you do not share our philosophy."

NCSEE, of course, shares the "philosophy" of the WEEA, the AAUW, the Wellesley Center, and the Ms. Foundation: the conviction that girls are academically shortchanged and personally demeaned by schools that favor boys, that boys are predatory and in need of rigorous antisexist training, the earlier the better. It is true that I disagree with this perspective on boys and girls. For example, I object to the way NCSEE members deploy terms such as "equity" and "bias": any advantage boys enjoy (such as better scores on standardized math tests or greater participation in sports) constitutes gender bias that must be aggressively combated; any advantage girls enjoy (such as better scores on standardized reading tests or greater college attendance) constitutes a triumph of equity. In addition, unlike the NCSEE conference organizers, I am seriously concerned about boys' academic deficits. Nevertheless, there was much to interest me at this gathering.

In dozens of workshops spread over four days, NCSEE participants sat in circles, shared their feelings, and performed exercises designed to help the nations' girls find their voices in the classroom. Leading workshops were prominent figures such as Nan Stein and Sue Sattel. There was a promotional session to introduce the K-3 antiharassment guide *Quit It!* WEEA representatives hosted a roundtable and made a presentation urging conference participants to help them meet the demands of their new five-year contract with the Department of Education.

In one workshop, Peggy Weeks, the diminutive gray-haired director of gender equity for the Nebraska Department of Education, wrote her formulas for achieving nonsexist, bias-free schools on a large sheet of paper with a green felt-tip pen. "Do you know why I am using a green pen?" she asked. "Because green is the color of hope." She then stood aside while her copresenter wrote the following six words vertically on the board.

Sexism
Homocentrism
Ablism
Racism
Elitism
Disablism

Her assistant explained that the initial letters of these "isms" spell out SHARED. "That is powerful!" exclaimed Weeks to the appreciative audience of teachers, school administrators, and government officials.

A gender-equity instructor from New York University, Dr. Susan Levin Schlechter, addressed the call-out gap, the "problem" of boys getting more teacher attention than girls. She suggested that teachers "create a community of learners" by calling on students alternately: "boy-girl, boy-girl."[45] A vigilant diversity officer from the Aurora public schools in Colorado chastised her: she should have put it "girl-boy, girl-boy."

At another workshop, Victoria Warner, an Ohio State University doctoral candidate, reported on a large-scale, seven-year gender-equity project she and her colleagues had just completed. It involved eleven "gender-equity modules" (GEMS, for short), each consisting of a small packet of practice quizzes, worksheets, class activities, assessments, and "fact" sheets designed to "develop gender equity competencies."

Warner broke us down into small groups to practice a sample GEM exercise called the Bean Strategy. She distributed Baggies filled with beans. Some contained only two beans, others as many as ten. We were instructed to hold a discussion, but each time we spoke, we had to give up one of our beans. Once your bag was empty, you had to remain silent. This meant that some members could speak a lot more than others. (Gender-equity activists believe that boys always get "more beans" than girls do.) Later, we shared our feelings about what it had been like to be silenced or privileged in a discussion. Both can be upsetting, we learned.

I asked whether at any time during or after the seven-year development of the project there had been a follow-up evaluation of the GEMS to learn whether the activities actually improved student achievement or succeeded in reducing children's bias. The good-natured Warner smiled and said disarmingly, "We have never done that. I have no idea if this stuff works."

Although the NCSEE conference ignored boys' academic failings, it did not ignore the menace boys pose. Male violence was a major topic of concern. On the first day, Jackson Katz, a self-described male feminist, led a three-hour workshop on "gender violence prevention." He spent the first hour teaching participants how to avoid what he called the "patriarchal universe of discourse."

Katz distributed a handout that included a lot of alarming (but false) statistics on domestic violence (including some of WEEA's specious numbers). When my friend Sally politely pointed out the factual errors, Katz and several audience members were indignant. "This is not a discussion about statistics!" cried one angry woman. The group, including Katz, was far more appreciative of a remark by another participant: "Men fear that women will laugh at them; women fear that men will kill them." At the end of his three hours, Katz told us, "I know very few healthy men."

Katz announced that he and Nan Stein were inaugurating a new equity program called Gender Justice: Boys Speak Out. Despite its name, this is not a program to give boys a forum to talk about how schools may be failing them. Instead, Boys Speak Out honors boys "who have distinguished themselves in their schools or communities by supporting girls." [46] The purpose of Boys Speak Out is to encourage boys and young men to become feminist activists. That is the gender-equity movement's idea of a suitable program for boys.

Barbara Sprung, cofounder and codirector of Educational Equity Concepts and coauthor of *Quit It!*, gave the keynote speech, "Addressing Gender Equity in Early Childhood Education." It was Sprung who spoke of children's "malleability," and the "incredible opportunity" that malleability presents to educators. To dramatize the urgency of small children confronting pernicious gender stereotypes, she reported a window display she had seen the day before while strolling past F.A.O. Schwarz in Kansas City. She described a window full of Barbie dolls: "It was replete with everything you don't want—including Rapunzel Barbie." The audience was suitably aghast.

During the question-and-answer period, an audience member asked whether Sprung ever loses hope. A thoughtful Sprung replied, "Social change is hard. . . . Look at Seneca Falls. It is a long, long struggle."

THE TRUTH ABOUT MALE VIOLENCE

THE GIRL-CRISIS advocates have succeeded in projecting an image of males as predators and females as hapless victims. They have convinced school administrators, leaders of teachers' unions, and officials in the U.S. Department of Education to support them and fund them. They have been able to implement their curricula and policies in many of the nation's classrooms. They could hardly have done these things if they were not addressing genuine problems that school officials are trying to solve.

Sex differences in violence are very real: physically, males *are* more aggressive than females. [47] Cross-cultural studies confirm the obvious: boys are universally more bellicose. In a classic 1973 study of the research on male-female differences, Eleanor Maccoby and Carol Jacklin conclude that, compared to girls, boys engage in more mock fighting and more aggressive fantasies. They insult and hit one another and retaliate more quickly when attacked: "The sex difference [in aggression] is found as early as social play beings—at 2 or 2½." [48] The equity specialists look at these insulting, hitting, chasing, competitive creatures and see them as proto-criminals.

It is precisely in drawing this conclusion that they go badly wrong, for they fail to distinguish between healthy and aberrant masculinity. Criminologists distinguish between "hypermasculinity" (or "protest masuclinity"), on the one hand, and the normal masculinity of healthy young males, on the other. Hypermasculine young men do, indeed, express their maleness through antisocial behavior—mostly against other males, but also through violent aggression toward and exploitation of women. Healthy young men express their manhood in competitive endeavors that are often physical. As they mature, they take on responsibility, strive for excellence, achieve and "win." They assert their masculinity in ways that require physical and intellectual skills and self-discipline. In American society, healthy, normal young men (which is to say, the overwhelming majority) don't batter, rape, or terrorize women; they respect them and treat them as friends.

Unfortunately, many educators have become persuaded that there is truth in the relentlessly repeated proposition that masculinity per se is the cause of violence. Beginning with the factual premise that most violence is perpetrated by men, they move hastily (and fallaciously) to the proposition that maleness is the leading cause of violence. By this logic, every little boy is a potential harasser and batterer.

Of course, when boys are violent or otherwise antisocially injurious to others, they must be disciplined, both for their own betterment and for the sake of society. But most boys' physicality and masculinity are not expressed in antisocial ways.

It is very rare these days to hear anyone praising masculinity. The dissident feminist writer Camille Paglia is a refreshing exception. Her observations are effective antidotes to the surfeit of disparagements. For Paglia, male aggressiveness and competitiveness are animating principles of creativity: "Masculinity is aggressive, unstable, combustible. It is also the most creative cultural force in history." [49] Speaking of the "fashionable disdain for 'patriarchal society' to which nothing good is ever attributed," she writes, "But it is patriarchal society that has freed me as a woman. It is capitalism that has given me the leisure to sit at this desk writing this book. Let us stop being small-minded about men and freely acknowledge what treasures their obsessiveness has poured into culture." [50] Men, writes Paglia, "created the world we live in and the luxuries we enjoy" [51]: "When I cross the George Washington Bridge or any of America's great bridges, I think—*men* have done this. Construction is a sublime male poetry." [52]

BOYS BEHAVING BADLY

ALL THE SAME, Paglia's praise of males may sound irrelevant to administrators who have hard-core disciplinary problems in their schools. Much antisocial student behavior is sexual. Much of it perpetrated by males. The equity specialists may have a twisted understanding of masculinity; they may be routinely guilty of misrepresenting the facts and unfairly putting men and boys in a bad light; but they are not wrong when they point out that our schools are plagued with sexually crude, disrespectful, and untoward behavior. They at least have a plan for coping with some of the violence. Why should anyone object to their concerted attempt to deal with the problem?

Activists from NOW and the Wellesley Center are at their most persuasive about the need to resocialize boys when they cite harrowing cases of young men tormenting female students. Katie Lyle of Duluth, Minnesota, for example, was viciously humiliated by a group of boys who wrote obscene messages about her in the school bathrooms. Graffiti such as "Katie Lyle is a slut" and "Katie Lyle had sex with my dog" kept being eradicated and reappearing. This went on for weeks. Boys would taunt her on the bus with comments such as "Oh, Katie, do me" and "Are you as good as everyone says?"

Tawnya Brady, a high school student in Petaluma, California, faced a gauntlet of malicious boys who would moo at her whenever she passed, making remarks about the size of her breasts. In both cases, the school administrators failed to offer the girls effective protection. Examples such as these, which are not rare, strongly suggest that something is badly awry—with our schools and with our boys. They suggest the need to take resolute action. So we ask: What is wrong with sexual harassment programs that teach boys to respect girls? What is wrong with pursuing a vigorous policy of curbing boys' aggressive misogyny?

The answer is that boys do, indeed, need to be educated and civilized. They need to be turned into respectful human beings. One must show them, in ways that leave them in no doubt, that they cannot get away with bullying or harassing other students. Boys need strong moral guidance. Our schools should implement firm codes of discipline and clear and unequivocal rules against profanity, incivility, and hurtful behavior. Teachers and administrators have to establish a school environment that does not tolerate any variety of egregious meanness and incivility—sexual or nonsexual. Boys badly need moral education and discipline. So do girls.

But school behavior problems have very little to do with misogyny, patriarchy, or sex discrimination. They have everything to do with children's propensity to bully and be cruel. In coping with the generic problem of hurtful misconduct, schools must socialize children to be moral and considerate. And they must be prepared to enforce moral codes by bearing down hard on trespassers.

Children need a moral environment. They do not need gender politics. They do not need workshops that give primacy to sexual harassment and sexual violence as the foremost moral questions that citizens of our society face. Nor do children of any age need specious advocacy statistics that sensationalize the horrid things some men do to women.

Too many of our schools are rife with incivility, profanity, and bullying; most of the hurtful behavior and intimidation is in fact nonsexual. And girls do their share of it. Almost any junior high school girl will tell you that girls can create as much misery as boys, especially among other girls.

What we are facing in the schools transcends sex. But even when the misconduct is specifically sexual, it is not a manifestation of the sexist oppression of women. *Hostile Hallways* is the best-known study of harassment in grades eight through eleven. It was commissioned by the AAUW in 1993 and is a favorite of many harassment experts. But this survey revealed that girls do almost as much touching, grabbing, and graffiti writing as boys. According to the study, "85 percent of girls and 76 percent of boys surveyed say they have experienced unwanted and unwelcome sexual behavior that interferes with their lives."[53] Four scholars at the University of Michigan did a careful follow-up study of the AAUW data and concluded, "The majority of both genders (53%) described themselves as having been both victim and perpetrator of harassment—that is, most students had been harassed and had harassed others."[54] And these researchers draw the right conclusion: "Our results led us to question the simple perpetrator-victim model."[55] The simple male perpetrator/female victim model is, of course, the bread and butter of the gender-equity activists.

Consider another celebrated school harassment case, this one also in Petaluma, California. Students at Kenilworth Junior High spread a rumor that seventh-grader Jane Doe had "had sex with a hot dog." Jane could not walk in the hall without someone making the accusation. By eighth grade the hot dog taunts became so bad that Jane's parents were forced to move away from the district. They eventually sued the school for violating Title IX of the Education Act by failing to protect Jane from sexual harassment. The case was settled out of court.

But when *Los Angeles Times* writer Nina Easton took a closer look at the case, she discovered that Jane's worst tormentors were other girls.[56] According to Easton, "Jane's lawsuit focuses on the behavior of boys, but it is clear from her own words that the most vicious bullies were the Kenilworth girls who wore Raiders jackets and too much makeup and ran together as the tough crowd." Why did she become a target? Easton explains, "One former Kenilworth student said in a deposition that Jane became a target simply because she had started the [hot dog] rumor about someone else the year before. In her deposition, Jane acknowledged hearing the rumor from an out-of-state friend and passing it on to girlfriends."

BULLIES

SCHOOLYARD BULLYING is the generic problem of which sexual harassment is only one species. Bullying is a moral problem, and its effects on a child can be appalling. Consider the case of Curtis Taylor, an honor student at Oak Street Middle School in Burlington, Iowa. Here is a description of his plight that appeared in *Psychology Today:*

> For three years other boys had been tripping him in the hallways, knocking things out of his hands. They had even taken his

head in their hands and banged it into a locker. Things were now intensifying. The name-calling was harsher. Some beloved books were taken. His bicycle was vandalized twice. Kids even kicked the cast that covered his broken ankle. And in front of his classmates, some guys poured chocolate milk down the front of his sweatshirt. . . . Curtis blamed himself for other kids not liking him. That night, Curtis went into a family bedroom, took out a gun, and shot himself to death.[57]

Of course, this is an extreme example of schoolyard sadism. All the same, it's the sort of thing that can go on when teachers, administrators, and parents abdicate their responsibility to shape the moral atmosphere of a school. In too many schools, bullying goes unchecked by authorities. Most bullying and harassment are nonsexual in nature. But their effects, as this example shows, can be devastating.

Dan Olweus, a psychologist who has done some of the most careful research on bullying, estimates that "eight or nine percent of kids are the targets of bullies."[58] Boys are targeted more often than girls but, as we see from cases such as those of Katie Lyle, Tawnya Brady, and Jane Doe, girls too are maliciously victimized. Schools today are not meeting their responsibilities to protect our children from peer cruelty. The girl advocates have succeeded in calling attention to the sexual mistreatment of girls, and they have succeeded in getting many anti–sexual harassment programs into the schools, but they have done so at the cost of distracting us from the generic problem of incivility and active malice that make school life today a nightmare for many children.

In contrast to European schools, where programs devoted to the problem of bullying are commonplace, many American schools have allocated most of their moral budget to the problem of eliminating sexual harassment. It is as if all indignation must be directed at *sexual* slights and harms suffered by girls at the hands of boys, since such sufferings serve as examples of how "our sexist society" harms women. There are, in consequence, many anti–sexual harassment programs in the schools and few genuine antibullying programs.

In the past few years, some of the girl advocates have paid lip service to the generic problem of bullying. One very popular teachers' guide published by the National Education Association is *Bullyproof: A Teacher's Guide on Teasing and Bullying for Use with Fourth and Fifth*

Grade Students. (One Wellesley research associate estimates that it is used by approximately ten thousand teachers.)[59] But this supposed antibullying guide devotes more than half of its lessons to sexism and sexual harassment. Students using it practice writing protest letters about sexual harassment to imaginary perpetrators. They draft sexual harassment policies. The guide instructs teachers to "Ask students to read aloud from the sexual harassment handout and, as they read along, to circle words they do not understand."[60] Why should a curriculum designed to help ten- and eleven-year-old children cope with bullying and meanness be so resolutely focused on sexism and sexual harassment?

The answer is that the antibullying content is simply a cover under which the girl advocates promote their own disquieting view of social reality. Getting into the schools with their harassment prevention programs gives them a platform from which to teach boys and girls that our society is male-dominated and sexist. Although that gets the feminist point across, it is an ineffective, expensive, distracting, and socially divisive substitute for the kind of moral education and safe environment that children so badly need.

Unfortunately, a recent Supreme Court ruling makes it quite likely that children are going to get more divisive gender politics and less genuine ethics education—for the time being, anyway.

A VERDICT OF HER OWN

ON MAY 24, 1999, a bitterly divided Supreme Court ruled 5–4 in favor of applying sexual harassment laws to schoolchildren. In the case before the Court *(Davis v. Monroe County Board of Education)*, Aurelia Davis sued the Monroe [Georgia] School Board for half a million dollars because her daughter LaShonda, a ten-year-old in Forsyth, had suffered what she described as a five-month "barrage of sexual harassment and abuse" from a classmate, identified as G.F. According to Ms. Davis, ten-year-old G.F., who sat next to her daughter, had propositioned her, grabbed her breasts, and generally tormented her. The suit charges school officials with having failed to enforce LaShonda's civil rights to be protected from sexual discrimination as guaranteed under Title IX of the Education Amendments of 1972.

Justice Sandra Day O'Connor (joined by Justices Ruth Bader Ginsburg, Stephen Breyer, John Paul Stevens, and David Souter) wrote the majority opinion. "Students," she wrote, "must not be denied access to educational benefits and opportunity on the basis of gender." O'Connor pointed out that peer sexual harassment may be "so severe, pervasive, and objectively offensive that it effectively bars the victims' access to an educational opportunity or benefit."

Justice Anthony Kennedy was joined by Justices William Rehnquist, Clarence Thomas, and Antonin Scalia in opposing the decision. Kennedy, who wrote the dissent, was so outraged by the majority's decision that he took the unusual measure of standing up and reading passages of his dissenting opinion from the bench. (Justices do this on very rare occasions when they find the majority decision especially egregious.) The majority's decision, he said, "will breed a climate of fear that encourages school administrators to label even the most innocuous of child conduct sexual harassment." He predicted a flood of litigation. O'Connor answered that far from teaching little Johnny a "perverse lesson in federalism," as the dissenters alleged, the majority was simply trying to ensure "that little Mary may attend class."

Who could disagree with O'Connor? Who could argue against the principle that little Mary has the right to attend school in safety? However, this was not a case about children's safety. After all, school safety is as much or more a boy's issue as a girl's. When the Educational Testing Service asked eighth graders how safe they felt in school, it found that 7 percent of girls and 11 percent of boys "felt unsafe or very unsafe." [61] In another study, the U.S. Department of Education found that among students aged twelve to nineteen, 5.1 percent of males and 3.3 percent of females had experienced violent victimization at school. [62]

What O'Connor was called upon to explain was why threats to Mary's safety and peace of mind when she is bullied in a sexual way trigger federal action, but everyday threats to Johnny do not. The plain and simple fact is this: far more boys than girls face bullying that is "so severe, pervasive and objectively offensive that it effectively bars the victims access to an educational opportunity or benefit." If school safety is the issue, why is Mary's predicament more pressing to the Supreme Court than Johnny's?

Children torment and humiliate one another for all sorts of reasons; sex is just one of dozens. Kennedy noted as much in his dissent:

The girl who wants to skip recess because she is teased by the boys is no different from the overweight child who skips gym class because other children tease her about her size in the locker room; or the child who risks flunking out because he refuses to wear glasses to avoid the taunts of "four eyes"; or the child who refuses to go to school because the school bully calls him a "scaredy cat" at recess.

Justice Kennedy questioned the propriety and utility of labeling G.F.'s behavior "gender discrimination." Women's groups have a ready answer. They view sexual harassment as a kind of hate crime used by men to maintain and enforce the inferior status of women: little G.F. did not merely upset and frighten LaShonda, he demeaned her as a member of a socially subordinate group. The National Organization for Women explained clearly and succinctly why schoolyard harassment was discriminatory in its 1998 "Issue Report" on sexual harassment: "Sexual harassment is a form of violence against women used to keep women 'in their place.' . . . Our schools, in many respects, are training grounds for sexual harassment. Boys are rarely punished . . . while girls are taught that it is their role to tolerate this humiliating conduct."[63]

The theory that sexual misconduct in our schools is part of a general endeavor by males to keep women socially subordinate is not far short of paranoid. Moreover, it conveniently ignores the fact that girls do almost as much harassing as boys. It assumes that boys have more power than girls in our schools. But boys are just as insecure as girls and just as vulnerable to humiliation and mistreatment. The root problem in our schools is poor discipline and too many children acting maliciously with impunity.

By interpreting peer sexual harassment as a form of sexual discrimination, the Supreme Court seems implicitly to accept something like NOW's official view that "harassment is . . . used to keep women 'in their place.'" But why would five justices adopt the logic of the women's advocacy groups instead of the commonsense view voiced by Justice Kennedy?

The answer is simple: gender politics. Dozens of partisan groups have spent the past decade disseminating false statistics "showing" how vulnerable girls are, dramatizing their educational deficits, explaining how our schools are "training grounds for domestic violence," how "violence is the leading cause of death to women," how the status of girls is an "unacknowledged American tragedy." The precarious condition of the American girl is now part of the conventional wisdom. In this climate, in which our government and judiciary also live, it only seems right and just for little Mary to have a Supreme Court ruling of her very own.

The Court must always be fair. As matters now stand, the courts and the government, in effect, discriminate against boys on a fundamental issue: girls, being default victims of "discrimination," have a mantle of federal protection for their right to attend class that boys don't have. Moreover, with the new decision, boys are worse off than ever before. Schools, fearful of ruinous lawsuits, will treat normal boys as proto-harassers.

The Supreme Court ruling will no doubt generate more *Quit-It!*s, more workshops with "rape-imaging" exercises, and more readings on temporary restraining orders for seventh-graders. Groups such as NOW, the Wellesley Center, the AAUW, and the WEEA, ever eager to enter the nation's schools and take on the job of educating the nation's children about "gender equity," will be even more welcome.

The Supreme Court made a serious mistake in the *Davis* case. This is the same Court that in 1997 badly underestimated the disruptive effect of a harassment lawsuit on the normal functioning of the presidency. Now it has decided that applying sexual harassment laws to children will not disrupt the schools. It could not be more wrong.

WHAT IS IN STORE FOR BOYS?

WE WILL BE on the road to genuine fairness when school boards, principals, and teachers begin to focus in an objective way on the moral and cognitive development of all the children in their care. Children and teenagers need strong moral guidance. They need firm codes of discipline in a school environment that does not tolerate egregious meanness or gross incivility, whether sexual or nonsexual. They do not need divisive sexual politics, court judgments, and school policies that bear down hard on boys.

If parents begin to stand up for their sons, if they refuse to allow schools to subject them to the tender mercies of the self-styled equity specialists, the prospects of America's boys will brighten immeasurably. In the meantime, the undeclared war on boys continues to gather force.

CHAPTER THREE

GUYS AND DOLLS

IN THE SUMMER OF 1997, I took part in a television debate with feminist lawyer Gloria Allred.[1] Allred was representing a fourteen-year-old girl who was suing the Boy Scouts of America for excluding girls. Girls fifteen and older can join the Explorer Scouts, which are coed, but Allred was outraged that girls younger than fifteen are not allowed in. She referred to same-sex scouting as a form of "gender apartheid."

I pointed out that younger boys and girls have markedly different preferences and behaviors, citing the following homespun example: Hasbro Toys, a major toy-manufacturing company, tested a playhouse the company was considering marketing to both boys and girls. But it soon emerged that girls and boys did not interact with the structure in the same way. The girls dressed the dolls, kissed them, and played house; the boys catapulted the toy baby carriage from the roof. A Hasbro general manager came up with an explanation: boys and girls are different.[2]

Allred flatly denied that there are any innate differences. She seemed shocked by the boys' catapulting behavior. Apparently, she took it as a sign of a propensity to violence. She said, "If there are some boys who catapult baby carriages off the roofs of dollhouses, that is just an argument why we need to socialize boys at an earlier age, perhaps, to be playing with dolls. . . ."

Allred has powerful allies. Resocializing boys in the direction of femininity is now high on the educational agenda of many educators, women's institutes, and government officials. Notably active on this front of the undeclared war against boys are the Harvard Graduate School of Education, the Wellesley College Center for Research on Women, and the U.S. Department of Education.

A WELLESLEY COLLEGE EQUITY SEMINAR

IN 1998, THE WELLESLEY COLLEGE CENTER for Research on Women sponsored a daylong teacher-training seminar entitled "Gender Equity for Girls *and* Boys: A Conference for K–12 Teachers and Administrators." It attracted two hundred teachers and administrators from the Northeast. By attending the conference, teachers could receive state credits toward recertification. One session, "Dolls, Gender and Make-Believe: Gender Equity in the Early Childhood Classroom," was concerned with sex stereotypes and how to defeat them. It was led by Dr. Nancy Marshall, a senior research scientist and associate director of the Wellesley Center, and two of her associates.

According to Marshall, a child's sexual identity is learned by observing others. As she noted, "When babies are born, they do not know about gender." Since babies know very little about anything, Marshall's comment was puzzling. They don't know their blood type either, after all, but they still have one. Marshall explained that gender, which is indeterminate at birth, is formed and fixed later by a process of socialization that guides the child to adopt a male or a female identity. According to Marshall and her colleagues, a child learns what it means to be a boy or girl between the ages of two and seven. In those early years the child develops a "gender schema": a set of ideas about appropriate roles, attitudes, and preferences for males and females. The best prospects for influencing the child's gender schema are in these early, malleable years: these years are the opportunity zone.

Marshall and her associates presented a slide show, explaining, "A young mind is like Jell-O: you learn to fill it up with all the good stuff before it sets." What counts as "good stuff" for the Wellesley pedagogues is making children as comfortable as possible participating in activities traditionally associated with the other gender. One favorite slide (to which they came back several times) showed a preschool boy dressed up in high heels and a dress. "It's perfectly natural for a little boy to try on a skirt," they said. Perhaps, but what is the teacher who is promoting this activity trying to achieve?

The group leaders suggested that teachers "use water and bathing" to encourage boys to play with dolls. Acknowledging that preschoolers tend to prefer same-sex play, which reinforces "gender stereotypes," they advised teachers in the audience to "force boy/girl mixed pairs."

In a follow-up discussion, one of the participating teachers boasted of her success in getting boys in her kindergarten class to dress up in skirts. Another proudly reported that she makes a point of informing boys that their action figures are really dolls.

At no time during this eight-hour conference did any of the two hundred participating teachers and administrators question the assumption that gender identity is a learned characteristic. Nor did anyone mention the large and growing body of scientific literature from biologists and developmental psychologists, which I will survey later in this chapter, showing that many male-female differences, beyond the obvious physical ones, are natural, healthy, and, by implication, best left alone. On the contrary, everyone assumed that preschool children are as malleable as putty and can easily be socialized to adopt one or the other gender identity to suit the ends of equity and social justice.

EARLY INTERVENTIONS

THE U.S. DEPARTMENT OF EDUCATION is very involved in promoting "gender equity" in the schools. The Women's Educational Equity Act Publishing Center (the national resource center for "gender-fair materials" maintained by the Department of Education) distributes pamphlets that confidently assert the social origins of gender. Here, for example, is a passage from the center's guide entitled *Gender Equity for Educators, Parents, and Community:* "We know that biological, psychological, and intellectual differences between males and females are minimal during early childhood. Nevertheless, in our society we tend to socialize children in ways that serve to emphasize gender-based differences."[3]

In fact, "we know" no such thing. A recent special issue of *Scientific American* reviewed the growing evidence that children's play preferences are, in large part, hormonally determined.[4] Doreen Kimura, a psychologist at Vancouver's Simon Fraser University, writes, "We know, for instance, from observations of both humans and nonhumans that males are more aggressive than females, that young males engage in more rough-and-tumble play, and that females are more nurturing. . . . How do these and other sex differences come about? . . . It appears that perhaps the most important factor in the differentiation of males and females is the level of exposure to various sex hormones early in life."[5]

Department of Education personnel engaged in promoting gender equity in the schools ignore this scientific research, assuming along with Allred and the Wellesley Center experts that typical male and female play preferences are caused by faulty socialization. The Department of Education's Office of Educational Research and Improvement, for example, supported the development of a model curriculum guide for day care teachers, *Creating Sex-Fair Family Day Care,* which offers concrete suggestions on how to change current male and female sex-role "stereotyping" in early childhood.[6] The guide points out that the report was funded by the Department of Education and distributed under the auspices of its Women's Educational Equity Act, adding, however, that "no official endorsement of the Department should be inferred." Nevertheless, with "Office of Educational Research & Improvement, U.S. Department of Education" on the front cover, most readers will naturally assume that the booklet has the imprimatur of the government. Indeed, it is easy to mistake it for an official government document.

The central thesis of the guide is that the one and only way to defeat harmful gender roles is by intervening in the process of gender stereotyping of boys and girls as early in the children's lives as possible, preferably in infancy. Masculine stereotypes receive the lion's share of attention. Getting little boys to play with dolls is a principal goal. The 130-page guide includes ten photographs: two show a little boy with a baby girl doll; in one, he is feeding her, in the other, kissing her. The guide urges day care teachers to reinforce the boys' nurturing side: "It is important for both boys and girls to learn nurturing and sensitivity, as well as general parenting skills. Have as many boy dolls available as girl dolls (preferably anatomically correct). Boys and girls should be encouraged to play with them."[7] Just as little girls greatly enjoy the exaggerated femininity and glamour of Barbie, so little boys enjoy the exaggerated masculinity of G.I. Joe. But in the name of "nonsexist child rearing" the manual asks day care providers to "avoid highly feminine dolls such as Barbie or highly masculine dolls such as G.I. Joe."[8] Ever on the alert for "gender stereotypes" in dolls, the guide warns child care workers to "be wary of charming Momma Bears . . . wearing little aprons and holding a broom in one hand."[9]

A vigilant egalitarianism is the order of the day. One nursery rhyme recommended by the guide is a second verse for the popular "Jack and Jill" rhyme. In addition to being egalitarian (the second stanza evens things out by putting Jill's name first), it has the virtue of promoting safety awareness, something glaringly missing in the first verse:

> *Jill and Jack went up the track*
> *To fetch the pail again.*
> *They climbed with care, got safely there*
> *And finished the job they began.*[10]

This government-sponsored day care guide also urges vigilant monitoring of children's fantasy play: "Watch your children at play. Are stereotypes present in the fantasies and situations they act out? Intervene to set the record straight. 'Why don't you be the doctor, Amy, and you the nurse, Billy?'"[11] The end to be achieved justifies the interventions: Unless we practice nonsexist child rearing, "we cannot fulfill our dreams of equality for all people."[12]

GIRLS AND BOYS "DECIDED" TO SWITCH GENDER ROLES

LINDA KEKELIS and Barbara Buswell are AAUW-funded workshoppers who tour schools in Northern California instructing parents and teachers on how to help young children "grow beyond gender."[13] In their ninety-minute sessions they tell their audiences how parental conditioning causes children to develop different play preferences. According to Kekelis, "Girls are praised when they play with dolls, while boys are likely to be ignored by their parents when displaying nurturing behavior." Such gender-specific play, they point out, is constraining and limiting and an obstacle to true equity.

One Kekelis/Buswell workshop inspired Janice Lillard of Glenview Elementary School in Oakland to help her second-graders become more gender-conscious.[14] She reported unexpected success when the boys and girls decided to swap roles in their traditional end-of-the-year class play. "The remarkable thing," says Lillard, "is that they came up with the idea of switching roles completely on their own."[15]

Well, hardly on their own. The lessons inculcated all year by Lillard must surely have conveyed to her seven-year-old pupils that the sex-role reversal would be just the thing to please her. Indeed, the truly "remarkable thing" is that Lillard could deceive herself into thinking that the children's decision to switch boy-girl roles was spontaneous and not caused by indoctrination. Such self-deception is common among equity educators. It never seems to occur to them that they are tampering with children's individuality or intruding on their privacy.

Elisabeth Krents, admissions director at Dalton, one of New York City's elite private schools, boasts of her school's determination to get rid of conventional boy-girl behaviors: "We don't say, 'Okay, boys into the dress-up corner, girls into the block area,' but we build it into everything we do. In second grade, right now, they are studying Grimms' fairy tales, analyzing the gender stereotypes."[16]

In one class, the second-graders act out and analyze *Rumpelstilt-skin* using "gender blind" casting.[17] If the miller's daughter succeeds in spinning the straw into gold the king (played by a girl) will marry her. If she fails, he will have her killed. With the aid of the dwarf Rumpelstilt-skin, she succeeds. "Do you think this is a good marriage for her?" the teacher asks the class. One girl points out that "she has a husband who almost killed her." And the teacher drives home the point: "There are three men who have power over her life. A real patriarchal situation."

It is hard to imagine seven-year-old boys and girls enjoying such a didactic exercise. It conjures up images of children in China during the Cultural Revolution "analyzing" stories for themes of capitalist imperialism.

WILLIAM'S DOLL

BOYS WHO are subjected to the practice of "nonsexist child rearing" sometimes openly resist it. In their 1994 book, *Failing at Fairness*, Myra and David Sadker describe a fourth-grade class in Maryland in which the teacher worked with the boys to help them "push the borders of the male stereotype."[18] She asked them to imagine themselves as authors of an advice column in their local newspaper. One day they receive the following letter:

> Dear Adviser:
> My seven-year old son wants me to buy him a doll. I don't know what to do. Should I go ahead and get it for him. Is this normal, or is my son sick? Please help!

The nine-year-old "advisers" were extremely unsympathetic to the boy. The teacher then read aloud from a popular feminist book, *William's Doll*. It is a story about a boy who wants a doll "to hug it and cradle it in his arms."[19] His father refuses and tries instead to interest him in a basketball or an electric train. But William persists in wanting the doll. When his grandmother arrives, she gently scolds the father for thwarting William's wish. She takes William to the store and buys him "a baby doll with curly eyelashes, and a long white dress with a bonnet." William "loved it right away."[20]

The story did little to change the fourth-graders' minds. According to the Sadkers, "Their reaction was so hostile, the teacher had trouble keeping order."[21] A few reluctantly agreed that the boy could have a doll—but only if it was a G.I. Joe. The Sadkers were surprised that boys so young could be so inflexibly traditional: "As we observed her lesson, we were struck by how much effort it took to stretch outmoded attitudes."[22]

William's Doll has been made into a play. Boston University professor Glenn Loury tells of sitting through a production at his son's elementary school in Brookline, Massachusetts, in 1998. Loury, father of two boys (one was starring in the play), was not impressed, "First of all, what is wrong with wanting your boy not to play with a doll but to play baseball? I mean, there is nothing that needs to be fixed there."[23]

Loury speaks for many fathers and mothers. However, his voice and sensibility count for naught with the "gender scholars" in our schools of education or the equity experts at Wellesley and Harvard and in the U.S. Department of Education who are determined to release boys from their "straitjacket of masculinity." These reformers shape the attitudes and policy of an increasingly large number of schools. They are convinced that breaking down male stereotypes, starting in preschool, is good for society. None of them openly wonders whether encouraging boys to be more feminine is good for them or whether boys' resentment of the pressure to be more feminine is anything more than "backlash" or the expression of "outmoded attitudes."

In day care centers and elementary schools, the children targeted for resocialization are unaware of their teachers' intentions; nor have the taxpayers, who subsidize the equity workshops, the WEEA guides, and the myriad "gender-is-a-social-construction" college courses, been informed about this project. Nor, in particular, is this attitude known to that segment of the public who take their little boys to school every day, unaware that their "gender schemas" are to be modified by the boy reformers in ways conducive to achieving "our dreams of equality for all people."

Ms. Logan's Classroom

A LOT CAN BE LEARNED by looking into classrooms where teachers are actively attacking the "gender schemas" of their pupils. Peggy Orenstein's *SchoolGirls: Young Women, Self-Esteem, and the Confidence Gap* was written in association with the American Association of University Women.[24] Just after the AAUW had alerted the country to the plight of its shortchanged adolescent girls, Orenstein visited several middle schools to see at first hand how they were coping with the confidence gap. As a trusted insider, Orenstein was given full access to classrooms where teachers are preoccupied with raising the gender consciousness of students. From her detailed report, we get a good understanding of how the new gender specialists view boys and what they have in mind for them.

The climactic section of *SchoolGirls* is entitled "Anita Hill Is a Boy: Tales from a Gender-Fair Classroom." There Orenstein describes the classroom of Ms. Judy Logan, an award-winning English and social studies teacher at the Everett Middle School, a public school in San Francisco. Logan has gone as far as anyone in transforming her classroom into a woman-centered community of learners. Indeed, Logan is something of a pedagogical legend among girl-partisan activists. Jackie DeFazio, former president of the AAUW, says that a teacher like Logan, "who puts equity at the center of her classroom," fills her with hope.[25] Mary Pipher, author of *Reviving Ophelia*, praises Logan for offering "a new vision of what our schools can give to our children."[26]

Susan Faludi, author of *Backlash: The Undeclared War Against Women* and *Stiffed: The Betrayal of the American Man*, urges everyone who cares about "the future of our next generation" to read Orenstein's book, saying it "powerfully illuminates the forces that . . . break the precarious confidence of American girls."[27] I agree it should be read, but for reasons different from Faludi's: *SchoolGirls* is must reading for anyone who cares about the future of the nation's boys.

When Orenstein stepped into Logan's classroom for the first time, she found it "somewhat of a shock." There are images of women everywhere:

> The faces of Abigail Adams, Rachel Carson, Faye Wattleton, and even a fanciful "Future Woman" smile out from three student-made quilts that are draped on the walls. . . . Reading racks overflow with biographies of Lucretia Mott, Ida B. Wells, Sally Ride and Rigoberta Menchú. . . . There is a section on Pele, the Hawaiian goddess of volcanoes.[28]

At first Orenstein found herself wondering "Where are the men?" But then, in one of those characteristic "click" moments that feminists often report, the explanation dawned and all became clear: "In Ms. Logan's class, girls may be dazzled by the reflection of the women that surround them. And, perhaps for the first time, the boys are the ones looking through the window."[29]

In her sixth-grade social studies class, Logan asked each student to assume the role of a prominent African American and to deliver a dramatic monologue in that person's voice. She found that boys never chose to be women, so she started requiring two presentations: one as a woman, the other as a man. When Orenstein visited the class, it was Jeremy's turn to perform.

Jeremy had chosen blues singer Etta James as his subject. He spoke of her great achievements in music as well as her struggles with drugs. He then turned on a tape recorder and began to lip-synch a song. Some of the boys could not resist giggling, and soon Jeremy himself dissolved in laughter. Ms. Logan was not pleased, saying, "Class, I'd like you to understand the interaction between the audience and the performer. If you laugh it is very hard for Jeremy to stay in character, but if you support him, he can take risks."[30]

Soon it was Nick's turn. This "thin boy with carrot-colored hair, milky skin and freckles," had chosen to be Anita Hill. He ended the monologue by declaiming, "I had to have the courage to speak out against sexual harassment for other women in this country. So they could speak out too, and become strong."[31]

Logan was overjoyed. "Dr. Hill," she said to Nick, "I am a great admirer of yours. . . . Give her a hand, everyone." And Orenstein comments, "Even though she is gesturing to a boy—who in most cases would undoubtedly be ashamed to be called 'her' in front of forty peers—no one even flinches. Instead, the students burst into applause. And Nick, who has, if only for a few minutes, lived the experience of a sexually harassed woman, takes a seat."[32]

Logan's classes are unusual and fun. She is popular with her students. But according to Orenstein, many students complain that she is unfair to boys. One sixth-grader, Holly, said, "Sometimes I worry about the boys, that they kind of get ignored." Another said that her brother had taken one of Ms. Logan's classes, "and all she ever talked about was women women women. And he did not like it." Even the girls get tired of all the women-centeredness. Orenstein reports one as complaining, "Ms. Logan, I feel like I am not learning anything about men and I do not think that is right." Orenstein attributes the girls' objections to their low self-esteem; because of the "hidden curriculum," girls "have already become used to taking up less space, to feeling less worthy of attention than boys."

In one history class, the girls take over the discussion and go after the boys for being sexual predators. As the girls get angrier, Logan gets more animated. The girls' anger is the sign that her pedagogy is working: "This is a very important, scary, and profound conversation you are having."[33] What do the boys have to say for themselves?

One boy tries to placate the girls: "It's true that some guys are assholes in school. But there are nice people too."[34] During a subsequent male-bashing session, a Latino girl points out that though sexual harassment happens to girls more often, girls do it to boys as well: "We go up and feel on guys too."[35]

"That's a good point," says Logan—but not one she chooses to pursue. She soon stops the discussion: "We've gotten a lot done on this, but the class isn't about sexual harassment. It's American Women Making History."[36] But later she will return to the topic of sexual harassment and explain to her students how it is a part of a "hidden curriculum" that teaches girls to be second-class citizens: "They learn to become silent, careful, not active or assertive in life."[37]

Logan's pedagogy turns out to have its own hidden curriculum, which she teaches in every class, no matter what the subject. It is unflattering to males, and they learn the lesson. Luis, a seventh-grader, later confessed to Orenstein, "I couldn't really defend myself, because it's true. Men are pigs, you know?"[38]

As a final "unifying project," Logan's sixth-grade social studies class made a quilt to celebrate "women we admire." Logan was alarmed by Jimmy's muslin square. He had chosen to honor the tennis player Monica Seles, who, in 1993, was stabbed on court by a deranged man. Jimmy had stitched a bloody knife on a tennis racquet. It's not the sort of thing a girl would think of. Jimmy's square may be unique in the history of quilting, but Ms. Logan did not appreciate its originality. She insisted he start again and make an acceptable contribution to the class quilt.

I can see why Logan did not want Jimmy's square on the quilt. But what I think Jimmy was doing was looking for some way—within the oppressive confines of a feminist quilting environment—to assert his young maleness, which was under direct assault by his teacher.

Logan, clearly exasperated, did not see it that way. She confided to Orenstein, "When boys feel like they're being forced to admire women they try to pick one that they think behaves sort of like a man." Jimmy is left looking "despondently" at his rejected square.

Jeremy, the boy who portrayed Etta James, showed more progress. He had recently written an essay in praise of Anita Hill, which he had submitted to the regional National Organization for Women essay contest on "Women We Admire." His muslin quilting square celebrating Rosa Parks had been done to Logan's specifications. When he handed it in, Logan turned to Orenstein, saying, "This is how you teach about gender. You do it one stitch at a time."[39] Much taken by that remark, Orenstein used it to end her book.

FEMINIZING BOYS

JUDY LOGAN openly practices a feminizing pedagogy that embodies the goals and ideals of the gender-equity movement. If that movement continues in its current direction, more and more schools will be valorizing females, teaching history in a woman-centered way, inspiring boys to revere Anita Hill and to "enjoy" quilting. Few teachers are as extreme or committed as Logan, but the world of gender-equity workshops is her world, and teachers everywhere are exposed to it and encouraged to move in this direction. In practice, this comes down to monitoring and policing boys' stereotypical masculine behavior and getting them to participate in characteristically feminine activities. In the name of gender equity, the tolerant adage "Boys will be boys" is being replaced by "Down with *la différence!*"

Here is how *The Boston Globe* describes one gender-fair school in Lexington, Massachusetts.

> Four years after it created its gender equity committee, Fiske Elementary is rife with signs of raised awareness of gender. A quilt of famous women, sewn by fifth-grade boys and girls, is displayed in the front hall. A wood sign on principal Joanne Benton's door declares this to be the "Princessipal's Office." Benton proudly maintains that "we have no single-sex table in our lunch room, and at recess, boys and girls play kickball together."[40]

Fiske Elementary encourages boys to engage in activities traditionally associated with girls, such as sewing quilts. At the same time, the school discourages activities that are natural and traditional to boys, such as congregating together in the playground to play ball with one another.

The pressures for social egalitarianism are unremitting and take various forms. Alex Longo, a second-grade boy in East Windsor, New Jersey, was not allowed to pass out invitations to his birthday party; he had invited only boys, and his teacher and school principal deemed this sexist and discriminatory. Alex still does not understand his offense. Incidents such as this rarely become public, but in this case the father complained, and the story got into the press. When a reporter asked the little boy how he felt about the episode, he said, "I went in the cloak closet and cried. I felt really bad." [41]

An education professor at the University of North Carolina (Greensboro) and three coinvestigators observed a class of fifth-graders at the elementary school in Guilford, North Carolina. Here are some "inequitable interactions" they noted in *Education Leadership:* "We stayed for lunch that day and observed a sex-segregated fifth grade in the school cafeteria: boys at one table and girls at another. At recess boys played kickball and girls huddled around the sidewalk and talked with one another. But as the AAUW pointed out in 1992, most of the students did not show dissatisfaction with the way things were." [42]

The observers regarded the children's lack of dissatisfaction as something that needed to be corrected. For the next few months, they staged equity "interventions" designed to raise the children's gender consciousness. These researchers never questioned the doctrine that gender styles and preferences are socially determined. It did not seriously occur to them that the children's behavior might have little to do with the way they had been socialized and much to do with their nature as boys and girls. These teachers and school administrators—in Massachusetts, New Jersey, North Carolina, and New York—embrace the belief that gender-fair schools will require a new pedagogy that upsets and neutralizes many behavioral conventions associated with being a boy or a girl.

Shaping the gender identities of schoolchildren is a heady enterprise. And it is inspired and informed by the ideas of gender experts in some of our great universities. Preeminent among these is Carol Gilligan and her colleagues at the Harvard Graduate School of Education. They see themselves as participating in a profound revolution that will change the way society constructs young males. Once boys are freed of oppressive gender roles, they foresee a change in boys' play preferences.

In 1996, *The Boston Globe* described a joint lecture on boys by Gilligan and her associate Elizabeth Debold before "a standing-room-only crowd in the 250-seat auditorium" at a private school in Watertown, Massachusetts. [43] Gilligan and Debold explained that so-called male behaviors—roughhousing and aggressive competition—are not natural but are artifacts of culture. According to Debold, "Children don't start knowing what boys and girls are . . . it takes time to learn that boy/girl is a category." Superheroes and macho toys, she said, cause boys to be "angry and act aggressively." Showing the way to rectify this, Debold reported on their studies of three- and four-year-old boys who are comfortable playing dress-up and house with girls.

The idea that boys ought to be more comfortable in feminine activities is in vogue among academics in the emerging field of men's studies.[44] Like Gilligan and Debold, the practitioners of men's studies are concerned about the bad effects that masculine stereotypes have on the psyches of the nation's boys. According to William Pollack (director of the Center for Men at McLean Hospital and author of *Real Boys: Rescuing Our Sons from the Myths of Boyhood*) and Ronald F. Levant (a Boston University psychologist and cofounder of the Society for the Psychological Study of Men and Masculinity), the reconstructed psychologically healthy boys of the future will be raised without pressures to conform to masculine archetypes: "As we raise the next generation, the boys who will become men in the twenty-first century, we look forward to a time when these boys will be able to safely stay in the 'doll corner' as long as they wish, without being taunted. . . . "[45]

WHERE THE EQUITY ENTHUSIASTS GO WRONG

THE IDEA that girls and boys are the same and that masculinity and femininity are simply a matter of social conditioning have the status of first principles in schools of education, women's studies and gender studies departments, and the U.S. Department of Education. What follows from this is the notion that what society has constructed amiss can be torn down and reconstructed—in the *right* way. It is assumed that, at bottom, we are all essentially androgynous.

The feminist philosopher Sandra Lee Bartky speaks for many gender scholars when she says that human beings are born "bisexual" into our patriarchal society and then, through social conditioning, are "transformed into male and female gender personalities, the one destined to command, the other to obey."[46]

Even the so-called difference feminists—Carol Gilligan and her school, Sara Ruddick, and other feminist philosophers who celebrate certain feminine qualities, such as caring, nurturing, and social sensitivity—believe that these differences are socially constructed and should be constructed differently.

This doctrine does not stand up well under critical scrutiny. A growing body of empirical data that is rarely if ever mentioned in the gender-equity training seminars strongly supports the experience of parents and the wisdom of the ages: that many basic male-female differences are innate, hardwired, and not the result of conditioning. In the past few years, there have been important developments in neuroscience, evolutionary psychology, genetics, and neuroendocrinology that all but refute the social constructionist thesis and point to certain inborn gender differences.[47]

Males, for instance, are, on average, better at spatial reasoning than females.[48] They are more adept at rotating three-dimensional geometric figures in their minds, and they perform better on spatial manipulation tests. Males' superior skills in this area give them an advantage in math, engineering, and architecture. Of course, there are females with exceptional abilities in spatial reasoning, but, taken as a whole, males have a slight but distinct edge.

Females, on the other hand, have better verbal skills.[49] It has long been known that girls begin talking earlier and that speech and reading disorders such as dyslexia are more common in males. On most national assessment tests, females are well ahead of males in reading and writing. Unsurprisingly, many more females than males major in English, comparative literature, and foreign languages.

Girls' verbal skills may be responsible for their superior emotional expressiveness. Daniel Goleman, a science writer at *The New York Times* and author of *Emotional Intelligence,* reports on one explanation that ties early language facility to emotional style: "Because girls develop language more quickly than do boys, this leads them to be more experienced at articulating their feelings and more skilled than boys at using words to explore and substitute for emotional reactions such as physical fights."[50] Although Goleman believes girls' verbal skills may give them an emotional edge, he does not believe it makes them nicer than boys. As he sees it, girls' more rapid development of interpersonal skills and boys' physical superiority make for different styles of aggression: "By age 13 . . . girls become more adept than boys at artful aggressive tactics like ostracism, vicious gossip, and indirect vendettas . . . Boys, by and large, simply continue being confrontational when angered, oblivious to these more covert strategies."[51]

Go to any large toy mart and you will find sections for boys and sections for girls answering to their different preferences. For boys, gadgets and action are the things, while girls prefer dolls, glamour, and play-houses. Many a parent will tell you of failed efforts to get daughters interested in Lincoln logs and sons in sewing kits. Being differently talented and differently driven, the sexes have characteristically differ-ent behavior preferences. The gender-equity specialists believe that gender-distinct play preferences are purely a matter of social condition-ing. But researchers have confirmed what parents experience all the time: even without conditioning (indeed, even with countercondition-ing), boys and girls show different preferences and gravitate toward dif-ferent toys.

The exceptions only go to prove the rule. One group of girls does consistently prefer trucks over dolls: girls with congenital adrenal hy-perplasia (CAH). This is a genetic defect that results when the female fetus is subjected to abnormally large quantities of male hormones called adrenal androgens. CAH girls tend to grow up to be more aggressive than their non-CAH sisters. UCLA psychologists Sheri Berenbaum and Melissa Hines set up an experiment in which they observed the play be-havior of both CAH and non-CAH girls. They found that "the CAH girls spent significantly more time playing with boys' toys than did control girls."[52] CAH girls, incidentally, are also better at spatial rotation tests than their unaffected sisters.[53]

These sorts of findings, while not definitive, certainly do not square with the crude view that "gender is a social construct." If all gender dif-ferences were culturally determined, you would expect to find some so-cieties where females are the risk takers and males play with dolls. There would be societies in which females, on average, would do better in math and young males would be more verbally adept than females. But where are they? The social contructionists have no plausible explanation for the absence of such societies. But there are many plausible explanations for the distinctive gender differences in special aptitudes and characteristic behaviors that are grounded in biology, endocrinology, and evolutionary psychology. Quite apart from the sexual difference in reproductive func-tions, men and women are innately distinguished in "gender." Mother Nature is not a feminist.

The natural gender differences between men and women mean we cannot hope to get statistical male-female parity of competence and apti-tude in all fields. The same seems true of preferences: there will always be far more women than men who want to stay home with children; there will always be more women than men who want to be kindergarten teachers rather than helicopter mechanics. Boys will always be less interested than girls in dollhouses. This does not mean that our sex rigidly determines our future. The anthropologist Lionel Tiger has it right when he says, "Biology is not destiny, but it is good statistical probability."

INTERDICTED RESEARCH

ALTHOUGH COMMON SENSE is on the side of "la différence," scientists studying how physiological sex differences correlate with differences in preferences and aptitudes are subject to angry attacks. Feminist Gloria Steinem has called research on sex differences "anti-American." She says, "It is what is keeping us down." [54] According to Gloria Allred, such research simply should not be done: "This is harmful and dangerous to our daughters' lives, to our mothers' lives, and I am very angry about it." [55]

Laura Allen, a neuroanatomist at UCLA, is doing just the kind of work deplored by Steinem and Allred. She says, "As I began to look at the human brain, I kept finding differences. Seven or eight of the ten structures we measured turned out be different between men and women." [56] One example is the corpus callosum, a thick bundle of nerves that connects the two hemispheres of the brain. It is wider in the female brain, perhaps allowing for a better connection between the two hemispheres. But Allen reports that critics have warned her not to do this work. They say, "It's too provocative." [57]

Bennett and Sally Shaywitz, neuroscientists at Yale University, are also doing work that is unwelcome in many quarters. They are using new brain-imaging technologies—specifically functional magnetic resonance imaging (MRI)—to look for sex differences in the brain. In one experiment, they gave nineteen men and nineteen women volunteer subjects a simple language task (matching pairs of rhyming nonsense words). The results were striking and were featured on the cover of *Nature*. In both men and women, the front of the cortex in the left hemisphere lit up brightly, indicating that to be the area where this task is carried out. But in eleven of the nineteen women—and none of the men—an area in the right hemisphere also lit up. If two parts of the female brain focus on language, this might explain the female advantage in this area.[58]

Ruben and Raquel Gur and their colleagues at the University of Pennsylvania Medical School are also using the new imaging technology to study brain metabolism. In one 1995 study, men showed higher metabolic activity in the part of the brain known as the "old limbic system," a structure humans share with reptiles. Women showed greater activity in the cingulate gyrus, a "higher," more recently evolved part of the limbic brain that humans share with other primates. One journalist characterized the Gurs' findings this way: "The bottom line is that men are emotional reptiles—they tend to lash out when upset—whereas women are like monkeys: they sit down and chat about it."[59] When Raquel Gur presented her research to a group of female medical students, several approached her with the request that she not publicize her work.[60]

The precise significance of the findings of Allen, the Shaywitzes, and the Gurs on the nature/nurture question is yet to be determined. Because the early environment can change the brain, discoveries of anatomical and neurological differences do not decisively confirm a biological basis for behavior and psychological differences. Nevertheless, there is increasing evidence that some masculine and feminine traits may be hardwired.

But in the gender-equity workshops, the women's research institutes, and Department of Education publications, it is as if none of this evidence exists. Indeed, if some social constructionists could have their way, no such evidence *would* exist. For most of her career, Alice Eagly, a psychologist at Northwestern University, was a devout believer in what she now calls the "entrenched consensus": the view that sexual stereotypes and preferences are not biologically but culturally determined. In 1995, she published a kind of recantation in the *American Psychologist*, essentially saying that she and her colleagues had been in denial.[61] At an annual meeting of the American Psychological Association, Eagly presented the data that had persuaded her to abandon the entrenched viewpoint. The audience's reaction was stormy: "Some people were stamping their feet. Other[s] were glowering."[62] She now deplores the fact that many supposedly current contemporary psychology textbooks continue to inculcate the "outdated consensus."

MISOGYNIST PHILOSOPHERS

WHY DOES Gloria Steinem consider the study of sex differences to be un-American? Why is Gloria Allred so incensed? Why do Laura Allen, Raquel Gur, Alice Eagly, and their colleagues meet so much hostility from critics convinced that their research is "dangerous"? Why, in the face of so much persuasive counterevidence, do so many social theorists, psychologists, and educators persist in maintaining that gender is socially created?

The answer is fairly obvious: many fear that the findings of such research could be used against women. From a historical perspective, that fear is understandable. It wasn't all that long ago that intelligent men were deploying the idea of innate differences to justify keeping women down socially, legally, and politically. Before the women's movement took root in the nineteenth century, patriarchal thinking was the unchallenged norm. It was then taken for granted that women were not just innately different but naturally inferior and naturally subject to men.

Even an enlightened moral philosopher such as Immanuel Kant held the view that women by nature were ethically inferior to men. Kant believed that women have little respect for concepts such as right and obligation, which are at the very foundation of ethical living: "Women will avoid the wicked not because it is unright, but because it is ugly; and virtuous actions mean to them such as are morally beautiful. Nothing of duty, nothing of obligation! Woman is intolerant of all commands and all morose constraint. They do something only because it pleases them . . . I hardly believe that the fair sex is capable of principles." [63]

It was also widely believed that women are less intelligent than men. Stereotypes that demeaned women were commonly accepted, and women everywhere paid the price. Soon eminent scientists were weighing in to confirm women's alleged inferiority. In the nineteenth century, when anatomy and physiology were gaining scientific respectability, Paul Broca, a professor of clinical surgery and pioneer in brain anatomy, concluded that "the relatively small size of the female brain depends in part upon her physical inferiority and in part upon her intellectual inferiority." [64]

Gustave Le Bon, a French psychologist and contemporary of Broca, went further: "In the most intelligent races, as among the Parisians, there are a large number of women whose brains are closer in size to those of gorillas than to the most developed male brains. This inferiority is so obvious that one cannot contest it for a moment." [65]

Given the long history of how natural differences between men and women were constantly interpreted as proofs of male superiority, it is understandable that women such as Steinem and Allred react with suspicion to the suggestion that men and women are in any way innately different. Nevertheless, the corrective to that shameful history is not more bad science and rancorous philosophy; it is good science and clear thinking about the rights of all individuals, however they may differ.

CONFUSING EQUALITY WITH SAMENESS

HUMAN RIGHTS cannot depend on a denial of basic facts of human nature. We all have our rights, regardless of the differences that distinguish us. Moreover, women in most parts of the contemporary Western world are living proof that political and social equality can exist even though men and women are essentially different. We are, in fact, in a postegalitarian era, and the prospects for women have never been more exciting. Clare Boothe Luce, a conservative feminist who in her heyday in the 1940s was a well-known playwright and a member of the U.S. Congress, wrote and spoke about women at a time when the victory was not yet won. Her exemplary remarks on Mother Nature and sex differences are especially relevant today:

> It is time to leave the question of the role of women in society up to Mother Nature—a difficult lady to fool. You have only to give women the same opportunities as men, and you will soon find out what is or is not in their nature. What is in women's nature to do they will do, and you won't be able to stop them. But you will also find, and so will they, that what is not in their nature, even if they are given every opportunity, they will not do, and you won't be able to make them do it. [66]

WHEN TO KEEP NATURE AT BAY

OF COURSE, merely showing that a particular trait or disposition is genetic or hormonal is not the same as saying it should be encouraged. The social constructionists at Wellesley and elsewhere could still argue that even if male preferences are shaped by biology, they should be corrected. We are always improving on nature. Many medical problems, for example, are genetically transmitted, but we correct them. The analogy falters, however, when we talk about correcting a whole sex. If being a boy were a defect like being nearsighted, we could conceivably accept the need to correct it (perhaps with treatments controlling young males' "excessive" exposure to testosterone). But being a boy is not a condition or defect in need of a cure.

This is not to say there are never good reasons to work against nature in socializing boys and girls. We know, for example, that males are far more likely to pursue casual sexual encounters than females. (It is common throughout the world for males to frequent prostitutes; females rarely do it. A recent survey of college freshman found 53 percent of males endorsing casual sex; for females the figure was 28 percent.)[67] Male promiscuity is behavior we recognize as natural but that almost all societies, for good reasons, discourage and seek to curb. Untrammeled promiscuity ruins lives and is a disintegrative force in society. Although male promiscuity is natural, we socialize our boys to be sexually responsible. No one calls that an unwarranted interference with boys' nature.

But how much harm comes from allowing male-female differences to flourish in childhood? A great deal, the gender experts would have us believe, as we saw in Chapters 1 and 2. They talk of girls drowning and disappearing in a society that favors boys, of "gender apartheid," of the schoolyard as a training ground for incipient batterers. But these lurid claims are outrageously and recklessly false. At the same time, the would-be reformers completely ignore or arbitrarily discount all the good achieved by a tolerant policy that allows the sexes to freely pursue their different tastes in play.

No Running, No Jumping

CELESTE FREMON, a Southern California writer and mother of boys, was stunned when she was informed that one of her sons had been punished for running during recess. On another occasion, he was almost suspended because he jumped over a bench. The principal told her, "He knows that jumping over benches is against the rules, so this constitutes defiance."[68] Sad to say, normal youthful male exuberance is becoming unacceptable in more and more schools.

From the earliest age, boys show a distinct preference for active outdoor play, with a strong predilection for games with body contact, conflict, and clearly defined winners and losers.[69] Girls enjoy raucous outdoor play too of course, but they engage in it less often.[70] Deborah Tannen, professor of linguistics at Georgetown University and author of *You Just Don't Understand: Women and Men in Conversation*, sums up the research on male/female play differences: "Boys tend to play outside, in large groups that are hierarchically structured . . . Girls, on the other hand, play in small groups or in pairs; the center of a girl's social life is a best friend. Within the group intimacy is the key."[71]

Anthony Pellegrini, a professor of early-childhood education at the University of Minnesota, defines rough-and-tumble play (R&T) as a behavior that includes "laughing, running, smiling, jumping, open-hand beating, wrestling, play fighting, chasing and fleeing."[72] This kind of play is often mistakenly regarded as aggression, but according to Pellegrini, R&T is the very opposite. In cases of schoolyard aggression, the participants are unhappy, they part as enemies, and there are often tears and injuries. Rough-and-tumble *play* brings boys together, brings them joy, and is a critical part of their socialization. "Children who engaged in R&T, typically boys, also tended to be liked and to be good social problem solvers,"[73] says Pellegrini. Aggressive children, on the other hand, tend not to be liked by their peers and are not good at solving problems. He urges parents and teachers to be aware of the differences between R&T and aggression. The former is educationally and developmentally important—and should be permitted and encouraged; the latter is destructive and should not be allowed. Increasingly, however, those in charge of little boys, including parents, teachers, and school officials, are blurring the distinction and interpreting R&T as aggression. The failure of par-

ents and teachers to respect and understand the distinction poses a serious threat to boys' welfare and normal development. Teachers have always rightly prohibited rowdiness in their classrooms, but they made
proper allowances for it on the playground.

Today, many educators regard the normal play of little boys with
disapproval and some ban it outright. Carol Kennedy, a longtime teacher
and now principal of a school in Missouri, told *The Washington Post,*
"We do take away a lot of the opportunity to do things boys like to do.
That is be rowdy, run and jump and roll around. We don't allow that."[74]
One Boston-area teacher, Barbara Wilder-Smith, spent a year observing
elementary school classrooms. She reports that more and more "mothers and female teachers . . . believe that the key to producing a nonviolent adult is to remove all conflict—toy weapons, wrestling, shoving, and
imaginary explosions and crashes—from a boy's life."[75] She sees a growing chasm between the "culture of women and the culture of boys."[76]

Recess—the one time during the school day when boys can legiti-
mately engage in rowdy play—is now under siege and may soon be a
thing of the past. In 1998, Atlanta eliminated recess in all its elementary
schools. In Philadelphia, school officials have replaced traditional recess
with "socialized recesses" in which the children are assigned structured
activities and carefully monitored.[77] "Recess," reported *The New York
Times,* "has become so anachronistic in Atlanta that the Cleveland Avenue grammar school, a handsome brick building, was built two years
ago without a playground."[78] Dr. Benjamin Canada, the Atlanta school
superintendent, acknowledges that many parents "still don't quite get it.
They'll ask, 'So when are we getting a new playground?' And I'll say,
'There's not going to be a new playground.' "

The move to eliminate recess has aroused little notice and even less
opposition. It is surely not a deliberate effort to thwart the desires of
schoolboys. Just the same, it betrays a shocking indifference to boys' natural proclivities, play preferences, and elemental needs. Girls benefit
from recess—but boys absolutely need it.[79] Ignoring differences between boys and girls can be just as damaging as asserting differences that
do not exist. Boys, especially, are hit hard by any move to curtail or eliminate recess. Needless to say, school officials today would never act in a
manner equally dismissive of girls' characteristic desires and needs, for
they know they would immediately face a storm of justified protests
from women advocates. Boys have no such protectors.

Recess is also a time of sex segregation. But little boys playing kick ball together in the schoolyard are not only having a great deal of fun, they are forging friendships and bonding with other males in ways that are critical to their healthy development. Little girls who spend hours exchanging confidences with other girls or playing theatrical games are happily and actively honing their social skills. What these children are doing is developmentally sound. What justifiable reason can there be to interfere?

Of course, if it could be shown that "gender apartheid" in the playground had grievous social consequences, as male promiscuity does, an effort to curb it would be justified. But that has never been shown. Nor is there any reason to believe it will ever be shown. And in the absence of any proof that letting boys be boys is socially harmful, the initiative to change boys is an unwarranted and presumptuous attack on their boy natures.

LEARNING TO LOVE DARTH VADER

IN 1984, Vivian Gussin Paley, a beloved kindergarten teacher at the Chicago Laboratory Schools, published a highly acclaimed book about children's play entitled *Boys and Girls: Superheroes in the Doll Corner*. It is hard to imagine a book like that being well received in today's boy-averse environment. Her observations are worth dwelling on if only to remind ourselves how teachers used to talk about boys. Paley felt free to express her fondness for them *as they are*, warts and all. She also accepted and enjoyed the clear differences between the sexes; she has no illusions about the prospects of success for any efforts to do away with these differences: "Kindergarten is a triumph of sexual self-stereotyping. No amount of adult subterfuge or propaganda deflects the five-year-old's passion for segregation by sex." [80]

In one passage she describes the distinctive behavior of some nursery school boys and girls in the "tumbling room," a room full of climbing structures, ladders, and mats: "The boys run and climb the entire time they are in the room, resting momentarily when they 'fall down dead.' The girls, after several minutes of arranging one another's shoes, concentrate on somersaults . . . after a few somersaults, they stretch out on the mats and watch the boys." [81]

When the girls are left alone in the room without the boys, they run, climb, and become much more active; but then, after a few minutes, they suddenly lose interest and move on to other, quieter activities, saying "Let's paint" or "Let's play in the doll corner." Boys, on the other hand, *never* lose interest in the tumbling room. They leave only when forced to. "No boy," says Paley, "exits on his own." The "raw energy" of boys delights this teacher: "They run because they prefer to run, and their tempo appears to increase in direct proportion to crowded conditions, noise levels, and time spent running, all of which have the opposite effect on the girls." [82]

At the time Paley wrote her book, Luke Skywalker and Darth Vader were all the rage with the boys in her kindergarten class. The more she studied and analyzed the boys' play, the more she grew to understand and accept it; she also learned to be less sentimental about what the girls were doing in the doll corner, and to accept that as well. Not all in the doll corner was preparation for nurturing and caring. She learned that girls were interested in their own kind of domination: "Mothers and princesses are as powerful as any superheroes the boys can devise." [83]

The boys' imaginative play involves a lot of conflict and violence; girls' play, on the other hand, seems to be much gentler and more peaceful. But as Paley looked more carefully, she saw that there was, in fact, a great deal of conflict, discord, and antisocial behavior in girls' fantasies. The doll corner was in fact a center of "jealousy-ridden, disagreeable, exciting" play. "All sorts of pesty characters have tantrums: sisters quarrel, babies cry and throw dishes on the floor, pets topple chairs, mothers threaten and spank." [84]

Refreshingly, Paley does not have the urge to reform the kindergarten to some accepted specification of social justice or gender equality. In particular, she no longer feels the need to step in to guide boys to more caring ways of playing: "Let the boys be robbers, then, or tough guys in space. It is the natural, universal and essential play of little boys. Everything is make-believe except the obvious feelings of well-being that emerge from fantasy play." [85]

There are any number of fine teachers like Vivian Paley. But today they rarely give voice to their enthusiasm for boys, for that is not welcomed. More welcome and customary are the voices telling the public about how boys are "a danger to themselves and to society." The activist reformers who find boys in their natural state unsatisfactory have been successful in shaping the current attitude to boys. In the drumbeat of boy criticism, the message of teachers who feel as Paley does about boys is no longer getting through.

AN AUTHORITARIAN EQUALITY

STEINEM, ALLRED, and others who upbraid scientists for studying sex/gender differences are persuaded that such study is dangerous and unethical. I would argue that turning a blind eye to real differences and dogmatically insisting that masculinity and femininity are "created by culture" pose even more serious dangers of their own.

For as we have seen, there are all too many educators and social activists who believe they can do a better job of constructing our children's "gender identity" than is now done by benighted parents and "our sexist culture." This movement to change our children's concept of themselves is unacceptably invasive—indeed, it is deeply authoritarian. It cannot be justified as furthering any valid social ideal. Yet we find well-intentioned public servants in powerful federal government departments encouraging teachers to modify the gender concepts of the nation's children in order to achieve a new egalitarian social order. This is quite chilling.

It is also profoundly unnecessary. Most Americans regard the movement for women's equality as perfectly compatible with an understanding that men and women are innately different and must be allowed to develop in ways that accept and respect that difference. The kind of equality of the sexes most Americans embrace and hold dear is the equality demanded by the founders of the women's movement in the mid-nineteenth century: for women and men to be equal before the law and to be allowed the same freedoms, privileges, and rights. That kind of equality required the vote. It required equal access to public institutions such as universities. But it did not require the kind of social androgyny that is the ideal of so many high-minded contemporary reformers. And it is light-years away from the effort to "raise boys more like we raise girls." The reformers who promote their arcane and undemocratic notion of equality in our schools represent no one but themselves. But they speak with confidence about gender justice, and many American educators have become persuaded that eliminating "masculine stereotypes" is prerequisite to fulfilling the promise of a democratic equality.

The pressure on teachers to eliminate stereotypes in the lower schools is, so far, without effective opposition. Though few teachers or administrators are as single-minded as Judy Logan, Princessipal Benton, or the Dalton School's Elisabeth Krents, many are supportive, *and almost all are acquiescent.* They leave the initiative to all the self-styled "change agents" inside organizations such as the AAUW and the Wellesley Center, and reform-minded officials in the U.S. Department of Education, all of whom are diligently promoting an agenda aimed at transforming the nation's schoolchildren into egalitarian citizens of a future "gender-fair" community. Since these determined reformers are rarely challenged, their influence can only be expected to continue to grow. After all, who will stand up to oppose the cause of gender equity? Most parents haven't the slightest idea of what their children are facing. As for the children themselves, they are in no position to complain.

How did we get here? How did the legitimate cause of achieving educational equity in our schools get transformed into a mission to feminize boys? There was more than one step. But it all began with the assumption that our "patriarchal" society conspires to favor boys and to keep girls down by depleting them of their self-confidence. If we had to choose one person most responsible for promoting the idea that our culture is targeting girls for second-class citizenship, that person would be Carol Gilligan, professor of gender studies at the Harvard Graduate School of Education. Gilligan is the theorist who, almost single-handedly, initiated the fashion of thinking about American girls as victimized, silenced Ophelias. Her views on male and female development are beacons for gender-equity activists and teachers everywhere. She, more than anyone else, has inspired and given intellectual respectability to reformers' efforts to reconstruct children's gender identities. It is impossible to understand the war against boys without considering Gilligan's unique role.

CHAPTER FOUR

CAROL GILLIGAN AND THE INCREDIBLE SHRINKING GIRL

IN NOVEMBER 1994, *The Atlantic* magazine published an article by Gary Taubes debunking the claim that electrical power lines are significantly linked to cancer. Taubes, a contributing correspondent to *Science*, put the findings on electromagnetic fields (EMF) into the perspective of the history of science, which, he said, is "littered with examples of what Irving Langmuir, the 1932 Nobel prize winner in chemistry, called 'pathological science'—or the 'science of things that aren't so.' "[1]

Pathological science occurs when researchers report the existence of an illusory effect. According to Langmuir, "These are cases where there is no dishonesty involved but where people are tricked into false results . . . being led astray by subjective effects, wishful thinking or threshold interactions." A recent celebrated example is cold fusion. Pathological science, as Langmuir noted, never produces a fruitful research program. No new discoveries are made; pathological science gets nowhere, it just "goes on and on."

Quite often it is kept alive by journalists who prefer disseminating sensational claims to looking for dissenting voices. In the early 1990s, fear of electrical power lines was pervasive because of alarming stories in popular magazines.[2] In 1992, Keith Florig, an engineer and public policy analyst at Carnegie Mellon University, estimated that the cost of public anxiety over EMF "exceeds $1 billion annually."[3]

In 1996, by congressional request, the National Academy of Sciences reviewed more than five hundred studies of the health effects of electromagnetic radiation. It concluded that "the current body of evidence does *not* show that exposure to these fields presents a human-health hazard."[4] An editorial in *The New England Journal of Medicine* called for an end to research that "has produced considerable paranoia, but little insight and no prevention."[5] Then, in the summer of 1999, a federal investigation revealed that the original research linking power lines with cancer had ignored data that controverted the claim.[6] According to the Office of Research Integrity at the Department of Health and Human Services, the researcher had "engaged in scientific misconduct in biomedical research by falsifying and fabricating data and claims about the purported cellular effect of electromagnetic fields."

But as the University of Maryland physicist Robert Park notes, the deceptions are frequently unintentional. "It is often not deliberate fraud," he told *The New York Times*. "People are awfully good at fooling themselves. They are so sure they know the answer that they do not want to confuse people with ugly-looking data."[7]

The mix of bad science, self-deception, and uncritical journalism is even more potent in the human sciences. Carol Gilligan's purported discovery that adolescent American girls are in crisis (their confidence shattered when they "hit the wall of Western culture") is a case in point. In that instance, women's advocacy groups joined in sounding the alarm, and the "discovery" became politically unassailable. Public reaction to the news that our culture was demoralizing its girls has proved far more costly in social terms than the EMF hysteria—with schoolboys bearing the brunt of the costs.

Gilligan is Harvard University's first professor of gender studies. Journalists routinely cite her "landmark" or "ground-breaking" research on women's distinctive moral psychology.[8] She was *Ms.* magazine's Woman of the Year in 1984, and *Time* magazine put her on its shortlist of the most influential Americans in 1996. In 1997, she received the $250,000 Heinz Award for "transform[ing] the paradigm for what it means to be human."[9]

Gilligan's reputation as a media figure is not in doubt. Her scholarly reputation, however, is quite another matter. "Transforming the paradigm for what it means to be human" would certainly be a feat of great historical importance. But any such achievement would, at the very least, require a great deal of empirical evidence in support of the new paradigm. Gilligan, who compares her methodology to Darwin's, presents very little in the way of data to back up her claims. Most of her published research consists of anecdotes that are based on a small number of interviews. Apart from these interviews, her data (as we shall see) are unavailable for review, giving rise to some reasonable doubts about their merits and persuasiveness.

Despite the glaring lack of published data, Gilligan's conclusions have largely gone unchallenged. The skeptical judgments of the many scholars who don't take Gilligan seriously are buried in obscure academic journals.[10] Meanwhile, her bold theories and the "groundbreaking" empirical research that presumably backs them up are widely referred to and routinely celebrated in the popular media.

A LAVISH TRIBUTE

IN JANUARY 1990, *The New York Times Magazine* published a flattering feature story on Gilligan.[11] The article, entitled "Confident at 11, Confused at 16," reported that Gilligan had tracked the psychological development of girls as they entered adolescence and had uncovered the dismaying phenomenon of girls' being silenced, "going underground," and no longer knowing what they once knew. The piece mentioned in passing that Gilligan's research "provoked intense hostility on the part of academics" but provided few details. The message that came through was that an eminent Harvard scholar had made a shocking and important empirical discovery: as girls move into adolescence, our society pushes them into the background.

Once again, pathological science had met credulous journalism. This *New York Times Magazine* profile quickly generated a panicky concern for girls that would profoundly affect education policy in the 1990s. The alarming "discovery" that America's girls were suffering a loss of voice and a drain of confidence was similar to the electromagnetic-field scare in producing "considerable paranoia, but little insight." At a time when an educational gender gap was opening up with girls well in the lead, boys became objects of neglect as the educational establishment kept looking for ways to compensate the afflicted girls.

In her *New York Times Magazine* story on Gilligan, the author, novelist Francine Prose, speculated that Gilligan's new work on girls "may well oblige traditional psychology to formulate a more accurate theory of female adolescence." According to Prose, Gilligan believes that girls are pained and frightened by their own insights into the culture. "During adolescence girls . . . begin to see that their insights into clear-sightedness may be dangerous and seditious." [12] Gilligan called this "the moment of resistance," after which girls lose their confidence. Prose cited what became oft-quoted words of Gilligan's: "By 15 or 16 . . . [girls] start saying, 'I don't know, I don't know, I don't know.' They start not knowing what they had known." [13]

In 1990, when the *Times Magazine* article appeared, Gilligan had not yet studied boys. The article gave the impression that boys, beneficiaries of the male culture that drives girls underground, were doing comparatively well. A few years later, Gilligan would announce that boys too were victims of the dominant culture, being forced in early childhood to adopt masculine stereotypes that cause a host of ills, including their own loss of "voice." But that came later. In the early nineties, her focus was exclusively girls.

Prose did not deem Gilligan's neglect of boys a failing. On the contrary, she treated it as a virtue: "By concentrating on girls, the project's new studies avoid the muddle of gender comparisons and the issue of whether boys experience a similar 'moment of resistance.' Gilligan and her colleagues are simply telling us how girls sound at two proximate but radically dissimilar stages of growing up." [14]

What Prose considered a muddle to be avoided is clearly a crucial part of any research on adolescent development. For how, in the absence of comparative studies, can we possibly know whether what Gilligan described is specific to girls? Perhaps the loss of confidence that Gilligan discerned in girls is something boys undergo as well. Perhaps what Gilligan called a loss of voice and confidence is a necessary and even healthy aspect of maturation as children grow into adolescence. Perhaps at that period males as well as females find they know far less than they thought they knew, and their childish optimism and false self-esteem give way to a more realistic assessment of themselves.

Prose is a novelist and not a social scientist; she may be forgiven for failing to see that without comparative observations of boys, Gilligan's findings cannot be assessed, indeed cannot be taken seriously. Gilligan might at least have warned Prose of the limitations of her findings. Quite apart from Gilligan's scholarly obligation to give us a comprehensive picture of adolescence as a backdrop for her assertions about girls, she should have taken care that the public was not misled. Instead, her inattention to boys invited the conclusion that girls were in distress because the system was biased in favor of boys. And indeed, many of her readers (including some who are in charge of important women's organizations) did take Gilligan's work as supporting the view that our society favors boys and "shortchanges" girls.

SEVEN WOMEN AND A FAX MACHINE

PROSE'S ARTICLE announcing that a distinguished Harvard University scholar had discovered that the self-esteem of America's girls was being shredded dazzled progressive journalists and activists. Marie Wilson, president of the Ms. Foundation, described the reaction of her colleagues: "The research on girls struck a chord (perhaps a nerve) with the women at the Ms. organization. It resonated deeply and profoundly." [15]

Gilligan was soon to come down from her ivory tower to discuss her research with Ms. activists. Wilson recalls their first meeting: "The two of us met soon after the [Times Magazine] article appeared. The more we talked, the more we became determined to get this information out to the world."

So Gilligan, who had herself described her findings as "new and fragile," nevertheless joined Ms. staffers in their mission to alert "the world" to the plight of girls. Together they brainstormed on what practical measures to take to help restore girls' self-confidence and voice. Marie Wilson writes, "The more we read and learned, and the more we collaborated with the Harvard researchers, the more often we said: Yes, that was me—confident at 11, confused at 16. . . . What if this confidence could be tapped—and maintained? What if girls didn't have to lose self-esteem? Our blood quickened." [16]

The mood at Ms. was tense but excited. What should be done to help stem the terrible drain of girls' self-confidence? It was in pondering this question that Wilson, Gilligan, and Nel Merlino, a public relations specialist, hit on the idea of a school holiday exclusively for girls. What became Take Our Daughters to Work Day would achieve two purposes. First, an unprecedented girls-only holiday (the boys would stay in school) would raise public awareness about the precarious state of girls' self-esteem. Second, it would address that problem by taking a dramatic step to alleviate the drain of confidence girls suffer. As Ms. explained: for one day, at least, girls would feel "visible, valued and heard."

Looking back to the beginnings of a school holiday now observed by millions, Wilson and Gilligan are understandably self-congratulatory: "Miracle of miracles, seven women and a fax machine at the Ms. Foundation for Women pulled off the largest public education campaign in the history of the women's movement. In a nutshell, that's how Take Our Daughters to Work Day was born."[17]

Gilligan's "exposé" of the grim fate of American girls' self-esteem is central to the rationale for TODTWD. Here is the sort of information the sponsors now disseminate in their information packet: "Talk to an eight-, nine-, or ten-year-old girl. Chances are she'll be BURSTING WITH ENERGY. . . . Young girls are confident, lively, ENTERPRISING, straightforward—and bent on doing great things in the world."[18] But, as the guide points out, this does not last: "Harvard Project members found that by age 12 or 13 many girls start censoring vital parts of themselves—their honesty, insights, and anger—to conform to cultural norms for women. What has happened? Gilligan described girls coming up against a 'wall'—the wall of culture that values women less than men."[19]

Recall, in this connection, that it was Gilligan's theories of adolescent girls' development that also quickened the blood of the staid leaders of the American Association of University Women, prompting them in 1991 to undertake their famous self-esteem survey, which Gilligan herself helped to design. The AAUW then moved quickly into the political arena, successfully lobbying Congress for legislation to address the problem of equity for girls in the nation's schools.

It is not hard to understand why Gilligan's message "resonated deeply and profoundly" with many women's groups. They were clearly moved by her account of girls as silenced victims of the "male-voiced" culture. That charge against the patriarchy was not new, but Gilligan was the first to confer on it the cachet of a scientific finding backed by research, and this was music to orthodox feminist ears. Now the message would have to be taken seriously by others. Carol Gilligan was, after all, the acclaimed Harvard scholar who had done landmark research on women's moral psychology.

WOMEN'S DISTINCTIVE VOICE

IT WAS IN 1982 that Carol Gilligan's *In a Different Voice* presented the provocative thesis that men and women have distinctly different ways of dealing with moral dilemmas. Relying on data from three surveys she had conducted, Gilligan found that women tend to be more caring, less competitive, less abstract: they speak "in a different voice." [20] They approach moral questions by applying an "ethic of care." In contrast, men tend to approach moral issues by applying rules and abstract principles; theirs is an "ethic of justice." Gilligan argued further that women's moral style had been insufficiently studied by professional psychologists. She complained that the entire field of psychology as well as the field of moral philosophy had been built on studies that excluded women.

In a Different Voice was an instant success. It sold more than 600,000 copies and was translated into nine languages. A reviewer at *Vogue* explained its popular appeal: "[Gilligan] flips old prejudices against women on their ears. She reframes qualities regarded as women's weaknesses and shows them to be human strengths. It is impossible to consider [her] ideas without having your estimation of women rise." [21]

The book received a mixed reaction from feminists. Some (such as philosophers Virginia Held, Sara Ruddick, and others who would come to be known as "difference feminists") were tantalized by the idea that women were different from—and quite probably better than—men. But many academic feminists, who were then in a "men-and-women-are-exactly-the-same" phase, attacked her for reinforcing stereotypes about women as nurturers and caretakers.

Academic psychologists, feminist and nonfeminist alike, found Gilligan's specific claims about distinct male and female moral orientations unpersuasive and ungrounded in empirical data. In a 1984 review article in *Child Development*, Lawrence Walker of the University of

British Columbia reported on 108 studies of sex difference in solving moral dilemmas. What he found was that "sex differences in moral reasoning in late adolescence and youth are rare."[22] In 1987, three psychologists at Oberlin College attempted to test Gilligan's hypothesis. They administered a moral reasoning test to one hundred male and female students and concluded: "There were no reliable sex differences . . . in the directions predicted by Gilligan."[23] Concurring with Walker, the Oberlin researchers pointed out that "Gilligan failed to provide acceptable empirical support for her model."

That is putting it charitably. The more appropriate question is whether she had *any* significant empirical support for her model. If so, she had a duty to present it. Research in the human sciences is notoriously difficult—all the more reason to present what evidence one has so that others can evaluate it and attempt on their own to replicate it in their research.

The thesis of *In a Different Voice* is based on three empirical studies Gilligan conducted: the "college student study," "the abortion decision study," and the "rights and responsibilities study." Here is how Gilligan describes the last:

> This study involved a sample of males and females matched for age, intelligence, education, occupation, and social class at nine points across the life cycle: ages 6–9, 11, 15, 19, 22, 25–27, 35, 45, and 60. From a total sample of 144 (8 males and 8 females at each age) including a more intensely interviewed subsample of 36 (2 males and 2 females at each age) data were collected on conceptions of self and morality, experiences of moral conflict and choice, and judgments of hypothetical moral dilemmas.[24]

This puzzling description is all we ever learn about the "study." The study itself seems to have no proper name; it was never published, never peer-reviewed. It is, in any case, very small in its scope and the number of its subjects. Do the data actually exist? If they do, they are tantalizingly inaccessible. In September 1998, my research assistant, Elizabeth Bowen, called Gilligan's office and asked where she could find copies of the three "studies" that had been the basis of *In a Different Voice*. Gilligan's assistant Tatiana Bertsch told her they were unavailable. She explained that the "studies" were not in the public domain. Because of the "sensitivity" of the data (especially the abortion study), the information had been kept confidential. When Elizabeth asked where the studies were now kept, Bertsch explained that the original data were being prepared to be placed in a Harvard library: "They are physically in the office. We are in the process of sending them to the archives in the Murray Center."

In October 1998, Hugh Liebert, a sophomore at Harvard (who had been my research assistant the previous summer), spoke to Bertsch again. This time, she told him the data would not be available until the end of the academic year, adding, "They have been kept secret because the issues [raised in the study] are so sensitive." Bertsch suggested he check back occasionally. He tried again in March. Ms. Bertsch informed him, "They will not be available anytime soon."

On September 21, 1999, Liebert tried one last time. He sent an e-mail message directly to Dr. Gilligan, but it was Bertsch who sent back this reply:

> None of the *In a Different Voice* studies have been published. We are in the process of donating the college student study to the Murray Research Center at Radcliffe. But that will not be completed for another year, probably. At this point Professor Gilligan has no immediate plans of donating the abortion or the rights and responsibility studies. Sorry, that none of what you are interested in is available.

So, more than fifteen years after the publication of *In a Different Voice*, the data on which its bold thesis was based had never been available for public review, peer review, or any other kind of review. Nowhere in the book does Gilligan inform the reader of the whereabouts of the data. Because the book was published by Harvard University Press and because its author is a professor at that premier university, readers naturally assume that she did genuine studies, with the usual controls and professional review.

Brendan Maher is professor emeritus at Harvard and former chairman of the Psychology Department. I told him about the inaccessibility of Gilligan's data and the explanation that their sensitive nature precluded public dissemination. He laughed and said, "It would be extraordinary to say [one's data] are too sensitive for others to see." He pointed out that there is a standard way of handling confidential materials in research: you leave out the names but report the raw scores. You must do that "so others can see if they can replicate your study." You also must disclose such details as how you chose your subjects, how the interviews were recorded, and the method by which you derived meaning from them (your coding system). There is a real risk of bias and prejudice in coding, so it is critical to have two or three people code the same interview to see if you have "interrater reliability." Even with all these controls, there is no guarantee that your research is significant or accurate. But "without them, what do you have?"

What you have are unpublished, unexamined, uncriticized data that are nevertheless deemed to be of such historical importance to merit being donated to a prestigious Harvard research center for posterity. No doubt Gilligan will insist on continued "confidentiality." There is little reason to believe that the research that forms the basis of her distinctive views will ever be available for scholarly scrutiny.

Over the years, scholars have criticized Gilligan for her cavalier way with research data. In 1986, Tufts University professor Zella Luria commented on the elusive character of Gilligan's "studies": "One is left with the knowledge that there were some studies involving women and sometimes men and that women were somehow sampled and somehow interviewed on some issues. . . . Somehow the data were sifted and somehow yielded a clear impression that women could be powerfully characterized as caring and interrelated. This is an exceedingly intriguing proposal, but it is not yet substantiated as a research conclusion." [25]

In 1991, Faye Crosby, a Smith college psychologist (now at the University of California Santa Cruz), rebuked Gilligan for creating this "illusion of data": "Gilligan referred throughout her book to the information obtained in her studies, but did not present any tabulations. Indeed, she never quantified anything. The reader never learns anything about 136 of the 144 people from the third study, as only 8 are quoted in the book. One probably does not have to be a trained researcher to worry about this tactic." [26]

These are serious complaints of a type that, in disciplines that respect scholarly standards, have been known to lead to censure—or worse. Why has so little notice been taken of the sparsity of Gilligan's evidence? I see at least two explanations. First of all, in the Harvard Graduate School of Education, where Gilligan holds her professorship, the standards for acceptable research are very different from those in other Harvard departments. Second, Gilligan writes on "gender theory," which immediately confers ideological sensitivity on her findings. The political climate makes it very awkward for anyone (especially a man) to criticize her. Apart from the small group of feminist critics who bristled at her suggestion that men and women are different, few academics have dared to suggest that the empress had no clothes.

Gilligan's defenders will argue that to criticize her for her short-comings as an empirical psychologist is to miss the point. The true power of *In a Different Voice*, they say, has little to do with proving this or that claim about male and female behavior. It is "landmark research" because it advanced the idea that past psychological research was largely a male-centered discipline based on the experiences of only half the human race. Gilligan revolutionized modern psychology by introducing women's voices into a social science tradition that had systematically ignored them.

There is some merit to this argument. To be sure, Gilligan was not the first to urge that women be studied directly, rather than by way of male models. But it is certainly true that she has been more effective than anyone at getting that message through to both scholars and the wider public. For this she deserves credit. Moreover, at a time (in the early eighties) when women's scholarship was blinkered by the dogma that men and women were not significantly different, Gilligan's "difference feminism" was refreshing. Again, she warrants praise for bucking the tide of methodological androgyny. But questions persist about her claims of having made substantive discoveries about women's ways of making moral judgments.

In a Different Voice gives readers the impression that these claims are empirically based. Gilligan was not merely critiquing psychological methodology for being unconsciously sexist and male-centered, she was announcing a discovery of a distinctive way in which women approach moral dilemmas. That discovery turned out to be nothing more than a seductive hypothesis, without evidential basis.

For fifteen years after *In a Different Voice* was published, Gilligan would be regarded as having made original discoveries in the field of women's psychology. She has been acclaimed not merely as a political heroine who exposed sexist bias in the social sciences but as someone who has enriched developmental psychology by careful and fruitful studies of girls and women.

With the success of *In a Different Voice* and with the considerable resources available to her at Harvard, Gilligan might have gone on to answer her scholarly critics. She might have refined her thesis about male and female differences in moral reasoning and done the genuine research scholars expected of her. She might have tried to put her purported discoveries on a scientific footing. But that is not what she did. In the years since the publication of *In a Different Voice*, Gilligan's methods have remained anecdotal and impressionistic—with increasingly heavy doses of psychoanalytic theorizing and gender ideology.[27]

Her own subsequent work is not a good example of the type of scholarship that one must do to redress the neglect of women in social science and developmental psychology. The gloomy picture of adolescent girls that she presented to Ms., the AAUW, and a concerned public is every bit as distorted as any ever presented by social scientists using (in Gilligan's words) "androcentric and patriarchal norms."[28]

How Girls Are Squelched

By the mid-eighties, Gilligan was focusing more on the developmental psychology of adolescent girls. In 1990, she and two colleagues published *Making Connections: The Relational Worlds of Adolescent Girls at Emma Willard School.*[29] Sixteen authors, including Gilligan, interviewed Emma Willard students about how they felt growing into adolescence. The school, located in Troy, New York, takes both boarding and day students and is one of the oldest private girls' academies in the country. Gilligan explains in the prologue that the studies in the collection were not intended as a "definitive statement about girls." Instead, they were "offered in the spirit of celebration" to honor the 175th anniversary of the Emma Willard School.[30]

On one hand, the book is indeed nothing like a definitive study. On the other, there seems to be little cause for celebration. The claims made are large and disturbing. But here at least Gilligan's data are not sequestered. In the preface, Gilligan states the main "finding" starkly and dramatically, talking about how America's girls are in danger of drowning or disappearing in "the sea of Western culture," and claiming that she has discovered a progressive "self-silencing" of girls as they move into adolescence.

Preteen girls, Gilligan writes, are open and forthcoming; they are "stalwart resisters." They speak their minds. They don't tell you what they think *you* want to hear but what *they* want to say. "Eleven-year-olds are not for sale," says Gilligan.[31] But, by age twelve or thirteen, things change for the worse. Entering adolescence, girls become aware that they are in possession of subversive insights that threaten "male-voiced" patriarchal society. To protect themselves, they begin to hide the vast well of knowledge they possess about human relations. Many bury it so deep inside themselves that they lose touch with it. Says Gilligan: "Interviewing girls in adolescence . . . I felt at times that I was entering an underground world, that I was led in by girls to caverns of knowledge, which then suddenly were covered over, as if nothing was known and nothing was happening."[32]

Gilligan's metaphors are always mesmerizing. But what is it these girls know? What are they burying in those "caverns of knowledge"? According to Gilligan, girls possess an uncanny understanding of the "human social world . . . compelling in its explanatory power and often intricate in its psychological logic."[33] The sophisticated understanding of human relations that girls have but do not show they know, she says, rivals that of trained professional adults: "Much of what psychologists know about relationships is also known by adolescent girls."[34]

UNFAIRNESS AND NOT LISTENING

WHAT SORT of experiments did Gilligan and her colleagues carry out at the Emma Willard School that led to the discovery of girls' acute insights into human relations? A chapter called "Unfairness and Not Listening: Converging Themes in Emma Willard Girls' Development" gives a fair idea of Gilligan's methods and style of research. Gilligan and her coinvestigator, Elizabeth Bernstein, asked thirty-four girls to describe an occasion of someone "not being fair" and an occasion when someone "didn't listen."[35] Here are some sample replies of the Emma Willard girls:

Barbara, twelve-grader
Unfairness: "We had three final assignments . . . knowing the students were feeling very burdened, it was unfair of her [the teacher] to contribute to that."

Not listening: "She did not seem terribly moved by how the class was feeling."

Susan, eleventh-grader

Unfairness: "A friend of mine was kicked out because . . . she had a friend of hers who got 600s on the SATs go in and take them [for her] . . . I understand punishing her, but I don't think her life should be ruined. It makes me angry, I think they should have had her come back here. . . . I don't think they cared."

Not listening: "We were going to spend a weekend at a boys' school and [the dean] said I understand you are going to do some drinking. I was just so mad. . . . I said, 'I will follow the rules.' But she didn't listen. I didn't like her getting involved in my plans, because *I didn't think that was fair.*" [36]

To the untrained observer, these teenage girls don't sound exceptionally insightful. On the contrary, Susan appears to be immature and ethically clueless. She seems not to understand the ramified seriousness of the SAT deception; she is indignant that the dean of her boarding school, concerned about underage girls drinking, is so "involved" in her plans. But Gilligan and her colleague Bernstein seem never to notice the moral shortcomings of their subjects. Instead they tell us that girls such as Susan and Barbara are "unsettling" conventional modes of thinking about morality. They credit their callow subjects with exceptional moral insight: "The convergence of concerns with fairness and listening in older girls, for the most part, gives rise to a moral stance of depth and power." [37] Normally, write an excited Gilligan and Bernstein, we dissassociate the concepts of fairness and listening, but "remarkably, for these girls fairness and listening appear to be intimately related concepts." [38]

But how remarkable is it that the girls, asked by an interviewer to say something (a) about unfairness and (b) about not listening, got the idea that they were expected to describe instances in which they had felt that they were unfairly treated and their views were ignored?

I find Gilligan's sentimental, celebratory, valorizing descriptions of adolescent girls implausible and inaccurate. Her study of "unfairness and not listening"—despite its charts, graphs, and tables—is a caricature of research. Most of the girls' comments are entirely ordinary. Gilligan inflates their significance by reading profound meanings into them.

GILLIGAN'S EXPLANATION OF VOICE

GILLIGAN'S WORK is all about "voice," "listening," and how girls are "silenced" and "not listened to." In ordinary parlance, having a voice is having a say in some matter. Gilligan extends this meaning for her own purposes. She does not, however, succeed in making her own meaning reasonably clear.

Gilligan's new preface to *In a Different Voice* (written in 1993) contains a rather lengthy explanation:

> I [now] find it easier to respond when people ask me what I mean by "voice." By voice I mean voice. Listen, I will say, thinking that in one sense the answer is simple. And then I will remember how it felt to speak when there was no resonance, how it was when I began writing, how it still is for many people, how it still is for me sometimes. To have a voice is to be human. To have something to say is to be a person. But speaking depends on listening and being heard: it is an intensely relational act.[39]

Gilligan herself is aware that she has not (yet) offered an enlightening definition of voice, for she continues her explanation beyond the tautology:

> When people ask me what I mean by voice and I think of the question more reflectively, I say that by voice I mean something like what people mean when they speak of the core of the self. Voice is natural and also cultural. It is composed of breath and sound, words, rhythm, and language. And voice is a powerful psychological instrument and channel, connecting inner and outer worlds. Speaking and listening are a form of psychic breathing. This ongoing relational exchange among people is mediated through language and culture, diversity and plurality.[40]

The trouble now is that this talk about the "core of the self" and "psychic breathing" relies partly on metaphors whose meaning is even more mysterious than what they are supposed to define and partly on

literal statements—voice is "composed of breath, sound," and so on—
that are mere banalities.

Mistakenly believing she has supplied a cogent clarification of her
concept, Gilligan sums up its importance, saying, "For these reasons,
voice is a new key for understanding the psychological, social and cultural order—a litmus test of relationships and a measure of psychological health." [41]

Whatever Gilligan's credulous disciples and admirers—from the
editors of *Time* to the board members of the Heinz Family Foundation—
may say, it is embarrassingly clear that "voice," as Gilligan explains it
here (and she offers no clearer explanation in any of her other writings),
is a complete muddle without application to real people. Gilligan has not
provided a new key to social understanding. Instead, she has produced an
influential ideological perspective that sees girls as victims. Only the
most devoted disciples can be cheered by Gilligan's celebrations of
women and girls as heroic casualties of the male-voiced culture and find
illumination in her descriptions of social and psychological reality.

Although Gilligan fails to define her key concept, she does use the
term "voice" very effectively to drive home the point that those who lack
it are being unfairly subordinated by the dominant culture. In a recent
address, she asserted that her uncovering of the inner experiences of
women had initiated a "paradigm shift" in psychology. That immodest
claim is so revealing of what Gilligan herself believes she has contributed
that it too is worth quoting at some length:

> To me, the different voice signified a paradigm shift because it
> revealed a dissociation . . . at the core of a patriarchal, racist so-
> cial order [that had] ushered in an ideology and a psychology
> of separation as to be read as natural, normal, necessary and in-
> evitable. The dissociation from relationship and specifically
> from relationship with women and from vast reaches of the
> inner world hid the experiences, the thoughts and the feelings
> of all people who were considered to be lesser, less developed,
> less human, and we all know who these people are: women,
> people of colour, gays and lesbians, the poor and the disabled. [42]

Herein lies Gilligan's hidden appeal: her indictment of the way girls
are reared taps into the large reservoir of resentment of patriarchal

Western culture. All the same, her specific contention that contemporary American culture is silencing girls is odd. It is, after all, in Western cultures that girls are the most outspoken and free. Try speaking your mind in some Eastern cultures!

GIRLS, GIRLS, GIRLS

GILLIGAN WOULD HAVE US believe that preteen girls are cognitively *special*. But what about boys? Do boys of eleven also make "outrageously wonderful statements"? Are they also spontaneous and incorruptibly frank? Or does Gilligan believe that, unlike girls, eleven-year-old boys *are* "for sale"? As boys move into adolescence, do they too suffer a loss of openness and frankness? Are they too diminished in their teen years? Could it be that girls' specialness consists of their sophistication when compared with relatively clueless boys?

To establish her thesis that our culture silences adolescent girls, Gilligan would need to identify some clear notions of candor and measures of outspokenness, then embark on a massive, carefully designed study of many thousands of American boys and girls. Anecdotal methods—especially anecdotal methods applied to one sex—cannot begin to make the case. Moreover, Gilligan does not offer even anecdotal evidence that preteen boys and girls differ in natural wisdom and forthrightness.

It might actually be that preteen boys are just as astute and alive as preteen girls. That would have several possible implications for Gilligan's theory. Perhaps, like girls, adolescent boys are silenced and "forced underground." But if that is the case, sex is not a decisive factor; instead we are dealing with the familiar problem of adolescent insecurity that afflicts both girls and boys, and Gilligan's sensational claim that girls are at special risk would turn out to be false.

Alternatively, it may be that *only* girls "sell out" and become inarticulate and conformist; that adolescent boys remain independent, honest, and open interpreters of social reality. This too doesn't seem right; certainly Gilligan, would reject any alternative that valorized boys as being more candid and articulate than girls.

Unlike Gilligan, the rest of us enjoy the option of discarding gender games and returning to the conventional view that normal girls and boys do not differ significantly in respect to astuteness and candor. Both pass from childhood to adolescence by becoming less narcissistic, more reflective, and less sure about their grasp of the complex world that is opening up to them. Leaving junior high school, both boys and girls emerge from a "know-it-all" stage into a more mature stage in which they begin to appreciate that there is a vast amount they do not know. If so, it is not true that "girls start not knowing what they had known," but rather that most older children of both sexes quite sensibly go through a period of realizing that what they thought they knew may not be true at all—and that there is a lot out there to be learned.

The Tyranny of Nice and Kind

GILLIGAN'S MORE RECENT work continues her indictment of the male culture for the way it undermines girls. In *Meeting at the Crossroads*,[43] the book that followed *Making Connections*, Gilligan and her coauthor, Lyn Mikel Brown, remind us that "women's psychological development within patriarchal societies and 'male-voiced' cultures is inherently traumatic."[44] American girls undergo various kinds of "psychological foot-binding." They discover that "people . . . [do] not want to hear what girls know."[45] As a result of all of this, girls lose their candor and begin to cultivate an oppressive "niceness and kindness."

Gilligan's idealized portrait of female children as noble, spontaneous, and naturally virtuous beings who are progressively spoiled and demoralized by a corrupting socialization was first drawn by the eighteenth-century philosopher Jean-Jacques Rousseau. Rousseau sentimentalized both boys and girls. The late Christopher Lasch has argued that both Rousseau and Gilligan are wrong. Real girls do not change from a Rousseauian ideal of spontaneous virtue to something more muted, conformist, and "nice." On the contrary, as Lasch pointed out, when child psychologists look at adolescent girls without Rousseauian preconceptions, they are often struck by a glaring absence of "niceness and kindness."[46]

In researching *Crossroads*, Gilligan and Brown followed approximately one hundred girls through their years as students at the Laurel School for Girls in Cleveland, Ohio, between 1986 and 1990. One of the subjects, Anna, is presented as something of a heroic figure. They call her a "political resister," which turns out to mean that she is resisting the "tyranny" of niceness and kindness. When they interviewed her at age thirteen, they found her to be like all the other "self-silenced" girls who had "gone underground." But in a follow-up interview the next year, they discovered that she had broken out and regained her voice. As the authors present her, Anna offers a rare glimpse of a valiant adolescent rebel daring to speak out: "Anna speaks what she thinks and expresses what she feels."[47] Anna proves that girls can resist the forces that silence them. Of course, as the authors sadly acknowledge, she pays a price. Anna is excluded from social clubs, and other students find her disruptive, infuriating, and even "crazy."[48]

But the more readers learn about Anna, the harder it is not to sympathize with her disapproving classmates. As an example of her newfound outspokenness, Anna describes what happened when her English teacher asked her to compose a legend about a hero: "I wanted to write it from a Nazi standpoint, like Hitler as a hero. And my teacher really didn't go for that idea at all. And I started writing and she like, I mean, she got really mad, it was really weird. . . . I ended up writing two papers, a ladeedah legend and the one I wanted to write."[49]

According to Brown and Gilligan, "The teacher warned Anna she would sound like a little Nazi." But Anna persevered. She insisted that Hitler had been a hero in German eyes and refused to accept her teacher's "narrow-minded" distinction between a hero and an antihero. Anna also told her interviewers about her dream of living at the bottom of a mountain in Montana to be—"just one of those weird people." And she shared her wish of giving "the best Senior Speech in the world in terms of shocking people."

Gilligan and Brown praise the maverick Anna unstintingly, taking no notice of her obvious shortcomings: her moral obtuseness, her unabashed desire to shock, her principled indifference to giving offense to friends and teachers: "Anna, willing to be outspoken and disruptive, openly resisting becoming Pollyanna . . . stays with what she feels and thinks and therefore knows."[50]

If Anna is fighting the tyranny of niceness, other Laurel girls are presented as being trapped in it. Neeti is one of these: "I feel good when there is a person and she doesn't have anybody to be with that day, so I stay with her and I feel good."[51] By the time Neeti is fourteen, she also has a 3.7 grade point average, is active in sports and other school activities, and is well liked by her classmates. But interviews reveal to Gilligan and Brown that she "increasingly has difficulty voicing anything but the nice and kind self she shows the world." [52]

Of the two, Gilligan and Brown regard Anna to be the healthy one: "Unlike Anna, whose disruption will continue to put her at political risk, Neeti's movement underground may eventually place her at risk psychologically." [53]

Anna may have "political" problems; we hear of no other kind. Gilligan and Brown's uncritical celebration of Anna's "voice" raises serious questions about their judgment, their common sense, and therefore about the value and cogency of their research methods and conclusions.

THE MASTER'S TOOLS

GILLIGAN, WHO SEEMS unruffled by scholarly criticism, shows little signs of changing her research methods. She boldly insists that to give in to the demand for conventional evidence would be to give in to the standards of the "dominant culture" she is criticizing. She justifies her lack of scientific proof for her large claims by quoting the late poet Audre Lorde: "The master's tools will never dismantle the master's house." [54]

Lorde's remark is often used to fend off "masculinist" criticism of unscientific feminist methods. One might well ask, especially if one's research is part of a larger antipatriarchal project aimed at "dismantling the master's house," what better way to accomplish that end than by using the master's own tools? More to the point, Gilligan's justification for deserting sound scientific method in establishing her claims is deeply anti-intellectual. She seems to be saying, I don't *have* to play by the rules; the men wrote them. That rejection of conventional scientific standards simply will not do: if Gilligan feels justified in abandoning the methods of social science, she has to critique them. She should tell us what's wrong with them and show us a better set of tools.

WHAT OTHER RESEARCHERS SAY

MEANWHILE, researchers who do play by the conventional rules of social science do not seem to be able to confirm Gilligan's hypothesis. Susan Harter, a psychologist at the University of Denver, is studying issues of adolescent development, "voice," and self-esteem. Using the common notion of voice as "having a say," "speaking one's mind," and "feeling listened to" and applying relatively objective measures, she and her colleagues recently tested the claims that adolescent girls have a lower "level of voice" than boys and that girls' level of voice drops sometime between the ages of eleven and seventeen.

In one study, "Level of Voice Among Female and Male High School Students," Harter and her colleagues distributed a questionnaire to 307 middle-class students in a high school in Aurora, Colorado (165 females, 142 males). The students were asked whether they felt they were able to "express their opinions," "say what is on their minds," and "express their point of view." The study looked for gender differences and for evidence of the claim that girls' "level of voice" declined through the grades. It also considered students' expressiveness in different relationships (for example, with parents, teachers, and friends). Harter concludes, "Findings revealed no gender differences nor any evidence that voice declines in female adolescents."[55]

In a second study, "Lack of Voice as a Manifestation of False Self-Behavior Among Adolescents,"[56] Harter and her associates looked at the responses of approximately nine hundred male and female students from grades six to twelve to see if they could find evidence of a decline in female expressiveness. Their conclusion is that "there is no evidence in our data for a loss of voice among female adolescents as a group." They could not even find a trend in that direction: "Gilligan's argument is that girls in our society are particularly vulnerable to loss of voice . . . Our cross-sectional data revealed no significant mean differences associated with grade level for either gender, nor are there even any trends, in either the co-educational or all-girl schools."[57]

Harter admires Gilligan and is careful to say that these studies are inconclusive and that Gilligan's predictions about loss of voice may be true in certain domains for a certain subset of girls. She also suggests that more in-depth interviews might lend support to Gilligan's claims that girls struggle more with conflicts over authenticity and voice. But for the time being, Harter cautions "against making generalizations about gender differences in voice."[58]

Nevertheless, the evidence that Gilligan is wrong about a nation of squelched girls was strong at the time she first announced the girl crisis, and it continues to get stronger. In a 1990 U.S. Department of Education study of several thousand tenth-graders, 72 percent of girls "agreed" or "strongly agreed" with the statement "Teachers listen to what I have to say"; for boys the figure was 68 percent.[59] Nor did Gilligan's portrait of adolescent girls "losing their voice" agree with the findings of the AAUW self-esteem research that she herself helped design. In that survey of children aged nine to fifteen, 57 percent said teachers call on girls more and 59 percent said that teachers pay more attention to girls.[60]

One question specifically tested Gilligan's hypothesis: "Do you think of yourself as someone who keeps quiet or someone who speaks out?"[61] Among elementary school girls, 41 percent said they speak out; for high school girls the number went up to 56 percent. For boys, the reverse was true: 59 percent of elementary school boys said they speak out, but by high school they were one point behind girls, at 55 percent. These differences are small and well within the margin of error for this survey of 2,942 students (2,350 girls and 592 boys), but the results should have prompted Gilligan to ask herself whether her claim that girls increasingly lose confidence as they move into adolescence could possibly be tenable.

The 1997 MetLife study of 1,306 students in grades seven through twelve and 1,035 teachers in grades six through twelve by Louis Harris Associates asked students to respond to the statement "I feel that teachers do not listen to what I have to say." Thirty-one percent of boys but only 19 percent of girls said the statement was "mostly true."[62] If Gilligan is right, we should expect more than 19 percent of girls to feel ignored, and certainly more girls than boys.

CONCLUSION

THE *New York Times Magazine* profile that played so large a role in popularizing Gilligan's views described her as having a "Darwinian sense of mission to excavate the hidden chambers of a common buried past." Gilligan herself is not averse to the comparison with Darwin. Recently *Education Week* asked me what I thought of Gilligan's work and claims. I said, "I'm not sure what she does has much status as social science." *Education Week* reported Gilligan's response to my remarks: "[I]f quantitative studies are the only kind that qualify as 'research,' then Charles Darwin, the father of evolutionary theory, would not be considered a researcher." [63]

Gilligan does actually see herself as pursuing a Darwinian method of inquiry. She informs us that when she read Darwin's *Voyage of the H.M.S. Beagle,* she wondered if she "could find some place like the Galapagos Islands" to do her research in developmental psychology.[64] She says she did: "I went to my version of the Galapagos Islands with a group of colleagues. . . . We travelled to girls in search of the origins of women's development." And in the inner world of adolescent girls, Gilligan found hidden caverns that had hitherto been undiscovered.

Even a casual look at Gilligan's "landmark" contribution to science suggests that comparisons to Darwin are, to say the very least, premature. Darwin openly presented masses of data. His main thesis has been confirmed by countless observations of the fossil record. By contrast, no one has been able to replicate even the three secret studies that were the basis for the central claims Gilligan made in her most influential book, *In a Different Voice.*

In sum, Gilligan's work is more ideological than objective. Her theories show all the signs of being a classic example of Irving Langmuir's "pathological science": "the science of things that aren't so," the fruitless science that leads nowhere but often just goes on and on.

Reading Gilligan on silenced girls, on the limits of "androcentric and patriarchal norms," on "psychic breathing," on the unfeeling nature of "Western thinking," I cannot help wondering: Does any of her work have scientific validity? Is it even respectable as informal social commentary? These questions are pressing and relevant to our central concern, since Gilligan's work has persuaded thousands of educators that girls are being diminished, and the resulting reforms continue to have an adverse effect on boys.

Most recently, and somewhat ominously, Gilligan has gotten boys in her sights. It now seems to her that boys are the victims of the male-dominated culture rather than its favored beneficiaries. She claims to have found that boys, at a very young age (two to three), are being disconnected from their feelings and forcibly separated from others, especially women. She and her associates have embarked on a large-scale program to save the boys of the future by changing the way we socialize them in what she calls the "patriarchal social order." [65]

Given Gilligan's extraordinary influence on American education, the doubts about her work become ever more pressing. Do American boys need to be saved? And are thinkers like Gilligan and her followers equipped by knowledge and temperament to save them?

CHAPTER FIVE

GILLIGAN'S ISLAND

In 1995, Carol Gilligan and her colleagues at the Harvard Graduate School of Education inaugurated the Harvard Project on Women's Psychology, Boys' Development and the Culture of Manhood, a three-year program of research on boys. Within a year, Gilligan was announcing a boy crisis that was as bad as or worse than the one afflicting girls: "Girls' psychological development in patriarchy involves a process of eclipse that is even more total for boys."[1]

Gilligan claims to have discovered "a startling pattern of developmental asymmetry": girls undergo trauma as they enter adolescence; for boys the period of crisis is early childhood.[2] Between the ages of three and seven, she says, boys are pressured to "take into themselves the structure or moral order of patriarchal civilization—to internalize the patriarchal voice."[3] This masculinizing process is traumatic and damaging. "At this age," says Gilligan, "boys show a high incidence of depression, out of control behavior, learning disorders, even allergies and stuttering."[4]

Gilligan's views on boys' traumatic entry into a harmful masculine identity build on earlier psychological theories of female and male development, in particular the theories of feminist psychoanalyst Nancy

Chodorow, which Gilligan made use of in her 1982 book, *In a Different Voice*.[5] In Chodorow's 1978 book, *The Reproduction of Mothering*, she argued that traditional masculine and feminine roles are rooted not so much in biology as in a self-perpetuating sex/gender system that is universal to human societies: "Hitherto . . . all sex/gender systems have been male-dominated."[6] The sex/gender system, says Chodorow, is the way society has organized sexuality and reproduction to perpetuate the subordination of women. The system keeps women down by permanently assigning to them the primary care of infants and children, while men dominate the public sphere.

Because mothers do almost all of the nurturing, all children start out life more strongly identified with their mothers than their fathers. That identification and attachment, says Chodorow, have profoundly different consequences for boys and girls. A girl grows up with a "sense of continuity and similarity to the mother." Boys, on the other hand, learn that to be masculine is to be very *unlike* their caregiver: "Women, as mothers, produce daughters with mothering capacities and the desire to mother. . . . By contrast, women as mothers produce sons whose nurturant capacities and needs have been systematically curtailed and repressed."[7]

According to Chodorow, women as well as men help to perpetuate male supremacy by the way they socialize boys: "Women's mothering in the isolated nuclear family of contemporary capitalist society" shows boys that nurturing is women's work.[8] This "prepares men for participation in a male-dominant family, and society, for their lesser emotional participation in family life, and for their participation in the capitalist world of work."[9] In this way, the social organization of parental roles supports a capitalist/patriarchal system that Chodorow finds exploitative and unfair—especially to women: "It is politically and socially important to confront this organization of parenting. . . . It can be changed."[10]

In a Different Voice cites Chodorow's view that "boys, in defining themselves as masculine, separate their mothers from themselves, thus curtailing their 'primary love and sense of empathetic tie.' "[11] Feeling no corresponding need to disconnect themselves from their mothers, "girls emerge with a stronger basis for experiencing another's needs or feelings as one's own."[12] These ideas on the different ways girls and boys develop—girls in "continuity" with their female nurturers, boys in forced "separation" from their nurturers—help Gilligan explain why women and men should have different moral styles, women having an empathetic morality of care, men having an abstract morality of duty and justice.

Chodorow believed that males and females have the same capacity to nurture. In males this capacity is repressed, largely because male-dominated societies find it expedient to assign the primary nurturing role to girls and women. In Chodorow's view, this social ordering of parenting not only can but should be changed. Permanent reform will mean a radical change in gender identities; it will require "the conscious organization and activity of men and women who recognize that their interests lie in *transforming the social organization of gender*"[13] (emphasis added).

Chodorow's call for the transformation of the patriarchal sex/gender system and her condemnation of the "capitalist world of work" do not resonate today as they did in the 1970s. Her theory of child development and the construction of gender is also dated because of its inattention to biology and physiology. The more we learn about fetal development, and about male-female differences in brain structure and process, the harder it becomes to think of sex differences the way Chodorow thought of them.

Hard, but not impossible. Having read Chodorow in the 1970s, Gilligan appears to have been convinced that her views on the harm inflicted on children by the culture were profoundly right. She would repackage them, giving them the powerful support of her beguiling metaphorical prose. Gilligan was especially impressed with Chodorow's idea that patriarchy dictates styles of child rearing that are responsible for developmental deformations in both males and females.

MASCULINITY IN A "PATRIARCHAL SOCIAL ORDER"

FOLLOWING CHODOROW, Gilligan claims that boys get the message that in order to be "male"—to become "one of the boys"—they must suppress those parts of themselves that are most like their mothers. Gilligan speaks of a "relational crisis" that very young boys undergo as part of their initiation into the patriarchy. In effect, says Gilligan, boys are

forced to "hide [their] humanity" and submerge their best qualit[y]—
"their sensitivity." [14] Though this diminishes boys psychologically and
morally, it does offer them the advantage of feeling superior to girls. But
the male culture that enthrones the boy is dangerously aggressive and
competitive. Boys cannot opt out of it without paying a prohibitive price,
writes Gilligan: "If boys in early childhood resist the break between the
inner and outer worlds, they are resisting an initiation into masculinity
or manhood as it is defined and established in cultures that value or valorize heroism, honor, war, competition—the culture of the warrior, the
economy of capitalism." [15] At the same time, the process of masculine ac-
culturation in the "patriarchal social order" is psychologically devastating for boys: "To be a real boy or man in such a culture means to be able
to hurt without feeling hurt, to separate without feeling sadness or loss,
and then to inflict hurt and separation on others." [16]

In 1997, *The New York Times Magazine* ran a second interview with
Gilligan. "Can we talk about your new work—your research on boys?"
she was asked. Gilligan described a boy she had observed the day before:
"His face was very still. It didn't register a lot of emotion. He was around
6, when boys want to become 'one of the boys.' They feel they have to
separate from women. And they are not allowed to feel that separation as
a real loss." [17] To this, her interviewer remarked. "Sounds as if you're
trying to discover in boys the reasons men feel compelled to adopt certain models of what it means to be a man—models that men feel to be
enslaving."

"That's exactly it," Gilligan replied. She then explained that this
must be changed: "We have to build a culture that does not reward that
separation from the person who raised them." She said she hopes to develop a research method, in particular a way of relating to her boy subjects, that "will free boys' voices, to create conditions that allow boys to
say what they know" [18] and allow her to learn what the boys are sup-
pressing. Through her earlier studies she claims to have learned how to
reach and "free" the repressed voices of adolescent girls; now she hopes
to repeat that feat with boys. The aim is to devise a new kind of socialization for boys that will make their aggressiveness and need for dominance
things of the past. Gilligan envisions a new era in which boys will not
be forced into a stereotypical masculinity that separates them from
their nurturers but will be allowed to remain "relationally connected"

to those close to them. Once boys are freed of oppressive gender roles, she feels, far fewer will suffer the early trauma that leads to so many disorders.

Gilligan and others at the Harvard Project see themselves as defining the principles of a needed revolution that will change the way young males are socially constructed. As Gilligan told *The New York Times Magazine*, "We might be close to a time similar to the Reformation, where the fundamental structure of authority is about to change." Gilligan has nailed her preferred structure of authority to the door of the Harvard Graduate School of Education. The stakes are high, she says. She is calling for a new and healing pedagogy to free boys from an errant masculinity that is endangering civilization: "After a century of unparalleled violence, at a time when violence has become appalling . . . [w]e understand better the critical importance of emotional intimacy and vulnerability."[19] Gilligan asks us to reflect on these vital questions: "What if the equation of civilization with patriarchy were broken? What if boys did not psychologically disconnect from women and dissociate themselves from vital parts of relationships?"[20]

But other questions could also be asked: What if Gilligan's theories about boys are a travesty of scientific objectivity? What if the programs and policies she and her colleagues recommend turn out to do more harm than good? And what, if anything, can be done to protect boys from the trusting educators who faithfully accept Gilligan's view that boys are too stereotypically male and need to have their "gender schemas" rearranged?

DO BOYS NEED TO BE SAVED?

GILLIGAN'S THEORY about boys' development includes three hypothetical claims: (1) that boys are being deformed and made sick by traumatic, forced separation from their mothers; (2) that seemingly healthy boys are cut off from their own feelings and are relationally damaged; and (3) that the well-being of society may depend on freeing boys from "cultures that value or valorize heroism, honor, war, competition—the culture of the warrior, the economy of capitalism." Let us consider each proposition in turn.

According to Gilligan, boys are at special risk in early childhood:

they suffer "more stuttering, more bed-wetting, more learning problems ... when cultural norms pressure them to separate from their
mother."[21] (Sometimes she adds allergies, depression, attention deficit
disorder, and attempted suicide to the list.)[22] She does not cite any pedi-
atric research that supports her theories about the origin of these various
early-childhood disorders. Is there a single study, for example, that
shows that young males who remain intimately bonded with their
mothers are less likely to develop allergies or wet their beds?

More boys than girls suffer from speech and learning disorders, but
many girls are similarly afflicted. Are these girls disconnected from their
mothers? The more plausible explanations for boys' greater vulnerability to language disabilities are neurological.[23]

Gilligan's speculative assertion that the "pressure of cultural
norms" causing boys to separate from their mothers generates a host of
early disorders is never tested empirically. She offers no indication of
how it *could* be tested. Gilligan herself does not seem to feel that her assertions need to be confirmed empirically. She is confident that boys
must be protected from what the culture is doing to them, a culture that
initiates them into a manhood that "valorizes" war and the economy of
capitalism, a culture that desensitizes boys and, by submerging their humanity, is the root cause of "out-of-control and out-of-touch behavior"
and the ultimate source of war and male violence.

But are boys aggressive and violent because they are psychically
separated from their mothers? Thirty years of research suggest that it is
the absence of the male parent that is more often the problem. The boys
who are most at risk for juvenile delinquency and violence are boys who
are *literally* separated from their fathers. The U.S. Bureau of the Census
reports that in 1960, 5.1 million children lived with only their mother;
by 1996, the number was more than 16 million.[24] As the phenomenon of
fatherlessness has increased, so has violence. As far back as 1965, Senator
Daniel Patrick Moynihan called attention to the social dangers of raising
boys without benefit of paternal presence. "A community that allows a
large number of young men to grow up in broken families, dominated by
women, never acquiring any stable relationship to male authority, never
acquiring any rational expectations about the future—that community
asks for and gets chaos."[25]

In *Fatherless America*, the sociologist David Blankenhorn notes
that "Despite the difficulty of proving causation in social sciences, the

wealth of evidence increasingly supports the conclusion that fatherlessness is a primary generator of violence among young men."[26] William Galston, a former domestic policy adviser to the Clinton administration (now at the University of Maryland), and Elaine Kamarck, a lecturer at Harvard's J. F. Kennedy School of Government, concur. Commenting on the relationship between crime and one-parent families, they say, "The relationship is so strong that controlling for family configuration erases the relationship between race and crime and between low income and crime. This conclusion shows up time and again in the literature."[27]

It showed up, for example, in 1998, when Cynthia Harper of the University of Pennsylvania and Sara McLanahan of Princeton University studied the incarceration rates of six thousand males aged fourteen to twenty-two between 1979 and 1993.[28] Boys who lived in homes without fathers were twice as likely to have spent time in jail. These results held even after the researchers controlled for race, income, and parents' education. (Having a stepfather did *not* decrease the likelihood of incarceration.)

Fathers appear to be central in helping sons develop a conscience and a sense of responsible manhood. Fathers teach boys that being manly need not mean being predatory or aggressive. By contrast, when the father is absent, male children tend to get their ideas of what it means to be a man from their peers. Fathers play an indispensable civilizing role in the social ecosystem; therefore, fewer fathers, more male violence.

According to Blankenhorn, effective fathers need not be paragons of emotional sensitivity. In fact, they may possess qualities that would distress the gender experts at the Harvard Graduate School of Education. The typically masculine dad who plays roughly with his kids, who teaches his sons to be stoical and competitive, who is often glued to the television set watching football or crime dramas—is in fact unlikely to produce a violent son. As Blankenhorn explains, "There are exceptions, of course. But here is the rule. Boys raised by traditionally masculine fathers generally do not commit crimes. Fatherless boys commit crimes."[29]

Given Gilligan's general animus toward the "patriarchal social order," it is not surprising that her research appears to attach no importance to fathers. All the same, the more we learn about the reasons for juvenile violence, the clearer it becomes that the progressive weakening of the family—in particular, the absence of fathers from the home—plays a major role.

Restoring fathers to the home is nowhere on Gilligan's list of priorities. Instead, Gilligan and her Harvard associates concentrate on changing things like boys' play preferences. In an interview for *Education Week* Gilligan talks of a moment when each little boy stands at a crossroad: "You see this picture of a little boy with a stuffed bunny in one hand and a Lego gun in the other. You could almost freeze-frame that moment in development." [30] The interviewer reports Gilligan's comment on this crucial development period in boys' lives: "If becoming a boy means becoming tough, Gilligan says, then boys may feel at an early age that they have to hide the part of themselves that is more caring or stereotypically feminine."

Recall the suggestion of Gilligan's colleague, Elizabeth Debold, that it is superheroes and macho toys that "cause [boys] to be angry and act aggressive." The patriarchal pressures on boys to hide their feminine side create the problem. This is something the Harvard team hopes a new "Reformation" will radically change.

Describing the purpose of the Harvard Project on Women's Psychology, Boys' Development and the Culture of Manhood, Carol Gilligan and her codirector, Barney Brawer, state the following "working theory":

- "that the relational crisis which men typically experience in early childhood occurs for women in adolescence"
- "that this relational crisis in boys and girls involves disconnection from women which is essential to the perpetuation of patriarchal societies"[31]

A project that posits a "crisis" engulfing both boys and girls, caused by a patriarchal order that perpetuates itself by forcing children to "disconnect" from women, is not about to take a serious look at the problem of absent fathers. In his contribution to the statement describing the purpose of the Harvard Project, Brawer seeks to address this point by "adding two additional questions to Gilligan's analysis":

First: How do we include in our view of boyhood and manhood not only the problems of the traditional model but also potential strengths?

Second: What is the particular conundrum of boys living *without* fathers *within a culture of patriarchy*?

To the first of Brawer's questions, the answer is, How indeed? Having identified the "traditional model" of manhood as the cause of boys' crisis, how can we now turn around to acknowledge that the traditional manly virtues (courage, honor, self-discipline, competitiveness) play a vital role in the healthy socialization of boys? The second question oddly hints that the problems being caused by fatherlessness are somehow due to the culture of patriarchy—the default villain of the piece. We can see why Brawer finds fatherlessness a conundrum. The puzzle is why, in a Gilliganesque world where the ills suffered by boys are caused by a male culture that forcibly separates boys from their mothers, the absence of fathers wouldn't be a blessing. In the real world, of course, widespread fatherlessness is not a conundrum but a personal and social tragedy.

In 1998, Brawer moved the Harvard Project to Tufts University and renamed it the Boys' Project. As he now describes it, it is a "collaborative community" of teachers, counselors, researchers, and parents who will develop new "experiments in connection." [32] Reconstructing boys is the ultimate aim. How to do so is still undetermined. [33] Back at Harvard, Gilligan, Judy Chu, and their colleagues are moving forward with their own well-funded studies on how to rescue boys from the harmful culture of boyhood. According to *The New York Times,* Gilligan's chair carries with it a half-million-dollar research endowment. [34]

BOYS OUT OF TOUCH WITH THEIR FEELINGS

OBLIVIOUS TO ALL the factual evidence that points to paternal separation as a significant cause of aberrant behavior in boys, Gilligan bravely calls for a fundamental change in the rearing of boys that would keep them in a more sensitive relationship with their feminine side: we need to free young men from a destructive culture of manhood that "impedes their capacity to feel their own and other people's hurt, to know their own and other people's sadness." [35] Since, as she has diagnosed it, the purported disorder is universal, the cure must be radical. We must change the very nature of childhood: we must find ways to keep boys bonded to their mothers. We must undercut the system of socialization that is so "essential to the perpetuation of patriarchal societies."

Gilligan's views are attractive to many who believe that boys could well profit by being more sensitive and empathetic. But before anyone enlists in Gilligan's project of getting boys in touch with their inner nurturer, he or she would do well to note that Gilligan's central thesis—that boys are being imprisoned by their conventional masculinity—is not a scientific hypothesis. It is an extravagant piece of speculative psychology of the kind that sometimes finds acceptance in schools of education but is not creditable in most professional departments of psychology.

On a less academic plane, we may simply fault Gilligan's proposed reformation for straining common sense. It is obvious that a boy needs his father (or a father figure) to help him become a young man and that the ideal of belonging to the culture of manhood is terribly important to every boy. To impugn his desire to become "one of the boys" is to deny that a boy's biology determines much of what he prefers and is attracted to. Unfortunately, when education theorists deny boys' nature, they are in a position to cause them much misery.

Gilligan talks about radically reforming "the fundamental structure of authority" by making changes that will free boys from the masculine stereotypes that bind them. But in what sense are American boys unfree? Was the young Mark Twain or the young Teddy Roosevelt enslaved by conventional modes of boyhood? Is the average Little Leaguer or Cub Scout defective in the ways suggested by Gilligan? In practice, getting boys to be more like girls means getting them to stop segregating themselves into all-male groups. That's the darker, coercive side of the project to "free" boys from their masculine straitjackets.

It is certainly true that a small subset of male children fit Gilligan's description of being desensitized and cut off from feelings of tenderness and care. However, these boys do not represent the sex as a whole. Gilligan speaks of boys in general as "hiding their humanity" and showing a capacity to "hurt without feeling hurt." This, she maintains, is a general condition brought about because the vast majority of boys are forced into separation from their nurturers. But the idea that boys are abnormally insensitive flies in the face of everyday experience. Boys are competitive and often aggressive. But anyone in close contact with them—parents, grandparents, teachers, coaches, friends—gets daily proof of most boys' humanity, loyalty, and compassion.

Gilligan appears to be making the same mistake with boys that she made with girls. She observes a few children and interprets their problems as indicative of a deep and general malaise caused by the way our society imposes sex-role stereotypes on them. By adolescence, she concludes, the pressure to meet these stereotypes has impaired, distressed, and deformed both sexes. In fact, with the important exception of boys whose fathers are absent and who get their concept of maleness from peer groups, most boys are not violent. Most are not unfeeling or antisocial. They are just boys—and being a boy is not in itself a defect.

Does Gilligan really understand boys? She finds boys lacking in empathy, but does *she* empathize with *them?* Is she free of the tiresome misandry that infects so many gender theorists who never stop blaming the "male culture" for all social and psychological ills? Nothing we have seen or heard offers the slightest reassurance that Gilligan and her colleagues are wise enough or objective enough to be trusted to lead the field in devising new ways of socializing boys.

We have yet to see a single reasonable argument for radically reforming the identities of boys and girls. There is no reason to believe that such reform is achievable, but even if it were, the attempt to obtrude on boys and girls at this level of their natures is morally wrong. The new pedagogies designed to "educate boys more like girls" (in Gloria Steinem's phrase) are not harmless. Their approach to boys is unacceptably meddlesome, even subtly abusive.

A Good Word for the Capitalist Patriarchy and Martial Virtues

GILLIGAN'S WORK on boys irresponsibly downplays biological factors and ignores problems caused by family breakdown. Instead, it is heavy on cultural ideology and speculative psychology and light on common sense. In particular, it displays little sympathy for the males she is seeking to help.

Consider her criticism of how American boys are initiated into a patriarchal social order that valorizes heroism, honor, war, and competition. In Gilligan's world, the military man is one of the potent and deplorable stereotypes that "the culture of manhood" holds up to boys as a male ideal. But her criticism of military culture is flawed in a number of ways. First, the military ethos that Gilligan castigates as insensitive and uncaring is probably less influential in the lives of boys today than at most periods in our history. At the same time, it needs to be pointed out, the American military and its culture are nothing to be ashamed of. Indeed, if you want to cite an American institution that inculcates high levels of human concern, cooperation, and sacrifice, you could aptly choose the military.

Anyone who has firsthand knowledge of American military personnel knows that most are highly competent, self-disciplined, honorable, and moral young men and women ready to risk their lives for their country. Gilligan and her followers are confused about military ethics. Yes, the military "valorizes" honor, competition, and winning. Offering no reasons for impugning these values, which in fact are necessary for an effective life, she contents herself with insinuating that they are dehumanizing by contrast with the values she admires: cooperation, caring, self-sacrifice. She seems unaware that the values she holds dear are also essential to the military ethos. To suggest that the military ethic promotes callousness and heedlessness is a travesty of the facts. To accuse the military of being uncaring is to ignore the selflessness and camaraderie that make the martial ethos so attractive to those who intensely desire to live lives of high purpose and service.

The historian Stephen Ambrose, who has spent half his career listening to the stories of soldiers, tells of a course on the Second World War he gave at the University of Wisconsin in 1996 to an overflow class of 350. Most students were unfamiliar with the salient events of that war. According to Ambrose, "They were dumbstruck by descriptions of what it was like to be on the front lines. They were even more amazed by the responsibilities carried by junior officers . . . who were as young as they . . . they wondered how anyone could have done it." [36]

Ambrose tried to explain to them what had brought so many men and women to such feats of courage, such levels of excellence. He told them it hadn't been anything abstract. It had involved two things: "unit cohesion"—a concern for the safety and well-being of their soldier comrades that equaled and sometimes exceeded their concern for their own well-being—and an understanding of the moral dimensions of the fight: "At the core, the American citizen soldiers knew the difference between right and wrong, and they didn't want to live in a world in which wrong prevailed. So they fought, and won, and we all of us, living and yet to be born, must be forever profoundly grateful."[37]

What Ambrose understands and Gilligan does not is that an over-arching ethic of duty encompasses the ethic of care. The so-called manly virtues of honor, duty, and self-sacrifice *are* caring virtues, and it is wrong to deride them as lesser virtues. Gilligan's depreciation of the military is academically fashionable. Ambrose says that after he finished college in the late 1950s, he too shared the antimilitary, antibusiness snobbery that prevails in many universities today. He writes:

> By the time I was a graduate student, I was full of scorn for [ex-GIs]. . . . But in fact these were the men who built modern America. They had learned to work together in the armed services in World War II. They had seen enough destruction: they wanted to construct. They built the Interstate Highway system, the St. Lawrence Seaway, the suburbs. . . . They had seen enough killing; they wanted to save lives. They licked polio and made other revolutionary advances in medicine. They had learned in the army the virtues of a solid organization and teamwork, and the value of individual initiative, inventiveness, and responsibility.[38]

Carol Gilligan's many disciples, who teach in schools of education, work in the U.S. Department of Education, and shape policy in the nation's lower schools, show little awareness of the noble and constructive side of the military ethos. They seem not to appreciate or even understand the manly virtues. The thought seems never to have crossed their minds that the military virtues—stoicism, honor, cooperation, sacrifice, striving for excellence—are the virtues that sustain our civilization.

GILLIGAN'S DIRECTION

FINALLY, WHAT are we to make of Carol Gilligan's contribution and influence? Her earlier work on the different moral voices of males and females had merit; her demand that psychologists and philosophers take into account the possibility that women and men have different styles of moral reasoning was altogether appropriate. As it turns out, the differences are less important than Gilligan predicted. All the same, her suggestive ideas on sex and moral psychology stimulated an important discussion. For that she deserved recognition.

Her later work on adolescent girls and their "silenced" voices shows us a different Gilligan. Her ideas were successful in the sense that they inspired activists in organizations such as the AAUW and the Ms. Foundation to go on red alert in an effort to save the nation's "drowning and disappearing" daughters. But all their activism was based on a false premise: that girls were subdued, neglected, and diminished. In fact, the opposite was true: girls were moving ahead of boys in most of the ways that count. Gilligan's powerful myth of the incredible shrinking girl did far more harm than good. It patronized girls, portraying them as victims of the culture. It diverted attention from the academic deficits of boys. It also gave urgency and credibility to a specious self-esteem movement that wasted everybody's time.

Gilligan's latest work on boys is even more reckless and removed from reality. The myth of the emotionally repressed boy has great destructive potential. If taken seriously, it could lead to even more distracting and insipid school programs designed to get boys in touch with their feelings. More ominously, it could lead to increasingly aggressive efforts to feminize boys—for their own sakes and the supposed good of society.

Gilligan's work on girls led to an outpouring of writing about the shattered Ophelias in our midst. We are now facing a second spate of Gilligan-inspired books and articles, this time sounding the tocsin about the plight of our nation's isolated, repressed, and silenced young males. Boys, we hear, are being traumatized by a culture of manhood that surrounds them with harmful "myths of boyhood."[39] Boys, like girls, need to be rescued from the male culture. In this call for deliverance, Gilligan has been joined by some prominent male disciples. I shall now consider their research, their claims, and their overwrought recommendations for restoring psychic health to a nation of stricken young Hamlets.

CHAPTER SIX

SAVE THE MALES

ON JUNE 4, 1998, McLean Hospital, the psychiatric teaching hospital of the Harvard Medical School, issued a two-page press release announcing the results of a new study of boys.[1] The release, headlined "Adolescence Is Time of Crisis for Even 'Healthy' Boys," reported that researchers at McLean and Harvard Medical School found that "psychologically 'healthy' middle-class boys" are anxious, alienated, lonely and iso-lated—"despite appearing outwardly content."[2]

The study, entitled "Listening to Boys' Voices," was conducted by Dr. William Pollack, codirector of the Center for Men at McLean Hospi-tal and assistant clinical professor of psychiatry at Harvard Medical School. Though McLean issued the press release in June 1998, Pollack, a psychologist, had already come out with a book publicizing these dis-maying findings entitled *Real Boys: Rescuing Our Sons from the Myths of Boyhood.*[3]

Real Boys had been moderately successful before the Columbine High School shootings in April 1999. But it really took off when a star-tled public, hungry for expert counsel on what was wrong with the nation's boys, saw in Pollack a confident authority. Pollack appeared on *Oprah, 48 Hours, CBS This Morning,* and *Dateline NBC* to tell about his research finding that a silent crisis was engulfing American boys. He joined Vice President Al Gore on CNN's *Larry King Live* for a program dedicated to understanding school violence. He spoke to principals, counselors, and PTA leaders. In May 1999, for example, he delivered a keynote address to a convention of more than fourteen hundred Texas elementary school counselors seeking to better understand the boys in their care. In June he addressed two thousand PTA leaders in Portland, Oregon.[4]

Referring to boys as "Ophelia's brothers," Pollack did for boys what Gilligan and Mary Pipher had done for girls: he brought news of diminished and damaged lives to a large public. *Real Boys* stayed on *The New York Times'* best-seller list for more than six months. What sort of research findings does Pollack bring in support of his portrait of a nation of dysfunctional unhappy boys? Let's go back to the McLean announcement of Pollack's discovery.

The press release listed the study's major findings. Among them:

- "As boys mature, they feel increased pressure to conform to an aggressive dominant male stereotype, which leads to low self-esteem and high incidence of depression."
- "Boys feel significant anxiety and sadness about growing up to be men."
- "Despite appearing outwardly content, many boys feel deep feelings of loneliness and alienation."

We must bear in mind that Pollack is not talking about a small percentage of boys who are seriously disturbed and lethally dangerous. He is attributing pathology to normal boys, and his conclusions are expansive and alarming. "These findings," he said, "carry massive implications for what appears to be a larger national crisis, one that we are now seeing can occasion serious violence."[5] This national emergency called for a major social reform: "The time has come to change the way boys are raised—in our homes, in our schools and in society."[6]

It is unusual to find such sensational claims and recommendations issued from a staid research institution such as McLean. McLean is routinely ranked among the top three psychiatric hospitals in the United States, and its research program is the best endowed and largest of any private psychiatric hospital in the country. Any study bearing its imprimatur automatically and deservedly receives respectful attention. But this one strained credulity.

I requested a copy of the "Listening to Boys' Voices" study from McLean. A few days later, a thirty-page typed manuscript arrived. It had not been published, nor was it marked as about to be published. It had none of the usual properties of a professional research paper. Unlike most scientific papers, which alert readers to their limits, Pollack's paper was unabashedly extravagant, declaring that "these findings about boys are unprecedented in the literature of research psychology."[7]

Pollack said he had been moved to do his research on boys in great part because of the "startling findings" of Gilligan and others on girls, which had awakened "our nation . . . from its gender slumbers," alerting us to "the plight of adolescent girls lacking for voice and a coherent sense of self . . . many sinking into a depressive joyless existence." Except for Pollack's adulatory references to Carol Gilligan and Nancy Chodorow for their "profound insights," the manuscript contains not a single footnote referencing other research. Its conclusion, which reports on a "national crisis" centering on boys, was based on a battery of vaguely described tests administered to 150 boys. Pollack gave no explanation of how the boys had been selected or whether they constituted anything like a representative sample.

Pollack's pronouncements on the psychic condition of America's boys were grim. But even if we disregard the limitations of the database, his research came nowhere near supporting a finding of a "silent crisis" national in scope. On several of the tests he and his group administered, most of the 150 boys showed themselves to be healthy and well adjusted. A self-esteem test found them confident. The Beck's Depression Inventory, a widely used psychological assessment tool, uncovered "little or no clinical depression."[8] In private interviews the boys said they were close to their families, and enjoyed strong friendships with both males and females. Something called the "King & King's Sex Role Egalitarian Scale" found the vast majority of them agreeing that "there should be equal pay for equal work," "men should share in the housework," and "men should express their feelings."[9]

Pollack, however, repeatedly warns readers not to be fooled by such seemingly encouraging results. By interviewing boys and giving them tests that measure "unconscious attitudes," he claims to have found a truer picture, one of forlorn, alienated, and unconfident boys: "The results of this study of 'normal' everyday boys were deeply disturbing. They showed that while boys on the surface pretend to be doing 'fine,' beneath the outward bravado—what I have called the 'mask of masculinity'—many of our sons are in crisis." [10]

In one probe of the boys' "deeper unconscious processes," Pollack used a "modified" Thematic Apperception Test (TAT). In TAT tests, subjects are asked to look at ambiguous drawings of people and describe them. It is assumed that subjects will project their hopes and fears into the pictures. Pollack and his colleagues presented the boys with a series of drawings and asked them to write stories about them. One drawing depicts a young blond-haired boy sitting by himself in the open doorway of an old wooden house. The sun is shining on the boy, but a shadow eclipses whatever it is that lies inside. Pollack was alarmed by the boys' responses.

"What was shocking," he wrote, "was that *sixty percent* interpreted the picture as that of an *abandoned boy*, an *isolated child* or a *victim* of adult mistreatment"[11] (emphasis in the original). Pollack saw the children's stories as corroboration of the Gilligan/Chodorow thesis about early maternal abandonment: "The high percentage of stories featuring themes of abandonment, loneliness, and isolation, I believe, is suggestive of subconscious memories of premature traumatic separation." [12]

Pollack called the test he administered to boys a "modified" TAT. Modified how? He did not say. Even if it were accurate to say that the boys' reactions to the picture suggested feelings of loneliness and isolation, it is quite a leap to attribute their response to an early separation trauma. Before concluding that the boys' stories are the effect of their premature forced independence from mothers, we need to know whether other groups—say, a group of girls or of adult female psychologists—would have similarly "shocking" reactions to Pollack's modified TAT. Pollack makes no mention of control groups. In any case, before projecting his findings onto the entire population of American boys, he would need to establish that the boys he was testing were a representative sample.

It is also worth mentioning that Pollack's claimed discovery of an early and devastating separation trauma for boys contradicts findings of the American Psychiatric Association. Its official diagnostic guidebook, *DSM-IV,* says that separation anxiety disorder afflicts no more than 4 percent of children and more girls than boys. Nor does the disorder appear to be related to being prematurely separated from one's mother.

"Children with [this disorder]" says *DSM-IV*, "tend to come from families that are close knit." [13]

Pollack also expressed concern about the boys' apparent confusion about masculinity. A high percentage of his boys agreed with statements such as

- "It is essential for a guy to get respect."
- "Men are always ready for sex." [14]

He pointed out that these are the very same boys who said they believed "men and women deserve equal pay" and "boys and girls should both be allowed to express feelings." Pollack took these responses as evidence that the boys are hostage to a "double standard of masculinity." He concluded, "These boys reveal a dangerous psychological fissure: a split in their sense of what it means to become a man." [15]

This is not persuasive. We might well find teenage girls telling us that "It is essential for a girl to get respect." As for "Men are always ready for sex," why should any psychologist find it startling that adolescent boys agree with that? There is massive evidence—anthropological, psychological, even endocrinological, abundantly corroborated by everyday experience—that males are, on the whole, primed for sex and more ready to engage in it casually than females. And this begins in adolescence.

One well-known experiment compared the responses of male and female college students to invitations to have casual sex from an attractive stranger of the opposite sex. Seventy percent of males said, "Okay, let's do it," and almost all seemed comfortable with the request. Of the females, 100 percent said, "No," and a majority felt insulted by the proposal.[16]

To recognize that males tend to welcome sexual opportunities is not to say that boys endorse an exploitative promiscuity. Given the biological changes boys are undergoing, their eagerness is natural and not unhealthy. On the other hand, society correctly demands that they suppress what is natural in favor of what is moral. So most parents try to teach their sons to practice responsible restraint. Pollack regards the boys' positive response to "Men are always ready for sex" as an indication that something is very wrong with them. While this response may indicate some confusion among today's young men about right and wrong, nothing in it suggests any kind of psychological disorder. Pollack's reaction tells us more about his own limitations as a reliable guide to the nature of boys than it does about what boys are really like.

In sum, Pollack's paper does not present a single persuasive piece of evidence for a national boy crisis. I do not know whether "Listening to Boys' Voices" has been submitted for publication in a professional journal. Its sparse data and its strident and implausible conclusions render it unpublishable as a scholarly article.

Why did a research institute such as McLean give what amounts to a seal of approval to such dubious research? The press release speaks of "findings" and "correlations" and gives readers the impression that "Listening to Boys' Voices" is a study that meets McLean/Harvard standards for responsible, data-backed research. McLean requires investigators to submit research projects to a twelve-member Institutional Review Board for approval. According to Geena Murphy, a member of this board, approval is granted "on the basis of the study's scientific merit."

Pollack's study, with its outsized claims and lack of evidence, could hardly have been approved on the basis of scientific merit. How did it get past the board? In conversations with psychiatrists, I learned that because of managed care, hospitals, administrators, and staff are continuously looking for ways to generate revenue and publicity for their institutions. Members of the McLean Institutional Review Board might have decided that an attention-grabbing "boys-are-in-crisis" study produced by McLean's Center for Men, which Pollack codirects, would bring favorable attention to the hospital. If so, scientific merit, usually indispensable for a McLean study, may have been compromised.

I asked Dr. Bruce Cohen, chief psychiatrist at McLean, how Pollack's "research" had managed to receive McLean's endorsement and was told, "I prefer not to talk about this at this time." Had he read Pollack's study? I asked. "I don't read every study that comes out of McLean," he answered. I explained that this study was quite unusual. Pollack claims to have uncovered a national crisis; his findings are "unprecedented in the literature of research psychology." Surely that must have come to Dr. Cohen's notice. I asked how it was that, without having reviewed Pollack's evidence, McLean had issued a press release giving Pollack's work the cachet of genuine science. Cohen told me someone would get back to me. But before he hung up, I asked him for his opinion "as a clinician" of Pollack's description of the nation's boys as "young Hamlets who succumb to an inner state of Denmark." "That's in there?" he asked, in the worried tone of a high school principal inquiring about what seniors have put in the yearbook.

The next day, I received a call from Roberta Shaw, director of public relations at McLean. She explained that the decision to issue a press release had been based on the "news value" of the study. "We ask ourselves, 'Is it of public interest?' " She also assured me that Pollack "had several journals interested in publishing his study." She didn't know what they were. She suggested I call him directly. I did, but he never returned the call.

When medical scientists and journalists see a McLean press release reporting a significant research finding, they assume that the research meets the standards for which McLean is noted. If that assumption is wrong, McLean's office of public relations should caution the public that a "McLean study" simply means a "newsworthy" finding. Alternatively and preferably, Dr. Cohen should change his institution's policy and make scientific soundness a necessary condition for McLean's stamp of approval.

Universities such as Harvard are clearly uncomfortable with the use of their names to confer prestige on dubious work. In October 1998, Harvard announced a new policy barring faculty members from labeling their work as having been sponsored or endorsed by Harvard without the express permission of the dean or provost. As the Associated Press reported, "many institutions in the Ivy League have found themselves . . . linked to disputed data or research." [17] Last year Yale faced the same problem, and now anyone who wants to use the phrase "Yale University study" must get permission from the university's director of licensing. McLean might consider establishing a similar requirement for its researchers.

THE MEDIA BLITZ

WELL BEFORE the shootings in Littleton, Colorado, news organizations around the country were carrying stories about new research on the nation's anguished boys, citing Harvard and McLean scholars as authorities. In March 1998, *The Washington Post* ran a front-page story about the "plight of young males." It quoted Barney Brawer, Carol Gilligan's former partner at the Harvard Project on Women's Psychology, Boys' Development and the Culture of Manhood, who said, "An enormous crisis of men and boys is happening before our eyes without our seeing it . . . an extraordinary shift in the plate tectonics of gender."[18]

In a May 1998 *Newsweek* cover story on boys, Pollack warned readers, "Boys are in silent crisis. The only time we notice is when they pull the trigger."[19] ABC's *20/20* aired a segment on Pollack and his disturbing message, "Why Boys Hide Their Emotions."[20] *People* ran a profile of Pollack in which he explained how boys who massacre their schoolmates are the "tip of the iceberg, the extreme end of one large crisis."[21]

On July 15, 1998, Maria Shriver interviewed Pollack on the NBC *Today* show.

He informed the program's mass audience of the results of his research:

> Shriver: You say there is really a silent crisis going on with, quote, "normal boys." As a parent of a young boy, that concerns me, scares me a lot.
>
> Pollack: Well, absolutely. In addition to the national crisis, the boys who pick up guns, the boys who are suicidal and homicidal, the boys next door or the boy living in the room next door is also, I have found in my research, isolated, feeling lonely, can't express his feelings. And that happens because of the way we bring boys up.

Pollack's easy slide from "boys who pick up guns" to "the boy next door"—who, he assures us, is not very different inside—scared a lot of parents. This slide from abnormal boy to normal one, is, of course, illegitimate. There is not a shred of evidence in Pollack's research that justifies his "tip-of-the-iceberg," "boys-are-in-crisis" hypothesis. Yet Pollack glibly tossed it into the media echo chamber.

In an earlier interview (March 28), Jack Ford, the cohost of NBC's *Saturday Today*, asked Pollack, "Should I sit down with my eleven-year-old son and say to him, 'Look at what happened here down in Arkansas. Let me tell you why. Part of it is your makeup, part of it is how we've been bringing you up. Now let's sort of work through this together,' or is it too late for that?"

Pollack did not tell Ford that it would be wrong to suggest to his son that he too is capable of killing people. Instead he replied: "I think we should do that with eleven-year-old boys. I think we should start with two- and three- and four- and five-year-old boys and not push them . . . from their mothers. . . ." [22]

This is a remarkable exchange—one that would be inconceivable if the children under discussion were girls. No one takes disturbed young women such as Susan Smith (who made headlines in 1994 when she drowned her two sons by pushing her car into a lake) or Melissa Drexler (the New Jersey teenager who, in 1997, gave birth to a healthy baby at her senior prom, strangled him, and threw him into a trash bin) as tip-of-the-iceberg exemplars of American young women. Girl criminals are never taken to be representative of girls in general. But when the boy reformers generalize from school killers to "our sons," they're including your son and mine as well as Jack Ford's and Maria Shriver's. Would it ever occur to Jack Ford to ask a psychologist whether he should sit down with his daughter and say to her, "Look at what happened at that New Jersey prom. . . . Part of it is your makeup, part of it is how we've been bringing you up. Now let's sort of work through this together"?

Pollack sees the killer boys at the extreme end of a continuum that includes "everyday boys." However, when one reviews the individual histories of boys who perpetrated the shootings, one quickly learns that they are very unlike most "seemingly normal" boys. The Jonesboro, Arkansas, killers were members of a satanic cult. Kip Kinkel, the Oregon boy who killed his parents and then shot his classmates, had a history of torturing animals and setting fires. Columbine killers Eric Harris and Dylan Klebold were admirers of Hitler, choosing his birthday as the day of their Götterdämmerung. Even among seriously disturbed children, Harris, Klebold, and the other school killers represent an extreme.

In putting all boys "pushed from their mothers" onto a continuum with the Littleton shooters, Pollack does not adequately distinguish between healthy and unhealthy children. Before we call for radical changes in the way we rear our male children, we ought to ask the boy reformers to tell us why there are so many seemingly healthy boys who, despite having been "pushed from their mothers," are nonviolent, morally responsible human beings. How do those who say boys are disturbed account for the fact that in any given year less than one half of 1 percent of males under eighteen are arrested for a violent crime? [23]

Pollack's explanation for adolescent male violence in schools contributes to the national climate of prejudice against boys. That is surely not his intention. It is, however, an inevitable consequence of his sensationalizing approach to boys, treating healthy boys as if they were abnormal and abnormal, lethally violent boys as "the extreme end of one large pattern."[24]

A NATION OF HAMLETS AND OPHELIAS

IN REGARDING SEEMINGLY NORMAL CHILDREN as abnormally afflicted, Pollack was taking the well-trodden path pioneered by Carol Gilligan and Mary Pipher. Gilligan had described the nation's girls as drowning, disappearing, traumatized, and undergoing various kinds of "psychological foot-binding." Following Gilligan, Mary Pipher, in *Reviving Ophelia*, had written of the selves of girls going down in flames, "crashing and burning." Pollack's *Real Boys* continues in this vein: "Hamlet fared little better than Ophelia. . . . He grew increasingly isolated, desolate, and alone, and those who loved him were never able to get through to him. In the end he died a tragic and unnecessary death."[25]

By using Ophelia and Hamlet as symbols, Pipher and Pollack paint a picture of American children as disturbed and in need of rescue. But once one discounts the anecdotal and scientifically ineffectual reports on the inner turmoil of adolescents that have issued from the Harvard Graduate School of Education and the McLean Hospital's Center for Men, there remains no reason to believe that girls or boys are in crisis. Mainstream researchers see no evidence of it.[26] American children, boys as well as girls, are on the whole psychologically sound. They are not isolated, full of despair, or "hiding parts of themselves from the world's gaze"—no more so, at least, than any other age group in the population.

One wonders why the irresponsible and baseless claims that girls and boys are psychologically impaired have been so uncritically received by the media and the public. One reason, perhaps, is that Americans seem all too ready to entertain almost any suggestion that a large group of outwardly normal people are suffering from some pathological condition. By 1999, best-selling books had successively identified women, girls, and boys as being in crisis and in need of rescue. Late in 1999, Susan Faludi's *Stiffed: The Betrayal of the American Male* called our attention to yet another huge segment of the population that no one had realized was in serious trouble: adult men.[27] Faludi claims to have unmasked a "masculinity crisis" so severe and pervasive that she finds it hard to understand why men do not rise up in rebellion.

Although Faludi seems to have arrived at her view of men without having read Pollack's analysis of boys, her conclusions about men are identical to his about boys. She claims that men are suffering because the culture imposes stultifying myths and ideals of manliness on them. *Stiffed* shows us the hapless baby-boomer males, burdened "with dangerous prescriptions of manhood,"[28] trying vainly to cope with a world in which they are bound to fail. Men have been taught that "to be a man means to be at the controls and at all times to feel yourself in control."[29] They cannot live up to this stoical ideal of manliness. At the same time, our "misogynist culture" now imposes its humiliating "ornamental" demands on men as well as women. "No wonder," says Faludi, "men are in such agony."[30]

What is Faludi's evidence of an "American masculinity crisis"? She talked to dozens of unhappy men, among them wife batterers in Long Beach, California, distressed male pornography stars, teenage sex predators known as the Spur Posse (how did she miss the Menendez brothers?). Most of Faludi's subjects have sad stories to tell about inadequate fathers, personal alienation, and feelings of helplessness. Unfortunately, the reader never learns why the disconsolate men Faludi selected for attention are to be regarded as representative.

If men are experiencing the agonies Faludi speaks of, they are doing so with remarkable equanimity. The National Opinion Research Center at the University of Chicago, which has been tracking levels of general happiness and life satisfaction in the general population since 1957, consistently finds that approximately 90 percent of Americans describe themselves as happy with their lives, with no significant differences between men and women.[31] I recently asked its survey director, Tom Smith, if there had been any unusual signs of distress among men in the last few decades (the years in which Faludi claims that a generation of men have seen "all their hopes and dreams burn up on the launch pad"[32]). Smith replied, "There have been no trends in a negative direction during those years." But Faludi believes otherwise and joins Gilligan, Pollack, and the others in calling for a "new paradigm" of how to be men.

Faludi cites the work of Dr. Darrel Regier, director of the Division of Epidemiology at the National Institute of Mental Health, to support her thesis that men are increasingly unhappy.[33] I asked Dr. Regier what he thought of her men-are-in-distress claim. "I am not sure where she gets her evidence for any substantial rise in male distress," he replied. He was surprised that one of his own 1988 studies had been cited by Faludi as evidence of an increase in "anxiety, depressive disorders, suicide." "Well," Dr. Regier said, "that is a fallacy. The article shows no such thing."[34] What does he think of these false mental health scares? I asked. "I guess they sell books," he said.

Apocalyptic alarms about looming mental health disasters do sell well. In a satirical article entitled "A Nation of Nuts," *New York Observer* editor Jim Windolf tallied the number of Americans allegedly suffering from some kind of mental disorder. He sent away for brochures and literature of dozens of advocacy agencies and mental health organizations. Then he did the math. Windolf reported, "If you believe the statistics, 77 percent of America's adult population is a mess. . . . And we haven't even thrown in alien abductees, road ragers, and internet addicts."[35] If you factor in Gilligan's and Pipher's hapless girls, Pollack's suffering and dangerous boys, and Faludi's agonized men, we seem to be a country going to Hell in a handbasket.

Perhaps this fin de siècle fashion in identifying large groups as mentally infirm will soon wane—it has nothing left to feed on. With women, girls, boys, and now men all identified as stricken populations, the genre seems to have run out of victims.

Gilligan, Pollack, and Faludi are the preeminent crisis writers. Each finds abnormality and inner anguish in an outwardly normal and happy population. Each traces the malaise to the "male culture," which is blamed for forcing harmful gender stereotypes, myths, or "masks" on the population in crisis (be it women, girls, boys, or men). Girls and women, they say, are constrained to be "nice and kind"; boys and men are constrained to be "in control" and emotionally disconnected. Each writer projects an air of sympathy; each sincerely wants to help the casualties of our patriarchal culture. Nevertheless, by taking an unhappy minority as representative of a whole group, each of these writers is less than respectful to the allegedly afflicted population. Pollack, who wants to rescue boys from the myths of boyhood, unwittingly harms them by arousing public fear, dismay, and suspicion. In characterizing boys as

"Hamlets," he stigmatizes an entire sex and a particular age group. His seemingly benign project of rescuing boys from "the myths of boyhood" by reconnecting them to their nurturers puts pressure on boys to be more like girls. The unintended effect is to put boys on the defensive. Gilligan, Pipher, and Faludi portray their disconsolate multitudes sympathetically—but at the price of presenting them as pitiable.

Boys Out of Touch

I HAVE INVEIGHED against the large, extreme, and irresponsible claims of the crisis writers, pointing out that no credible evidence backs them up. What about their more moderate and seemingly reasonable assertions? Gilligan and Pollack speak of boys as hiding their humanity and submerging their sensitivity. They suggest that apparently healthy boys are emotionally repressed and out of touch with their feelings. Is that true?

My own fourteen-year-old son, David, sometimes shows signs of the kind of emotional disengagement that worries the boy reformers. He came to me one evening when he was in the seventh grade, utterly confused by his homework assignment. Like many contemporary English and social studies textbooks, his book, *Write Source 2000,* was chock full of exercises designed to improve children's self-esteem and draw them out emotionally.[36] "Mom, what do they want?" David asked. He had read a short story in which one character always compared himself to another. Here are the questions David had to answer:

- Do you often compare yourself with someone?
- Do you compare to make yourself feel better?
- Does your comparison ever make you feel inferior?

Another set of questions asked about profanity in the story:

- How do you feel about [the main character's] choice of words?
- Do you curse? Why? When? Why not?
- Does cursing make you feel more powerful? Are you feeling a bit uneasy about discussing cursing? Why? Why not?

The *Write Source 2000 Teacher's Guide* suggests grading students on a scale from 1 to 10: 10 for a student who is "intensely engaged," down to 1 for a student who "does not engage at all." My son did not engage at all. Here is how he answered:

- Do you often compare yourself to someone else? "Sometimes."
- Do you compare to make yourself feel better? "No. I do not."
- Do your comparisons make you feel inferior? "No."

I was amused by his terse replies, but in the spirit of Gilligan and Pollack, the authors of *Write Source 2000* might see them as signs of emotional shutdown. Toy manufacturers know about boys' reluctance to engage in social interactions. They have never been able to interest boys in the kinds of interactive social games that girls love. In the computer game "Talk with Me Barbie," Barbie develops a personal relationship with the player: she learns her name and chats with her about dating, careers, and playing house. These Barbie games are among the all-time best-selling interactive games. But boys don't buy them.

Males, whether young or old, are less interested than females in talking about feelings and personal relationships. In one experiment, researchers at Northeastern University analyzed college students' conversations at the cafeteria table. They found that young women were far more likely to discuss intimates: close friends, boyfriends, family members. "Specifically," say the authors, "56 percent of the women's targets but only 25 percent of the men's targets were friends and relatives." [37] This is just one study, but it is backed up by massive evidence of distinct male and female interests and preferences. In another study, boys and girls differed in how they perceived objects and people. [38] Researchers simultaneously, presented male and female college students with two images on a stereoscope: one of an object, the other of a person. Asked to say what they saw, the male subjects saw the object more often than they saw the person; the female subjects saw the person more often than they saw the object. In addition, dozens of experiments confirm that women are much better than men at judging emotions based on the expression on a stranger's face. [39]

These differences have motivated the gender specialists at the Harvard Graduate School of Education, the Wellesley Center, the Boys' Project at Tufts, and McLean Hospital's Center for Men to recommend that we all try to "reconnect" boys. But do boys need to be more emotionally connected? Would boys be more connected if they were taught to be comfortable playing with "Talk with Me Barbie"? Are their behavioral preferences and emotional attitudes signs of insensitivity and repression, or are they normal manifestations of biological structures that determine the different ways in which boys and girls function?

If, as the evidence strongly suggests, the characteristically different interests, preferences, and behaviors of males and females are expressions of innate, "hardwired" biological differences, the differences in emotional styles will be difficult or impossible to eliminate. But then why should anyone make it their business to eliminate them?

The gender experts will reply that boys' relative taciturnity puts them and others in harm's way; in support they adduce their own research. But as I have tried to show, that research is flawed. There is no good reason to believe that boys as a group are emotionally endangered; nor is there reason to think that the typical male reticence is some kind of disorder in need of treatment. In fact, the boy reformers such as Pollack, Gilligan, and their acolytes need to consider the possibility that male stoicism and reserve may well be traits to be encouraged, not vices or psychological weaknesses to be overcome.

A PLEA FOR RETICENCE

THE ARGUMENT in favor of saving boys by reconnecting them emotionally rests on the popular assumption that repressing emotions is harmful, while giving discursive vent to them is, on the whole, healthy. Psychologists have recently begun to examine the supposition that speaking out and declaring one's feelings is better than holding them in. Jane Bybee, a psychologist at Suffolk University in Boston, studied a group of high school students, classifying them as "repressors," "sensitizers"(those keenly aware of their internal states), or "intermediates." She then had the students evaluate themselves and others using these distinctions. She also had the teachers evaluate the students. She found that the "repressors" were less anxious, more confident, and more successful academically and socially. Bybee's conclusion is tentative: "In our day-to-day behavior it may be good not to be so emotional and needy. The moods of repressed people may be more balanced." [40]

Her study is small and its findings are qualified, but it flies in the face of conventional "emotivist" doctrine; it is unconventional also in daring to put to the test of actual experience the popular and unquestioned assumption that emotional openness is beneficial. Nor is Bybee's the only study to question emotivist assumptions. In a 1997 article in *Lingua Franca*, writer Emily Nussbaum summarized the small but impressive body of psychological research that makes "the case for repression." [41] George Bonanno of Catholic University (now at Columbia University) has done several studies that challenge the commonly held assumption that venting negative emotions such as grief by talking about them openly is necessary for regaining mental health. [42] His research, in fact, showed negative effects: grieving individuals who expressed strong negative emotions about their loss were worse off than the so-called repressors, who recovered more rapidly. Bonanno checked his results by using "double-blind" and controlled methods. For example, he had outside psychologists examine his bereaved subjects and determine which were healthier in recovery. The ones who had repressed their grief turned out to be considerably healthier than the strong emoters. In more recent, as-yet-unpublished research, Bonanno and a team of researchers at the National Institutes of Health have found that among adolescent girls who have been sexually abused, those who showed emotional avoidance did better than those who expressed their anger and grief more openly.

Bonanno's work strikes at the contemporary axiom that talking things out is the way to mental health. So do some studies of Holocaust survivors. According to Hanna Kaminer and Peretz Lavie of the Israel Institute of Technology in Haifa, survivors who have been induced to talk it out fare significantly worse than repressors do. [43] "Repression has been understood as a pathological phenomenon," write Kaminer and Lavie. "Our findings contradict this assumption." [44] Their conclusion is the very opposite of the conventional one: "Help survivors to seal off the atrocities that they experienced."

Without presuming to judge the complex issues at stake, one must note that in most past and present societies, "repression" of private feelings has often been regarded as a social virtue. From a historical perspective, the burden of proof rests on those who believe that being openly expressive makes people better and healthier. That view has become a dogma of contemporary American popular culture, but in most cultures—including our own until quite recently—reticence and stoicism are regarded as commendable, while the free expression of emotions is often seen as a shortcoming.

Pollack, who is a champion of emotional expressiveness, instructs parents, "Let boys know that they don't need to be 'sturdy oaks.' " To encourage boys to be stoical, says Pollack, is to harm them: "The boy is often pushed to 'act like a man,' to be the one who is confident and unflinching. No boy should be called upon to be the tough one. No boy should be harmed in this way." [45]

But Pollack needs to show, not merely assert, that it harms a child to be "called upon to be tough." Why shouldn't boys—or, for that matter, girls—try to be sturdy oaks? All of the world's major religions place stoical control of emotions at the center of their moral teachings. For Buddhists, the ideal is emotional detachment; for Confucianism, dispassionate control. Nor is "Be in touch with your feelings" one of the Ten Commandments. Judeo-Christian teaching enjoins attentiveness to the emotional needs and feelings of others—not one's own.

In maintaining that being emotionally unreserved is beneficial, Pollack and his colleagues in the boy-reform movement rely on the same pop culture beliefs that are so often used to justify the unseemly and humiliating personal revelations elicited on television by the Jerry Springers and Jenny Joneses. But they are wrong to do so.

The insights of the save-the-male psychologists into the inner world of boys are by no means self-evident, nor is it at all obvious that their emotivist proposals would benefit boys. Boys' aggressive tendencies do need to be checked. But the boy reformers have not proved that they have the recipe for civilizing boys and restraining their rough natures. Before the gender experts at the Harvard Graduate School of Education and the practitioners of the new male psychology are given broad license to reprogram our sons to be "sensitizers" rather than repressors, they should first be required to show that the repairs they are so anxious to make are beneficial and not injurious.

These reform-minded experts should seriously consider the possibility that American children may in fact need more, not less, self-control and less, not more, self-involvement. It may be that American boys don't need to be more emotional—and that American girls do need to be less sentimental and self-absorbed. Maybe some of the crashing and disappearing selves that Pipher and Gilligan talk about are selves that have for too long been self-preoccupied, to the unhealthy exclusion of outside interests.

THE CULTURE OF THERAPY

THE BRITISH WRITER and social critic Fay Weldon has coined the useful, if somewhat ungainly, term "therapism" for the popular doctrine that almost all personal troubles can be cured by talk.[46] Weldon is more concerned with therapism as a pop phenomenon than an educational practice; but in either sphere, talk therapy, once primarily a private therapeutic technique, has gone public in ways undreamed of in Sigmund Freud's philosophy.[47]

Strangers, proudly in touch with their feelings, share their innermost thoughts and experiences with one another. Talk-show participants make intensely personal disclosures to wildly applauding audiences. The endless stream of confessional memoirs, the self-esteem movement, the textbooks and questionnaires that probe children's innermost feelings are all manifestations of a profound and rampant therapism.

The contemporary faith in the value of openness and the importance of sharing one's feelings is now so much a part of popular culture that we find even such staid organizations as the Girl Scouts of America giving "points" for being open about grief. *Lingua Franca* writer Emily Nussbaum reports that "a Girl Scout troop in New York instituted a 'grief patch' in 1993—troop members could earn this medal by sharing a painful feeling with one another, writing stories and poems about death and loss and meeting with bereavement counselors." [48]

One sector in our society has so far been highly resistant to therapism: little boys are no more interested in earning "grief patches" than they are eager to interact personally with dolls. When homework assignments require them to explore their deeper feelings about a text, it is likely that they will not engage. I suspect that efforts to get little boys to be more overtly emotional rarely succeed. But I do not discount the powers of the would-be reformers to do a lot of harm and cause a lot of grief by trying.

Having been taught to think of the children in their care as deformed by their conditioning and in need of "rescue," many educators, eager to help, feel justified in intruding into the children's psychic lives. Such intrusion is ethically questionable. First, few educators have the training or authority to approach children in the public sphere as healers. Second, when we consider the power teachers have over children, the therapeutic approach to children raises grave ethical issues.

The self-esteem movement, which is only now beginning to recede, has sinned massively in this regard. All through the 1990s, self-esteem was the education buzzword. Everyone needed it; many demanded it for their children or pupils as a right. But the excesses of those who promoted techniques for increasing students' self-esteem provide a cautionary example of what can happen when teachers, counselors, and education theorists, armed with good intentions and specious social science (for one thing, no one agrees on what self-esteem is or how to measure it), turn classrooms into encounter groups.

It has never even been shown that "high self-esteem" is a good trait for students to possess. Meantime, researchers have uncovered a worrisome correlation between inflated self-esteem and juvenile delinquency. As Brad Bushman, an Iowa State University psychologist, explains, "If kids develop unrealistic opinions of themselves and those views are rejected by others, the kids are potentially dangerous."[49]

John Hewitt, a University of Massachusetts sociologist, has examined the morality of the self-esteem movement in a fine scholarly book called *The Myth of Self-Esteem*. Hewitt documents the exponential growth of self-esteem articles and programs from 1982 to 1996.[50] He points to the ethical hazards of using the classroom for therapeutic purposes. In a typical classroom self-esteem exercise, students complete sentences beginning "I love myself because . . ." or "I feel bad about myself because . . ." Hewitt explains that children interpret these assignments as *demands* for self-revelation. They feel pressed to complete the sentences "correctly" in ways the teacher finds satisfactory. As Hewitt acutely observes, "Teachers . . . no doubt regard the exercises as being in the best interest of their students. . . . Yet from a more skeptical perspective these exercises are subtle instruments of social control. The child *must* be taught to like himself or herself. . . . The child *must* confess self-doubt or self-loathing, bringing into light the feelings that he or she might prefer to keep private"[51] (emphasis in original).

Far from being harmless, these therapeutic practices are unacceptably prying. Surely schoolchildren have a right not to be subjected to the psychological manipulations of both self-esteem educators and the reformers intent on getting boys to disclose their emotions in the way girls often do.

THERAPISM VERSUS STOICISM

THERE DOES NOT appear to be anything much wrong with the psyches of the vast majority of American children. On the other hand, there is strong evidence that they are morally and academically undernourished. Every society since the beginning of history has confronted the difficult and complex task of civilizing its young, teaching them self-discipline, instilling in them a sense of what is right and what is wrong, and imbuing them with a devotion to public duty and personal accountability. The problem is old, and the workable solution to it is known—character education in a sound learning environment. The known, tested solution does not include therapeutic pedagogies.

Children need to be moral more than they need to be in touch with their feelings. They need to be well educated more than they need to have their self-esteem raised. Children do not need support groups or twelve-step programs. They don't need to have their femininity or masculinity "reinvented." They don't need emotional fixes. Genuine self-esteem comes with pride in achievement, which is the fruit of disciplined effort.

American boys do not need to be rescued. They are not pathological. They are not seething with repressed rage or imprisoned in "straitjackets of masculinity." American girls are not suffering a crisis of low self-esteem; they are not being silenced by the culture. The vast majority of girls and boys are psychologically sound. But when it comes to the genuine problems that do threaten our children's prospects—their moral drift, their cognitive and scholastic deficits—the healers, social reformers, and confidence builders provide no solutions; on the contrary, they exacerbate the problems and stand squarely in the way of what needs to be done to solve them.

WHY JOHNNY CAN'T, LIKE, READ AND WRITE

THERE IS a much-told story in education circles about a now-retired Chicago public school teacher, Mrs. Daugherty. She was a dedicated, highly respected sixth-grade teacher who could always be counted on to bring out the best in her students. One year she had a class she found impossible to control. The students were noisy, unmanageable, and seemingly unteachable. She began to worry that many of them had serious learning disabilities. When the principal was out of town, she did something teachers were not supposed to: she entered his office, and looked in a special file where students' IQs were recorded. To her amazement, she found that a majority of the students were way above average in intelligence. A quarter of the class had IQs in the high 120s—128, 127, 129; several in the 130s—and one of the worst classroom culprits was in fact brilliant: he had an IQ of 145.

Mrs. Daugherty was angry at herself. She had been feeling sorry for the children, giving them remedial work, and expecting little from them. Things soon changed. She immediately brought in challenging work, increased the homework load, and inflicted draconian punishments on any malefactor. She ran the class with uncompromising discipline. Slowly but perceptibly, the students' performance improved. By the end of the year, this class of former ne'er-do-wells was among the best behaved and highest performing of sixth-grade classes.

The principal was delighted. He knew about this class and its terrible reputation. So at the end of the year, he called Mrs. Daugherty into his office to ask her what she had done. She felt compelled to tell him the truth. The principal heard her out and forgave her. He congratulated her. But then he said, "I think you should know, Mrs. Daugherty, those numbers next to the children's names—those are not their IQ scores. Those are their locker numbers."[1]

The moral of the story is clear: Strict is good. Demanding and expecting excellence can only benefit the student. These were once truisms of education. Even today, setting and enforcing high standards for students surely is uncontroversial. Who would question the need for challenging work, high expectations, and strict discipline? The sad answer is that a lot of education theorists are skeptical about these things. Rousseauian romanticism, in the form of progressive education, has long been a powerful force in American schools. The shift away from structured classrooms, competition, strict discipline, and skill-and-fact-based learning has been harmful to all children—but especially to boys.

DON'T FILL A VASE, LIGHT A FIRE

PROGRESSIVE PEDAGOGUES pride themselves on fostering creativity and enhancing children's self-esteem. Exacting discipline and the old-fashioned "dry-knowledge" approach are said to accomplish the opposite: to inhibit creativity and leave many students with feelings of inadequacy. Progressives frown on teacher-led classrooms with fact-based learning, memorization, phonics, and drills. Trainees in schools of education are enjoined to "Teach the student, not the subject!" and are inspired by precepts such as "[Good teaching] is not vase-filling; rather it is fire-lighting."[2]

In this "child-centered" model, the teacher is supposed to remain in the background so that students have the chance to develop as "independent learners." Drill and rote have no place in a style of education focused on freeing "the creative potential of the child." One well-known proponent of progressivism, Alfie Kohn, author of *The Schools Our Children Deserve* and *Punished by Rewards,* suggests that the modern cooperative classroom should resemble a musical jam session: "Cooperative learning not only offers instruments to everyone in the room, but invites jazz improvisation."[3]

Child-centered education has been prevalent in American schools of education since the 1920s. According to University of Virginia education scholar E. D. Hirsch, Jr., the "knowledge-based approach currently employed in the most advanced nations [has been] eschewed in our own schools for more than half a century."[4] Except for a brief period in the late fifties and early sixties (when the Soviet Union's success with *Sputnik* generated fears that an inadequate math and science curriculum was a threat to national security), the fashion in American education has been to downplay basic skills, knowledge acquisition, competitive grading, and discipline. This fashion has opened a worrisome education gap that finds American students near the bottom among advanced countries.[5]

In recent years, a growing number of British educators have become convinced that progressive methods in education are a prime reason their male students are so far behind the girls. There is now a concerted movement in Britain to improve boys' educational prospects by going back to a traditional pedagogy. Many British educational leaders believe that the modern classroom fails boys by being too unstructured, too permissive, and too hostile to the spirit of competition that so often provides boys with the incentive to learn and excel. Added to this is the national concern over the economic consequences of male underachievement. Stephen Byers, the British schools standards minister, says, "Failure to raise the educational achievement of boys will mean that thousands of young men will face a bleak future in which a lack of qualifications and basic skills will mean unemployment and little hope of finding work."[6]

By contrast, the looming prospect of an underclass of badly educated—even barely literate—American boys has yet to become a cause for open concern among American educators, not to speak of politicians. Nevertheless, the day of reckoning cannot be far away. Massachusetts Institute of Technology economist Lester Thurow observes, "Within the developed world, the under-educated and under-skilled are going to be left out, or perhaps more accurately, thrown out of the global game."[7] There are some disquieting voices. In a 1995 article in *Science,* University of Chicago education researchers Larry Hedges and Amy Nowell warned about the bleak employment outlook for the "generally larger number of males who perform near the bottom . . . in reading and writing."[8]

BOYS IN THE UNITED KINGDOM

LIKE AMERICAN BOYS, boys in Great Britain and Australia are markedly behind girls academically, notably in reading and writing. They too get most of the failing grades, and more of them lose interest in school. The big difference is that British educators and politicians are ten years ahead of Americans in confronting and addressing the problem of male under-achievement.

In 1988, a council of British headmasters organized a clearinghouse for information on effective classroom practices and programs for boys. Nearly a decade later, they published a booklet summarizing what they had learned. *Can Boys Do Better?* describes specific classroom activities and teaching styles that have been tried at British schools such as Moulsham High School in Chelmsford and Thirsk School in North Yorkshire.[9] Nearly every suggestion violates some hallowed progressive tenet. Here is a partial list of the approaches that these practitioners found work for boys:

- More teacher-led work
- A structured environment
- High expectations
- Strict homework checks
- Consistently applied sanctions if work is not done
- Greater emphasis on silent work
- Frequent testing
- One-sex classes

The British headmasters call for "silent" (solitary) reflection and study; they do not celebrate collaborative learning. The headmasters advise schools to avoid fanciful, "creative" assignments, noting, "Boys do not always see the intrinsic worth of 'Imagine you're a sock in a dustbin.' They want relevant work."[10] Nor are they concerned about the students' self-esteem. They know that boys do better than girls on self-esteem questionnaires, but that "gender gap" does not strike them as evidence that girls are being tragically shortchanged. As Peter Downes, former president of the Scottish Headmasters' Association Associates, dryly notes, "Boys swagger . . . while girls win the prizes."[11] He urges teachers to be brutally honest with boys about what life has in store for them if they continue to underperform academically.

Coed public schools throughout Great Britain are now experimenting with all-male classes. In 1996, Ray Bradbury, the head teacher of King's School in Winchester, was alarmed by the high failure rate of his male students. Seventy-eight percent of the girls were getting passing grades or better, but only 56 percent of the boys. Bradbury identified the thirty or so boys he thought to be at risk for failure and placed them together in a class. He chose an athletic young male teacher he thought the boys would find easy to like. The class was not "child-centered." The pedagogy was strict and old-fashioned. As Bradbury explained, "We consciously planned the teaching methodology. The class is didactic and teacher-fronted. It involves sharp questions and answers, and constantly checking understanding. Discipline is clear-cut—if homework isn't presented, it is completed in a detention. There is no discussion."[12]

Here is how one visiting journalist describes a typical class: "Ranks of boys in blazers face the front, giving full attention to the young teacher's instructions. His style is uncompromising and inspirational. 'People think that boys like you won't be able to understand writers such as the Romantic poets. Well, you're going to prove them wrong. Do you understand?' "[13]

The teacher finds that the boys in his single-sex class actively support one another with genuine team spirit: "When girls are present, boys are loath to express opinions for fear of appearing sissy." He chooses challenging but male-appropriate readings: "Members of my group are football mad and quite 'laddish.' In the mixed classes they would be turned off by *Jane Eyre*, whereas I can pick texts such as *Silas Marner* and The War Poets." The initial results have been promising. In 1996, the boys were far behind the girls. By 1997, after only a year in the special class, the boys had nearly closed the gap. As one of the boys said, "We are all working hard to show we can be just as successful as the other groups."[14]

The authors of *Can Boys Do Better?* are careful not to claim too much for their pedagogical practices: "It should be stressed that many of these strategies [to help boys do better] have only recently been implemented, and it is too early in many cases fully to evaluate their effective-ness."[15] However, a follow-up study by the National Foundation for Ed-ucation Research in 1999 (*Boys' Achievement, Progress, Motivation and Participation*) supported the headmasters' key propositions: "The fol-lowing items all emerge as being important: highly structured lessons, more emphasis on teacher-led work, clear and firm deadlines, short-term targets."[16] The same report noted that all-male classes and all-male schools may be "singularly well-placed to raise achievement among boys, as they could tailor their strategies directly to the needs of boys."[17] More recently, the cautious optimism of the boy-focused educators who have been advocating and practicing a more traditional pedagogy for boys was spectacularly vindicated.

In the fall of 1998, the British government introduced into primary schools a compulsory back-to basics program called the "Literacy Hour." Its explicit purpose was to narrow the achievement gap between boys and girls. The program incorporates practices that are antithetical to most of the hallowed precepts of progressivism: it is phonics-centered, whole-class, teacher-led, with old-fashioned emphasis on such things as grammar and punctuation. David Blunkett, the education secretary, also insisted that teachers find boy-friendly reading materials such as adven-ture, sports, or horror stories as well as nonfiction. "Boys like reading technical texts," Blunkett told a conference of school principals.[18]

The effects of the back-to-basics program on male literacy were im-mediate and dramatic. In the fall of 1999, British newspapers announced the good tidings: "Boys Close Literacy Gender Gap";[19] "Boys Catching Up with Girls Thanks to Literacy Hour."[20] According to the *Daily Mail:*

> While the girls are still ahead, the ability gap has dramatically narrowed. Education Secretary David Blunkett will see the new key state results as complete vindication of his back-to-basics policies in primary schools. . . . The figures suggest that the new regime is paying rich dividends. Last year just 64 per-cent of 11-year-old boys were proficient in reading. Today's figure is 78 percent. The remarkable improvement has ex-ceeded the wildest expectation of the government.[21]

To an American observer, the very fact that the plight of *boys* is making headlines is almost as remarkable as anything the British are doing to help them. Just as remarkable is that the initiatives to solve the problem of lagging boys are coming as much from the government as from the traditionalist forces in education. Success in helping boys has become a political imperative. *The Daily Telegraph* noted that Secretary Blunkett had "staked his political future" on the drive to narrow the gender gap: "Mr. Blunkett had promised to resign if 80 percent did not reach [proficiency] in the national curriculum English tests for 11-year-olds in 2002."[22]

Anyone who is aware of and concerned about the large number of outwardly confident but academically mediocre American boys will want to pay close attention to the initiatives unfolding in Britain. The U.S. Department of Education reports that "the gap in reading proficiency between males and females [favoring females] is roughly equivalent to about one and a half years of schooling."[23] The gap shows up early, and it remains large at every stage that children are tested. In 1998, for example, eighth-grade boys were 13 points behind girls on the National Assessment of Educational Progress. For twelfth-graders the gap was 15 points.[24] (The NAEP scale scores range from 0 to 500.) The 1994 Department of Education "Reading Report Card for the Nation and the States" showed that 47 percent of the nation's fourth-grade boys were "below basic" in reading; for females the figure was 36 percent.[25] American education officials know all about the problem of boys, but there is no visible effort to make the problem known to the public at large, nor is anyone openly committed to addressing and solving it.

By the time they reach college age, many American young men are outside the culture of the written word. In an annual survey of college freshmen conducted by the Higher Education Research Institute at UCLA, students are asked how many hours per week they spent reading for pleasure during the preceding year. The 1998 results were consistent with other years: 35 percent of males answered "none." Reading for pleasure is something these young men have never gotten used to. Among females, the figure was 22 percent.[26]

The debate between traditionalists and progressives over how to teach language skills is old. What is frustrating is that in the United States this debate has been carried on for decades without anyone taking serious notice of the fact that American boys were becoming significantly less literate than girls. Surely this fact is one to which attention must be paid; surely the question of what is a "best practice" in the teaching of reading and writing must consider how well it works for boys.

The federal government, state departments of education, and women's groups have been expending millions of dollars addressing a surreal self-esteem problem that allegedly afflicts girls more than boys. In the matter of literacy, we have a real and genuinely alarming difference between males and females. But this shows boys in trouble, and no one seems to want to talk about that, much less take concerted action to correct it. For while it is perfectly acceptable to say that boys are psychologically distressed and in need of rescue from the myths of boyhood, it is not popular to say that our educational system is shortchanging boys academically. So at the present time, we in the United States are taking no constructive action to aid the nation's underachieving boys.

THE WIDER BACKGROUND

A FRIEZE ON THE facade of the Horace Mann building of Columbia Teachers College celebrates nine great education pioneers. Among them are Johann Heinrich Pestalozzi (1746–1827), Johann Friedrich Herbart (1776–1841), and Friedrich Froebel (1782–1852). Few Americans know much about the profound influence that these eighteenth-century German and Swiss theorists have had on American education. Froebel, for example, is credited with inventing the concept of the kindergarten. The German word "Kindergarten" literally means a garden whose plants are children. Froebel regarded children as fragile young plants and the ideal teacher as a gentle gardener:

> To young plants and animals we give space, and time, and rest, knowing that they will unfold to beauty by laws working in each. We avoid acting upon them by force, for we know that such intrusion upon their natural growth could injure their development. Yet man treats the young human being as if it were a piece of wax, a lump of clay out of which he can mould what he will! . . . Education and instruction should from the very first be a passive, observant, protective, rather than prescribing, determining, interfering. . . . All training and in-

struction which prescribes and fixes, that is interferes with Nature, must tend to limit and injure.[27]

Froebel wrote these words almost two hundred years ago, but his
plant/child metaphor continues to inspire American educators. In the
most straightforward sense, the plant metaphor is profoundly antiedu-
cational; after all, you can't teach a plant; all you can do is help it develop.
Progressive educators oppose "interference" with the child's nature and
look for ways to release his or her creative forces. Teachers are urged to
build on the "natural curiosity children bring to school and ask the kids
what they want to learn."[28] All this is antithetical to classical education.
A traditional teacher such as Mrs. Daugherty establishes a strict curriculum based on requirements and standards that all students are expected
to satisfy. She knows what her students need to learn at each stage, and
there is little likelihood that she will ask them to choose what they
should take up next.

*Best Practice: New Standards for Teaching and Learning in
America's Schools* is a 1998 summary of the "emerging standards of
state-of-the-art teaching."[29] Its authors, three curriculum experts from
National-Louis University in Evanston, Illinois, are themselves progressives, but they base their recommendations on what "good teachers do."
Their list of "best practices" reflects what they say is the "unanimous"
opinion of leading education experts. As the authors explain:

> Whether the recommendations come from the National
> Council of Teachers of Mathematics, the Center for the Study
> of Reading, the National Writing Project, the National Council
> for the Social Studies, the American Association for the Ad-
> vancement of Science, the National Council of Teachers of
> English, the National Association for the Education of Young
> Children, or the International Reading Association, the funda-
> mental insights into teaching and learning are remarkably
> congruent. Indeed, on many key issues the recommendations
> from these diverse organizations are unanimous.[30]

What are the specific recommendations of these leading education
organizations? The authors of *Best Practice* draw up a list of the "new"
standards and practices. The list, in fact, is not new. It is a compendium of

the basic tenets of progressivism. It is also the exact opposite of what the British headmasters are recommending for boys. As the authors of *Best Practice* explain, our major teaching associations agree that our schools need:

- LESS student passivity: sitting, listening, receiving, and absorbing information
- LESS rote memorization of facts and details
- LESS emphasis on competition and grades in school
- MORE active learning in the classroom with all the attendant noise and movement of students doing, talking, and collaborating
- MORE cooperative, collaborative activity; developing the classroom as an interdependent community.[31]

Many of these recommendations reflect views put forward by Harold Rugg and Ann Shumaker in *The Child-Centered School,* a classic of progressivism written back in 1928.[32] As the education scholar Diane Ravitch explains, Rugg and Shumaker believed that the primary focus of education should be "freedom, activity and creative self-expression."[33] These ideas were also present in the works of Rugg's famous and influential contemporary William Heard Kilpatrick of Columbia University. They would return again in the 1960s, when A. S. Neill's *Summerhill* became a best-seller, and again in the writings of the "angry young educators" such as John Holt, Herbert Kohl, and Jonathan Kozol. Here is a précis of their contribution from a recent historical retrospective by Lynn Olson in *Education Week:* "They derided the meaningless routines, dehumanizing discipline, and lock step schedules of many schools; denounced the unbridled authoritarianism and the schools' role in perpetuating social inequities; and waxed eloquent over their own attempts at innovation.[34]

In 1986, an influential book, *Women's Ways of Knowing,* gave a feminist twist to the progressivist agenda. Its authors claimed that women learned best in a cooperative, collaborative classroom. They impugned competition and favored "connected learning"—a "warmer and fairer" teaching style that allows students to "empathetically enter into the subject they are studying."[35]

The authors of *Best Practice* boast that their recommendations are the expression of an "unrecognized consensus" stemming from a "remarkably consistent, harmonious vision of this 'best educational practice.' "[36] Altogether oblivious to the widening learning gap that is leaving American children far behind the children of other industrial countries, they celebrate the "potential transforming power" of progressivism's "harmonious vision." It is a vision that anyone concerned with the career prospects of American young people can no longer afford to trust. Treating children as plants unfolding "to beauty by laws working in each" has not succeeded. Basic intellectual skills such as reading and writing do not develop by way of laws working within. Literacy does not come naturally to human beings. It certainly does not come naturally to many little boys.

For some years now, British education officials have been complaining that the progressive approach to the teaching of language skills disadvantages boys. In 1995, School Standards Minister Stephen Byers said, "A return to more structured reading lessons will benefit both boys and girls, but the evidence shows that it is boys who have been most disadvantaged by the move away from phonics."[37]

Bonnie Macmillan, a British education scholar, has researched the decline in literacy in the primary grades. Her conclusion in *Why Schoolchildren Can't Read* is the same as Byers's: progressive education methods—especially whole language—put boys at special risk: "Boys are more likely than girls to have problems learning to read. . . . They may be more distracted by extraneous noise, particularly speech, during learning tasks, and may be more susceptible to picture effects, the wide range of bright and colorful illustrations in their readers distracting their attention from the decoding tasks."[38] And she concludes: "[S]ince . . . boys [are] are more susceptible to developing reading problems than girls, it seems likely that the lack of appropriate instruction will take more of a toll on the reading attainment of boys."[39]

As far as I know, no one in the United States has considered the problem of language teaching in this light. The idea that some approaches are better for one sex than the other is not in itself politically incorrect, provided they favor girls. For the time being we cannot expect our public officials to suggest that teachers assign more boy-friendly materials.

OTHER PEDAGOGICAL DERAILMENTS

THE BRITISH EXPERIENCE suggests that boys respond well to the older pedagogies. If that is right, it is boys who are paying the highest price for the current misguided fashions in education. One such fashion is the celebration of "cooperative learning" and the denigration of competition. The London *Daily Telegraph*'s education writer, Janet Daley, who thinks as well as she writes, correctly points out that boys have been adversely affected by the current trend to deemphasize the competitive elements in learning. "By rejecting the old-fashioned ladder of tests, measurable achievement and competition, incentives were lost that had once given school a comprehensible point to many pupils— particularly the male ones. [A] world in which no one can be called a winner and nothing counts as losing will have little call on the young male psyche."[40]

The movement to eliminate competitive rankings in American schools has made great headway in recent years. Pat Riordan, dean of admissions at George Mason University, researched class rankings for the National Association of Secondary Schools. She estimates that 60 percent of schools no longer use them.[41] At Community High, a public secondary school in Ann Arbor, Michigan, academic awards at graduation are kept a secret. There are no class rankings, no valedictorian. At graduation, everyone gets a turn to speak. As the guidance counselor explains, "Everybody is seen as an equal contributor to the class of '99."

WE HONOR ALL STUDENTS says a bumper sticker from Drew Elementary School in Arlington, Virginia. The implication is that schools with honor rolls dishonor those who do not qualify. Jim Mitchell, executive director of the Maryland Association of Elementary School Principals, explains the new hostility to the honor roll: "It flies in the face of the philosophy of not making it so competitive for those little kids. . . . We even frown on spelling bees."[42]

Throughout the country, battles are raging. Typically, school officials are seeking to eliminate competitive practices, and parents and school board members are fighting to reinstate them. After several schools in Prince William County, Virginia, tried to eliminate the honor roll, the school board intervened. In defending it, one board member, John Harper, Jr., expressed an opinion very much at odds with the spirit of progressivism but shared by many parents: "To me, competition is what America is all about. The more they compete, the better they become." [43]

Competition that provides incentives to excel is as natural to a successful classroom as it is to a successful sports team. Competition in matters of intellect is not harmful but essential to progress. The Talmudic sage who said, "The envy that scholars bear to one another increases the world's wisdom" had it right. Competitive learners have always been a driving force in the advancement of knowledge. Of course grades are competitive, but they "increase the world's wisdom." E. D. Hirsch, the educator and reformer from the University of Virginia, advises, "[I]nstead of trying fruitlessly to abolish competition as an element of human nature, we should try to guide it into educationally productive channels." [44]

A lot of what is now considered bad practice—an emphasis on skills and drills, a reliance on competitive motivations, a teacher-centered pedagogy—is unavailable in many of today's schools. Yet these practices may be especially effective in getting boys to learn and progress. American educators need to ask whether, in moving away from skills and drills, phonics, teacher-led discussions, competition, and same-sex classes, they have not inadvertently been moving away from what works for boys.

THE WAR AGAINST SINGLE-SEX EDUCATION FOR BOYS

As SOON AS they identified the gender education gap, British educators began seriously experimenting with same-sex classes in coed public schools as a way of helping to narrow it. This courted progressivist rancor. As the London *Times* pointed out in 1994, "The schools' proposal [for same-sex classes] challenges the progressive orthodoxy of the past 30 years that holds that single-sex is 'unnatural.' " [45] Marian Cox, headmistress at the Cotswold School, admitted that single-sex schools were an unorthodox measure, but, she said, "We have a national crisis with boys' under-achievement in English. Either we tackle it, or we put our heads in the sand and ignore it. We felt the time had come to bite the bullet." [46]

When American schools try to develop special programs for boys, they find groups such as the National Organization for Women and the American Civil Liberties Union poised to oppose them. In 1989, threats of lawsuits from both organizations prevented the Detroit public schools from proceeding with plans for all-male academies for at-risk urban youths. When schools in Dade County, Florida, were considering establishing two all-male classes for underachieving boys, the U.S. Department of Education's Office of Civil Rights blocked them.

In 1994, Senator John Danforth tried to address this impasse. He offered an amendment to an education bill proposing that ten school districts be permitted to experiment with same-sex classes without threat of lawsuit. The amendment passed the Senate but was rejected in conference with the House of Representatives. Says Danforth, "I was stunned at the organized opposition to the amendment. Opponents argued vehemently that the provision would result in injustice to young girls, despite the amendment's requirement that same-sex classes be offered to both boys and girls." [47]

The vehemence is supplied by girl-partisan groups such as NOW, which argues that "segregation" by sex is as pernicious as that by race. Anne Conners, president of the New York City chapter of NOW, has stated the organization's official position: "Public money should not be used to fund institutions segregated on the basis of sex." [48] But at least NOW is consistent: it applies the principle that "segregated schools and classes are bad" to both all-male and all-female programs. NOW has joined the ACLU in challenging the legality of the highly successful Young Women's Leadership School in East Harlem, a girls-only public school started in 1996.

Other women's groups, such as the National Women's Law Center, suggest that same-sex programs may be justifiable for girls, but not for boys. Deborah Brake, a senior counsel at NWLC, notes that the "considerable network" of federal, state, local, and private scholarships and programs for girls and women may be legitimate because of past inequities: "In light of the history of discrimination against women in education and the barriers that female students continue to face based on their gender, there [may be] a legitimate place for such programs." [49] Judith Shapiro, president of Barnard College, is less tentative. In a 1994 opinion piece in the Baltimore *Sun:* "In a society that favors men over women, men's institutions operate to preserve privilege, women's institutions challenge privilege and attempt to expand access to the good things of life." [50]

In fact, our society does not favor boys. It certainly does not favor the growing number of boys who are disengaged, barely literate, and without the prospects of going to college. These young men have very little access to "the good things of life." Unfortunately, elite educational leaders such as Shapiro and Brake, who oppose single-sex pedagogy for boys, have little interest in finding out whether all-male classes are useful for the many thousands of at-risk boys.

A SCHOOL IN BALTIMORE

HARFORD HEIGHTS ELEMENTARY SCHOOL, the largest elementary school in Maryland, is in a poor section of Baltimore. No one at the school has read the report of the British headmasters; but Harford teachers and administrators, determined to find ways to help young males succeed academically, have found their own way to many of the practices recommended in *Can Boys Do Better?*

Since the mid-nineties the school has experimented with same-sex classes for both boys and girls. These classes are optional. Parents and teachers jointly decide who will most benefit. In selecting students for the all-male classes, school officials give boys with behavior problems and boys from fatherless homes priority. (These two groups often overlap.)

As in Great Britain, the all-boy classes are taught by male teachers, and the boys' natural competitiveness and high-spiritedness are not discouraged but channeled to good ends. As the former principal who initiated the program said, "The boys become competitive rather than combative." [51]

Walter Sallee, who has taught an all-boys class at Harford Heights for three years, uses many of the old-fashioned methods favored by the British headmasters. His classes are highly structured. He teaches phonics, grammar, and diction. He carefully monitors student progress. He uses a lot of boy-friendly materials; for example, he has developed math lessons based on Jackie Robinson's baseball statistics. His students, like boys everywhere, are fascinated by sports and sports stars, so these lessons are a great success. In gym class, his focus is character education through sportsmanship.

Sallee works hard to exploit the boys' natural competitiveness to promoting academic achievement. He breaks his class (twenty-seven ten-year-old boys in 1998–99) down into "teams." He turns classroom activities into contests. There is an elaborate point system. There are prizes. School uniforms are optional at Harford, but most of the boys in Sallee's class choose to wear them. Teams get extra points when all members don the uniform.

The boys in his all-male classes are mostly poor and African-American. Sallee is concerned about their self-esteem and confidence; but he does not rely on gimmicks or therapeutic methods. The boys gain confidence by mastering skills, becoming good sports, being team players and young gentlemen. One of Sallee's primary aims is to help his students develop their social skills. They learn to express themselves with confidence, and they learn manners. Several times a year the all-boy and all-girl classes take part in shared events. One favorite occasion is a Thanksgiving banquet. The boys escort the girls to the table, help them into their chairs, and engage in polite conversation. The children love it—especially the girls.

Sallee's students are at risk for every kind of academic and behavioral problem. But in this all-male environment, such problems nearly vanish. Should a boy neglect to do his work or misbehave, he hurts his team and disappoints his teacher. School disengagement is a problem for many boys, but it is especially severe among young black males. The boys in Sallee's class are the very opposite of disengaged. They are enthralled. As Sallee told me, "They love the positive attention they get in the class. They look forward to it and hate to miss a single day."[52]

Harford Heights offers same-sex classes in grades three, four, and five. The classes are a great success with parents, who are asking for more of them. It is easy to see why. Millions of parents, rich and poor, from all ethnic backgrounds, would welcome an opportunity for their sons to attend a class like Mr. Sallee's. Boys everywhere need structure, phonics, diction, grammar, and a competitive environment. Mr. Sallee's deliberate efforts to teach ethics through sportsmanship and good manners could be the making of many boys. But the likelihood of many parents having such an opportunity is remote. The forces arrayed against public, same-sex education for boys are formidable indeed.

SOME PRIVATE BOYS' SCHOOLS

THE HEIGHTS SCHOOL is in the center of Potomac, Maryland, one of the wealthiest suburbs of Washington, D.C. In many ways, it could not be more unlike Harford. The students at Harford are mostly poor and black: at the Heights they are predominantly white and middle or upper middle class. Harford is in a run-down section of Baltimore. Heights sits on twenty wooded acres. Harford is a public elementary school. Heights is an independent all-male Catholic elementary and high school. But there are some striking similarities in the way the two schools educate boys.

The much-loved Heights headmaster (recently retired), Joseph McPherson, can sound very much like Sallee when talking about how boys learn. "Boys need games, and they thrive on competition," he explains. "Who can skip the rock the most number of times?" All twenty-seven teachers at the Heights are male. "Boys are much more docile to men," says McPherson. Yet the school is hardly macho. The younger boys (aged eight to ten) attend class in log cabins filled with collections of insects, plants, and flowers. They memorize poetry and take weekly classes in painting and drawing. The day I visited, I observed a class of well-behaved fifth-graders sitting in rows, wearing blue blazers, and taking turns performing scales on their recorders.

Competition is part of the everyday life of the school—there are lots of awards and prizes—but, as in Sallee's class, it is constrained by ethics. One favorite all-school game is "Capture the Flag": it's a war game, played with a great deal of team spirit and with an established tradition of the older boys protecting the younger ones.

For McPherson, the goal of educating children is not only to impart information and teach skills but to "provide them with a noble vision of life—to convey to them that they have to do something great with their lives." He believes that adult males are uniquely suited to impart this philosophy to boys. McPherson explains that male teachers can introduce boys to the world of ideas, of nature, art, poetry, and music, and generally "expand their range of interests without the boys feeling they are risking their masculinity."

Landon, another distinguished boys' school, is a few miles away from the Heights. The headmaster, Damon Bradley, explained to me that at all-male academies boys do things "they would never agree to do if girls were around." At Landon, 75 percent of the boys are involved in music and art. "Competition is something boys respond to," says the headmaster. But in a boys' school, competition takes place in unusual pursuits. One highly coveted honor at Landon is to be selected for the bell choir. Oddly enough, football players and other school athletes love the choir and vie for a place in it. It is hard to get into the choir, which is run like a team sport. Headmaster Bradley seems touched by all the burly choir members with their thick necks wearing white gloves. In his writings on boys' schools, Bradley dwells on the ancient view that manliness and virtue are intimately related:

> Our Latin teacher has explained to me that the Latin word for "man" (vir) can easily be recognized in the word *virtute*, as its root derivation, suggesting that "virtue" and "manliness" were integrally linked in the Roman mind. . . . [I]n the classical world—and arguably in boys' schools—manliness is defined more by virtue and less by might. . . . [T]he primary challenge of our schools is to help boys fuse "gentleness" with manliness.[53]

WHY SINGLE-SEX CLASSES ARE GENERALLY UNAVAILABLE

WHEN THE U.S. SUPREME COURT ruled in 1996 that the Virginia Military Institute was violating the Fourteenth Amendment to the Constitution by excluding women, it dealt an almost fatal blow to same-sex education *for boys.* In the majority opinion, written by Justice Ruth Bader Ginsburg, the Court retained full protection for any female-only programs that could be said to compensate for the disabilities women suffer: "Sex classifications may be used to compensate women 'for particular economic disabilities [they have] suffered,' to 'promote equal employment opportunity,' to advance the full development of the talent and capacities of our Nation's people. But such classifications may not be used, as they once were, to create or perpetuate the legal, social and economic inferiority of women." [54]

In light of this ruling, all-girls programs could still be seen as compensatory; all-boys programs, on the other hand, are regarded as discriminatory. The ruling puts a chill on all special initiatives for boys. However, while it discourages them, it does not strictly prohibit them. Programs that separate the sexes while offering each the same resources and opportunities remain permissible. At least, that is how the U.S. Office of Civil Rights seems to be interpreting the law. Programs in Maryland, Virginia, and California have so far survived legal challenges from the Office of Civil Rights because they cover both boys and girls and are voluntary. [55] In practice, however, single-sex education is an allowable option for girls, but rarely for boys.

In 1996, the California state legislature allocated $5 million toward the development of all-male and all-female "academies." These may be either separate schools or special programs within existing coed schools. [56] Sean Walsh, a spokesman for then-Governor Pete Wilson, who initiated the program, justified it as a corrective against the laissez-faire progressivism that has seen literacy plunge in the primary grades: "The [same-sex] academies will allow a more structured, more disciplined environment where kids could get a core curriculum, a sense of right and wrong, a sense of personal responsibility, a sense of duty." [57] The program is in its early stages, but it is already quite popular with parents and students. There is anecdotal evidence that it is succeeding, but a formal analysis of the program will be submitted to the state legislature in 2000.

Women's groups remain uneasy, however. In 1998, the American Association of University Women released *Separated by Sex: A Critical Look at Single-Sex Education for Girls*. The report, a compilation of essays by several scholars, turned out to be inconclusive. Most of the contributors agreed that more careful and systematic long-term research was needed. But the AAUW press release was categorically negative. "What the report shows is that separating by sex is not the solution to gender inequity in education," wrote Maggie Ford, president of the AAUW Educational Foundation. Critics soon pointed out the disparity between the full report and the press summary. [58] One of the contributing scholars, Cornelius Riordan, was stunned by the negative spin in the press release. He told the *Los Angeles Times* that the releases were "slanted" and "off the deep end." [59]

The episode should stand as a warning. In their laudable efforts to evaluate the efficacy of same-sex programs objectively, California legislators would do well to take precautions not to be pulled into the acrimonious misandrist maelstrom that this issue currently generates in this country. Otherwise, they'll find themselves in the position of Professor Riordan and Senator Danforth before him. I spoke to California Governor Pete Wilson in June 1999 about the evaluation. He was pessimistic about the prospects of a fair review. He believed the entire process was being compromised by politics and special agendas.

Meanwhile, the British experiment with all-male pedagogy is proceeding, with promising initial results. On July 14, 1997, *The Times* of London carried a story under the headline "Boys Do Better in Single-Sex Schools": "Boys gain more from single-sex education than girls, according to research that will ignite the debate over the advantages of segregating sexes at school. Boys in single-sex schools did about 20 percent better than those in mixed sex [classes]."[60]

This *Times* story reported the findings of a small study carried out by a research group commissioned by all-male British schools; its conclusions may not be relevant to American boys. At this time we simply don't know whether single-sex classes are the key to a better pedagogy for boys. Nor are we likely to find out in the near future so long as girl-partisan organizations effectively discourage research and debate on the same-sex solution to the problem of lagging boys.[61]

Coeducation is a strong tradition in the United States, and it is doubtful that we will ever adopt a single-sex system on a large scale. On the other hand, those who oppose it on ideological grounds should not be indulged. Single-sex classes do not cost substantially more than mixed classes. They seem to be working for privileged boys who attend private schools like Heights and Landon as well as for the disadvantaged boys in Mr. Sallee's class. The British headmasters believe in them. We need a national discussion of the merits of all-male classes. And we need to take care that groups such as NOW, the AAUW, and the National Women's Law Center do not control and shape that discussion.

SUPPOSE THE BRITISH HEADMASTERS and government officials are right in suggesting that boys would generally be much better off in a traditional learning environment. What are the chances that American schools will provide it? At present, the prospects for change do not look bright. To begin with, the academic plight of boys has not yet even been identified as a serious problem by either the government or the educational establishment. Boys are still not on the agenda. The media's interest in boys is focused not on their academic deficits but on their potential for violence. Then, too, the child-centered, therapeutic style of education under which boys do not do well appears deeply entrenched in many of our "best" school systems.

All the same, I am optimistic that change for the better will be coming rather quickly on the heels of a widespread public awareness that the future of our children, and especially of our sons, is in jeopardy. The onset of a galvanizing awareness (which the British already have) cannot be delayed here much longer.

I have been arguing that our educational system needs to address the problem of male underachievement. In the next chapter I shall turn to what our schools have been doing and failing to do for boys' moral development. The consequences of failure in this area have not escaped the notice of the public.

CHAPTER EIGHT

THE MORAL LIFE OF BOYS

BOYS WHO ARE morally neglected have unpleasant ways of getting themselves noticed. All children need clear, unequivocal rules. They need structure. They thrive on firm guidance and discipline from the adults in their lives. But it appears that boys need these things even more than girls do.

The Josephson Institute of Ethics conducts surveys on the moral attitudes of young people. These surveys show that girls routinely outperform boys in matters of honesty. For the *1998 Report Card on the Ethics of American Youth*, Josephson researchers polled a sample of ten thousand high school students. They found that significantly more boys "agree" or "strongly agree" that "I would be willing to cheat on a test if it would help me get into college" (44 percent of males, 27 percent of females). Thirty-three percent of high school boys said that in the past year they had shoplifted "two or more times"; for girls, the figure was 21 percent.[1]

The American Psychiatric Association defines a "conduct disorder" as "a repetitive and persistent pattern of behavior in which the basic rights of others, or other major age-appropriate societal norms or rules, are violated."[2] According to the APA, the prevalence of conduct disorder has increased since the 1960s. Far more males than females have the disorder: "Rates vary depending on the nature of populations sampled and the methods of ascertainment: for males under age 18 years, rates range from 6 percent to 16 percent; for females, rates range from 2 percent to 9 percent."[3] For conduct disorders severe enough to get the attention of the police, boys are even more predominant. According to the Justice Department's Office of Juvenile Justice and Delinquency Prevention Center, 73 percent of children aged ten to seventeen arrested for property crimes in 1993 were boys; of those arrested for violent crimes, 86 percent were boys.[4]

That the male's propensity for antisocial behavior is significantly greater than the female's holds true cross-culturally. A 1997 University of Vermont study compared parents' reports of children's behavior in twelve countries. The countries studied (which included the United States, Thailand, Greece, Jamaica, Puerto Rico, and Sweden) differed greatly in how they defined gender roles. Yet in every case boys were more likely than girls to fight, swear, steal, throw tantrums, and threaten others.[5]

Every new generation enters society unformed and uncouth. Princeton University demographer Norman B. Ryder speaks of "a perennial invasion of barbarians who must somehow be civilized . . . for societal survival."[6] Ryder views the problem from the vantage point of society. But when socialization is inadequate, the children also suffer. A society that fails in its mission to humanize and civilize its children fails its male children in uniquely harmful ways. The rise in conduct disorder is one indication that the socialization of males is increasingly ineffective.

Janet Daley, the education reporter at *The Daily Telegraph* in London, has written at length about how the lack of directive moral education harms boys more than girls:

> There is one indisputable fact with which anyone who is serious about helping young men must come to terms: boys need far more discipline, structure and authority in their lives than do girls. . . . Boys must be actively constrained by a whole phalanx of adults who come into contact with them—parents, teachers, neighbors, policemen, passers-by in the streets—be-

fore they can be expected to control their asocial, egoistic impulses.[7]

Many contemporary American children never encounter this "phalanx of adults." In fact, as I shall try to show, there are now a large number of adults who have defected altogether from the central task of civilizing the children in their care, leaving them to fend for themselves.

WHEN THE "BARBARIANS" DON'T GET CIVILIZED

IN THE LATE EIGHTIES and early nineties, newspapers carried shocking stories about adolescent boys exploiting, assaulting, and terrorizing girls. In the South Bronx, a group of boys known as the "whirlpoolers" surrounded girls in public swimming pools and sexually assaulted them. In Glen Ridge, New Jersey, popular high school athletes viciously raped a retarded girl. In Lakewood, California, a gang of high school boys known as the Spur Posse turned the sexual exploitation of girls into a sport.

Women's groups seized on these incidents as symptomatic of a violent misogyny pervading American culture. They blamed the stereotypical male socialization. Referring to the Glen Ridge case, Betty Friedan noted somberly that "machismo is a fertile breeding-ground for the seeds of evil."[8] Columnist Judy Mann wrote that the California Spur Posse case "contains all the ingredients of patriarchal culture gone haywire."[9] For Susan Faludi, the Spurs were "ground zero of the American masculinity crisis."[10]

Joan Didion wrote a lengthy piece on the Spur Posse for *The New Yorker,* and Columbia University journalism professor Bernard Lefkowitz spent six years researching the Glen Ridge case. In 1997, he published *Our Guys: The Glen Ridge Rape and the Secret Life of the Perfect Suburb.* Didion and Lefkowitz offer a detailed view of the lives of the young male predators. We can see for ourselves some of the forces that turned seemingly normal boys into criminals. Were they desensitized by being separated from their mothers at too early an age, as Pollack and Gilligan suggest? Are they products of conventional male socialization? Are they the offspring of what Judy Mann calls the "machocracy"?[11]

"OUR GUYS"

THE GLEN RIDGE rape was reported on May 25, 1989. Several popular high school athletes had lured a retarded girl into a basement, removed her clothes, and penetrated her with a broomstick and a baseball bat. Lefkowitz was intrigued by the question of how seemingly normal American boys had come to commit such acts: "This wasn't about just a couple of oddballs with a sadistic streak. . . . Thirteen males were present in the basement where the alleged rape occurred. There also were reports that a number of other boys had tried to entice the young woman into the basement a second time to repeat the experience. . . . I wanted to know more about how this privileged American community raised its children, especially its sons." [12]

According to Lefkowitz, these boys were "pure gold, every mother's dream, every father's pride. They were not only Glen Ridge's finest, but in their perfection they belonged to all of us. They were Our Guys." [13] What had gone wrong? To find out, he undertook "an examination of the character of their community and of the young people who grew up in it." [14]

Lefkowitz shares with Friedan and Mann the view that machismo created much of the evil:

> The Jocks didn't invent the idea of mistreating young women. The ruling clique of teenagers adhered to a code of behavior that mimicked, distorted, and exaggerated the values of the adult world around them. . . . But these misguided and ultimately dehumanizing values were not exclusive to this one small town. As the continuing revelations of sexual harassment and abuse in the military, in colleges, in the workplace . . . suggest, these values have deep roots in American life. [15]

Lefkowitz presents the Glen Ridge story as a modern morality tale about misogyny and the oppression of women. But the facts he powerfully reports sustain a very different interpretation of what happened. The real story is about how a group of adults—parents, teachers, coaches, community leaders—failed massively and tragically to carry out their responsibility to civilize the children in their care. The problem with these young male predators was not conventional male socialization but its absence.

All through elementary school and junior high, twins Kevin and Lyle Scherzer and Chris Archer, the three boys who would later be convicted of rape, had bullied other students and mistreated teachers. The "jocks," as their group was called, routinely disrupted class with outbursts and obscenities. They smashed up the science laboratory, trashed the Glen Ridge Country Club, stole from other students, and vandalized homes. All these actions apparently went unpunished. No charges were filed. No arrests were made. No athletic privileges were rescinded. No apologies were demanded or received. According to Lefkowitz, the jocks had such a bad reputation that twenty families withdrew their children from the school system during their reign.[16]

The history of abuse of the retarded girl, Leslie, goes back to Kevin and Lyle's early childhood. The girl's mother reports that when the twins were in kindergarten, they tricked her daughter into eating dog feces. Later, they fed her mud, pinched her arm until it was covered with welts, and routinely referred to her in public as "Brain-Les," "Head-Les," and "retard."

Again, it seems that the boys were never reprimanded or punished. Leslie's parents chose not to tell Kevin and Lyle's parents about the feces, the mud, and the welts. No one seemed to see the behavior in moral terms. Leslie's parents did consult a child psychologist, who blamed the incidents on the girl's immaturity—something she would grow out of. The active malice and cruelty of these boys were never regarded as serious problems to be stopped.

From the time they were small children, the boys who would later take part in the rape were opportunistically abusive and cruel to nearly anyone who crossed their paths. This pattern persisted through adolescence. It affected their peers regardless of sex. Later on, it affected their teachers and schoolmates. The glaring absence of any firm discipline, the failure of the adults in their lives to punish them for their actions, turned them into monsters.

By the time the Glen Ridge boys assaulted Leslie in the basement, they had had years of experience perpetrating mayhem and abuse—without suffering any consequences. Where were their parents? The school officials? The police? According to David Maltman, principal of the Glen Ridge Middle School, "These kids would act up in class, disrupt the learning situation, set other kids up, get in fights with them, go after them back and forth to school. By the fifth grade, they already had had a bad name for a long time." [17] Officials did attempt to intervene. Just before the unruly cohort entered high school, Maltman and the teachers developed a plan to introduce more discipline and order into the school. It had several features that are standard in many schools:

1. Students with learning and behavior disorders would be identified and put in special classes, and, where necessary, would be given professional treatment. (Kevin Scherzer, for example, had been classified as "neurologically impaired" in second grade. A child study team had given him the same classification as the retarded girl, Leslie. But his parents had always insisted that he be mainstreamed and treated as normal.)
2. The school would hire a crisis intervention counselor.
3. The school would institute an alcohol awareness program.
4. The school would draw up a new code of discipline, which it would strictly enforce.

Many Glen Ridge parents were incensed by these plans. They argued that hiring crisis intervention counselors and establishing an alcohol awareness program would give Glen Ridge a bad reputation. The very idea of having their children "classified" under some category of disorder made these parents angry. When Maltman presented the (mild) code of discipline at a parents meeting, "all hell broke loose." According to the principal, "The parents thought these were Gestapo methods." [18]

Lefkowitz's book describes boys raised so permissively, with so little moral guidance, that they ended up sociopaths. It is a tale of young barbarians who were never civilized, a suburban *Lord of the Flies*. The difference is that the feral English boys in William Golding's novel committed their atrocities when they were away from adults, stranded on an island after a shipwreck. What is so chilling about Glen Ridge is all the doting adults who had for years presided over their children's moral disintegration. The story behind the Lakewood, California, Spur Posse is very similar.

THE MORAL LIFE OF BOYS 185

"WHAT'S NOT TO LIKE ABOUT ME?"

THE SPUR POSSE, a popular high school clique that took its name from the San Antonio Spurs basketball team, consisted of twenty to thirty middle-class boys who competed with one another in "scoring" with girls. They especially targeted underage girls, and in March 1993 nine members were arrested and charged with a variety of crimes, ranging from sexual assault to rape. One of the alleged victims was a ten-year-old girl.

Eventually, most of the charges were dropped, but these swagger-ing, ignorant, predatory boys from "Rapewood" enjoyed a temporary celebrity. "We didn't do nothing wrong 'cause it's not illegal to hook up," an indignant nineteen-year-old Billy Shehan told *The New York Times*.[19] ("Hooking up" is a colloquial term for sexual intercourse; Billy was in the lead with sixty-seven "hookups.") The boys appeared on *Dateline* and the Maury Povich, Jane Whitney, and Jenny Jones shows, telling fas-cinated audiences about their sexual adventures.

Orthodox feminist writers such as Betty Friedan, Judy Mann, and Susan Faludi saw in the Spur Posse an embodiment of macho-patriarchal ideals. Less encumbered by a feminist framework, novelist and social critic Joan Didion saw them more conventionally as a group of socio-pathic boys. When Didion visited Lakewood in 1993 to do a story on them for *The New Yorker*, she noted that contempt for women was not all that the members of the Lakewood Spur Posse had in common. Like the Glen Ridge jocks, these boys had been permitted to terrorize a town with impunity for years. A member of the school board told Didion sto-ries of Spurs approaching nine- and ten-year-old children in play-grounds, stealing their baseball bats, and saying, "If you tell anyone, I'll beat your head in." The group had a long history of antisocial behavior, including burglary, credit card fraud, assault, arson, and even an at-tempted bombing.

Like the jocks, the Spur Posse had little sense of the harm and suf-fering they were causing and no feelings of remorse or shame. One thing they did seem to have was high self-esteem. Writing about them in her *New Yorker* piece, Joan Didion says: "The boys seemed to have heard about self-esteem, most recently at the 'ethics' assemblies . . . the school had hastily organized after the arrests, but hey, no problem. 'I'm definitely comfortable with myself and my self-esteem,' one said on *Dateline*."[20] When another interviewer asked a member of the group if he liked himself, the surprised boy replied, "Yeah, why wouldn't I? I mean, what is not to like about me?"

The then mayor of Lakewood, Marc Titel, rightly saw in this group of boys a deplorable failure of moral education: "We need to look at what kind of values we are communicating to our kids."[21]

Although boys are not morally inferior to girls, they are certainly more physically aggressive, more prone to violence, and less risk averse. It is precisely because boys are by nature more physically assertive that they so badly need a strict and explicit character education that places strong behavioral constraints on them, constraints that many progressive educators feel we have no right to "impose" on any child.

We gain little illumination by exotically talking about Glen Ridge and Lakewood in terms of "patriarchal culture gone haywire" or "ground zero of the American masculinity crisis." It is more to the point and less esoteric to regard them as examples of morally undeveloped boys and evidence of what can happen when adults withhold elementary moral instruction from the young males in their charge. The more one faults masculinity in itself, the farther one strays from acknowledging the failures of moral education in the last decades of the twentieth century. Talking about moral failure is less stylish than talking about the inimical workings of patriarchy. But it is far more to the point.

A SOCRATIC DIALOGUE

UNFORTUNATELY, even some moral philosophers are reluctant to talk in plain terms about right and wrong and to pronounce moral judgment in what look to be clear cases of moral callowness and immaturity. In the fall of 1996, I took part in a televised ethics program billed as a "Socratic dialogue." For an hour, I joined another ethics professor, a history teacher, and seven high school students in a discussion of moral dilemmas. The program, "Ethical Choices: Individual Voices," was shown on public television and is now circulated to high schools for use in classroom discussions of right and wrong.[22] Its message still troubles me.

In one typical exchange, the moderator, Stanford law professor Kim

Taylor-Thompson (now at New York University), posed this dilemma to the students: Your teacher has unexpectedly assigned you a five-page paper. You have only a few days to do it, and you are already overwhelmed with work. Would it be wrong to hand in someone else's paper?

Two of the girls found the suggestion unthinkable and spoke about responsibility, honor, and principle. "I wouldn't do it. It is a matter of integrity," said Elizabeth. "It's dishonest," said Erin. But two of the boys saw nothing wrong with cheating. Eleventh-grader Joseph flatly said, "If you have the opportunity, you should use it." Eric concurred: "I would use the paper and offer it to my friends."

I have taught moral philosophy to college freshmen for more than fifteen years, so I was not surprised to find students on the PBS program defending cheating. There are some in every class, who play devil's advocate with an open admiration for the Devil's position. But at least that evening, in our PBS "Socratic dialogue," I expected to have a professional ally in the person of the other philosophy teacher, Professor William Puka of the Rensselaer Polytechnic Institute. Surely he would join me in making the case for honesty.

Instead, the professor defected. He told the students that in this situation, it was the teacher who was immoral for having given the students such a burdensome assignment. He was disappointed in us for not seeing it his way. "What disturbs me," he said, "is how accepting you all seem to be of this assignment. To me it's outrageous from the point of view of learning to force you to write a paper in this short a time."

Through most of the session the professor focused on the hypocrisy of parents, teachers, and corporations but had little to say about the moral obligations of the students. When we discussed the immorality of shoplifting, he implied that stores were in the wrong for their pricing polices and talked about "corporations deciding on a twelve percent profit margin . . . and perhaps sweatshops."

The professor was friendly and to all appearances well meaning. Perhaps his goal was to "empower" students to question authority and rules. That, however, is something contemporary adolescents already know how to do. Too often, we are teaching students to question principles before they understand them. And in this case the professor was advising high school students to question moral teachings and rules of behavior that are crucial to their well-being.

Professor Puka's "hands-off" style has been fashionable in the public schools for thirty years. It has gone under various names: values clarification, situation ethics, self-esteem guidance. These so-called value-free approaches to ethics have flourished at a time when many parents are failing to give children basic guidance in right and wrong. Meanwhile, the courts have made matters worse. Since 1969, in cases like *Tinker v. Des Moines School District* and *Goss v. Lopez* (discussed below), the U.S. Supreme Court has greatly expanded the civil rights of children and diminished the power of teachers to enforce order and discipline.[23]

Educators such as the professor in that Socratic dialogue, as well as some Supreme Court justices, have turned many of our schools into value-free zones. As usual, their intentions were benign: to protect the liberty, autonomy, and self-expression of young people from adult authoritarian pressure. Unfortunately, these theorists and jurists are conceptually confused. And it is boys, more than anyone else, who suffer from their confusion.

The story of why so many children are being deprived of elementary moral training spans three or four decades of misguided reforms by educators, by parents, and by judges. Reduced to its philosophical essentials, it is the story of the triumph of Jean-Jacques Rousseau over Aristotle.

ARISTOTLE VERSUS ROUSSEAU

SOME 2,400 YEARS AGO, Aristotle articulated what children need: clear guidance on how to be moral human beings. What Aristotle advocated became the default model for moral education over the centuries. He showed parents and teachers how to civilize the invading hordes of child barbarians. Only recently have many educators begun to denigrate his teachings.

Aristotle regarded children as wayward, uncivilized, and very much in need of discipline. The early Christian philosopher Saint Augustine went further, regarding children's refractory nature as a manifestation of the original sin committed by Adam and Eve when they rebelled against the dictates of God. Each philosopher, in his way, regarded perversity as a universal feature of human nature.

Aristotle compared moral education to physical training. Just as we become strong and skillful by doing things that require strength and skill, so, he said, do we become good by practicing goodness. Ethical education, as he understood it, was training in emotional control and disciplined behavior. Habituation to right behavior comes before an appreciation or understanding of why we should be good. First, children must be socialized by inculcating into them habits of decency and using suitable punishments and rewards to discipline them to behave well. Eventually they will understand the reasons for and advantages of being moral human beings.

Far from giving priority to the free expression of emotion, Aristotle (and Plato too) taught that moral development is achieved by educating children to modulate their emotions. For Aristotle, self-awareness meant being aware of and avoiding behaviors that emotion dictates but reason proscribes: "We must notice the errors into which we ourselves are liable to fall (because we all have different tendencies) . . . and we must drag ourselves in the contrary direction." [24] Children with good moral habits will gain control over the intemperate side of their nature and grow into free and flourishing human beings. As Aristotle put it, "The moral virtues . . . are engendered in us neither by nor contrary to nature; we are constituted by nature to receive them, but their full development is due to habit. . . . So it is a matter of no little importance what sort of habits we form from the earliest age—it makes a vast difference, or rather all the difference in the world." [25]

Aristotle's general principles for raising moral children were unquestioned through most of Western history; even today his teachings represent commonsense opinion about child rearing. But in the eighteenth century, the wisdom of Aristotle was directly challenged by the theories of the Enlightenment philosopher Jean-Jacques Rousseau.

Rousseau denied that children are born wayward (originally sinful), insisting instead that they are, by nature, noble, virtuous beings who are corrupted by an intrusive socialization. The untutored child is spontaneously good and graceful: "When I picture to myself a boy of ten or twelve, healthy, strong and well built for his age, only pleasant thoughts arise. . . . I see him bright, eager, vigorous, care-free, completely absorbed in the present, rejoicing in abounding vitality." [26]

According to Rousseau, "the first education should be purely negative. . . . It consists not in teaching virtue or truth, but in preserving the heart from vice and the mind from error." [27] He rejects the traditional notion that moral education in the early stages must habituate the child to virtuous behavior: "The only habit a child should be allowed to acquire is to contract none. . . . Prepare in good time for the reign of freedom and the exercise of his powers, by allowing his body its natural habits and accustoming him always to be his own master and follow the dictates of his will as soon as he has a will of his own." [28]

Contrary to the received view, Rousseau believed the child's nature to be originally good and free of sin. As he saw it, a proper education provides the soil for the flourishing of the child's inherently good nature, bringing it forth unspoiled and fully effective. In his view, the goal of moral education is defeated when an external code is imposed on children. Rousseau was modern in his distrust of socially ordained morals as well as his belief that the best education elicits the child's own authentic (benevolent) nature. Rousseau emphatically rejected the Christian doctrine that human beings are innately rebellious and naturally sinful: "Let us lay it down as an incontestable principle that the first impulses of nature are always right. There is no original perversity in the human heart." [29]

Although Rousseau was against instilling moral "habits" into a free and noble being, he did allow that a child's development requires guidance and encouragement to elicit its own good nature. He urged parents and tutors to put the child's "kindly feelings into action." [30]

Other Christian and pagan thinkers were convinced that far more was needed. They insisted that virtue cannot be attained without a directed moral training that habituates the child to virtuous behavior. Saint Augustine and the orthodox Christian thinkers were especially pessimistic about the efficacy of putting kindly feelings into action. According to Augustine, not even the most disciplined moral education could guarantee a virtuous child; education without divine help ("grace") is insufficient. By contrast, not only do Rousseau's followers deny the Augustinian doctrine that our natures are originally sinful and rebellious, they go further by regarding "directive" moral education as an assault on a child's right to develop freely.

There is much to admire in Rousseau. He argued for humane child rearing at a time when rigidity and cruelty were common. Though his criticisms of the educational practices of his day were valid, his own recommendations have not proved workable. It is, perhaps, worth noting that he did not apply his fine theories to his own life; he was altogether irresponsible in dealing with his own children. [31] His theories, too, were marred by inconsistencies. On the one hand, he was firmly against instilling habits in a child; on the other, he dispensed a lot of sound Aristotelian advice to parents for habituating their children to the classical virtues: "Keep your pupil occupied with all the good deeds."

Despite his celebration of freedom, even Rousseau would have been appalled by the permissiveness we see so much of today. "The surest way to make your child unhappy," he wrote, "is to accustom him to get everything he wants." [32] All the same, he parted company with the traditionalists on the crucial question of human nature. For better or for worse, Rousseau's followers ignored his Aristotelian side and developed the "progressive" elements of his educational philosophy.

Though we would like to believe him, Rousseau's rosy picture of the child fails to convince. In "Émile," Rousseau states that although children may do bad deeds, a child can never be said to be bad, "because wrong action depends on harmful intention and that he will never have." [33] This flies in the face of common experience. Most parents and teachers will tell you that children often have harmful intentions. In perhaps the most famous description of children's "harmful intentions," Saint Augustine, in his *Confessions*, describes his boyhood pleasure in doing wrong—simply for the joy of flouting prohibitions:

> In a garden near our vineyard there was a pear tree, loaded with fruit that was desirable neither in appearance nor in taste. Late one night . . . a group of very bad youngsters set out to shake down and rob this tree. We took great loads of fruit from it, not for our own eating, but rather to throw it to the pigs; even if we did eat a little of it, we did this to do what pleased us for the reason that it was forbidden. [34]

Indeed, some parents and teachers might find Augustine's description of children's unruly nature understated. Some may find Golding's *Lord of the Flies* a more telling description of what children are naturally like than Rousseau's romantic ideal.

Who is right, Aristotle or Rousseau? Aristotle wins the argument in the court of common sense and historical experience. He certainly wins with most parents. Throughout the world, mothers and fathers never cease to work at habituating children to the exercise of self-control, temperance, honesty, courage.

But it is Rousseau who powerfully dominates the thinking of the theorists whose influence pervades modern schools of education. The educational philosophy of Rousseau inspired the progressive movement in education, which turned away from rote teaching and sought methods that would free the creativity of the child. Rousseau's ideas are also deployed to discredit the traditional directive style of moral education associated with Aristotelian ethical theory and Judeo-Christian religion and practice.

The directive style of education, denigrated as indoctrination, was cast aside in the second half of the twentieth century and discontinued as the progressive style became dominant. By the 1970s, character education had been effectively discredited and virtually abandoned in practice.

What happens when educators celebrate children's creativity and innate goodness and abandon the ancestral responsibility to discipline, train, and civilize them? Unfortunately, we know the answer: we are just emerging from a thirty-year experiment with moral deregulation. The ascendancy of Rousseau as the philosopher of education and the eclipse of Aristotle have been bad for all children, but they have been especially bad for boys.

VALUE-FREE KIDS

IN 1970, THEODORE SIZER, then dean of the Harvard Graduate School of Education, coedited with his wife, Nancy, a collection of ethics lectures entitled *Moral Education*.[35] The preface set the tone by condemning the morality of the "Christian gentleman," the American "prairie," *The McGuffey Readers*, and the hypocrisy of teachers who tolerate a grading system that is often the "terror of the young."[36] The Sizers were especially critical of the "crude and philosophically simpleminded sermonizing tradition" of the nineteenth century. They referred to directive ethics education in all its guises as "the old morality." According to the Sizers, leading moralists agree that that kind of morality "can and should be scrapped."[37]

The Sizers favored a "new morality" that gives primacy to students' autonomy and independence. Teachers should never preach or attempt to inculcate virtue; rather, through their actions, they should demonstrate a "fierce commitment" to social justice. In part, that means democratizing the classroom: "Teacher and children can learn about morality from each other."[38]

The Sizers preached a doctrine that was already being practiced in many schools throughout the country. Schools were scrapping the "old morality" in favor of alternatives that gave primacy to the children's moral autonomy. "Values clarification" was popular in the seventies. Proponents of values clarification consider it inappropriate for a teacher to encourage students, however subtly or indirectly, to adopt the values of the teacher or the community. The cardinal sin is to "impose" values on the student. Instead, the teacher's job is to help the students discover "their own values." In *Readings in Values Clarification* (1973), two of the leaders of the movement, Sidney Simon and Howard Kirschenbaum, explain what is wrong with traditional ethics education: "We call this approach 'moralizing,' although it has also been known as inculcation, imposition, indoctrination, and in its most extreme form, brainwashing."[39]

Lawrence Kohlberg, a Harvard moral psychologist, developed cognitive moral development, a second favored approach. Kohlberg shared the Sizers' low opinion of traditional morality, referring disdainfully to the "old bags of virtues" that earlier educators had sought to inculcate.[40] Kohlbergian teachers were more traditional than the proponents of values clarification. They sought to promote a Kantian awareness of duty and responsibility in students. They were also traditional in their opposition to the "moral relativism" that many progressive educators found congenial. All the same, they shared with other progressives a scorn for any form of top-down inculcation of moral principles. They too believed in "student-centered teaching," in which the teacher acts less as a guide than as a "facilitator" of the student's development.

Kohlberg himself would later change his mind and concede that his rejection of "indoctrinative" moral education had been a mistake.[41] But his admirable recantation had little effect. In the final decades of the twentieth century, the traditional indoctrinative (directive) approach to moral education had fallen into desuetude in most public schools and the negative views prevailed.

Ironically, the next fashion in progressive pedagogy, student-centered learning, was soon to leave the Kohlbergians and the values clarifiers far behind. The new buzzword was "self-esteem." By the late eighties, self-esteem education had become all the rage. Ethics was superseded by attention to the child's personal sense of well-being: the school's primary aim was to teach children to prize their rights and self-worth. In the old days, teachers would ask seventh-graders to write about

"The Person I Admire Most." But in today's "child-centered curriculum," they ask children to write essays celebrating themselves. In one popular middle school English text, an assignment called "The Nobel Prize for Being You" informs students that they are "wonderful" and "amazing" and instructs them to "create two documents in connection with your Nobel Prize. Let the first document be a nomination letter written by the person who knows you best. Let the second be the script for your acceptance speech, which you will give at the annual award ceremony in Stockholm, Sweden."[42] For extra credit, students can award themselves a trophy "that is especially designed for you and no one else."

Throughout most of human history, children learned about virtue and honor by hearing or reading the inspiring stories of great men and women. By the 1990s, this practice, which many educators regarded as too directive, was giving way to practices that suggested to students that they were their own best guides in life. This turn to the autonomous subject as the ultimate moral authority is a notable consequence of the triumph of the progressive style over traditional directive methods of education.

It's hard to see how the Harvard theorists who urged teachers to jettison the "crude and philosophically simpleminded sermonizing tradition" of the nineteenth century can defend the crude egoism that has replaced it. Apart from the philosophical niceties, there are concrete behavioral consequences. The moral deregulation that the New England educators called for took hold in the very decades that saw a rise in conduct disorders among boys in the nation's schools. No doubt much, perhaps most, of this trend can be ascribed to the large social changes that weakened family and community. But some of the blame can be laid at the doors of the well-intentioned professors who helped undermine the schools' traditional mission of morally edifying their pupils.

Few thinkers have written about individual autonomy with greater passion and good sense than the nineteenth-century philosopher John Stuart Mill. But Mill makes it clear that he is talking about adults. "We are not speaking of children," he says in *On Liberty*. "Nobody denies that people should be so taught and trained in youth as to know and benefit by the ascertained results of human experience."[43]

Mill could not foresee the advent of thinkers such as the Sizers and the values clarificationists, who would glibly recommend "scrapping" the old morality.

ROUSSEAU IN THE COURTS

IN RECENT DECADES, the courts have done their share to erode teachers' and school officials' power to enforce traditional moral standards and discipline. In 1969, in *Tinker v. Des Moines School District*, the U.S. Supreme Court ruled that Iowa school authorities had violated students' rights by denying them permission to wear protest armbands to school. Justice Abe Fortas, in the majority opinion, found the action of the school authorities unconstitutional: "It can hardly be argued that students shed their constitutional rights to freedom of speech or expression at the schoolhouse gate."[44]

Justice Hugo Black dissented. Though a great champion of First Amendment rights, he pointed out that schoolchildren "need to learn, not teach." He wrote, presciently, "It is the beginning of a new revolutionary era of permissiveness in this country fostered by the Judiciary. . . . Turned loose with lawsuits for damages and injunctions against their teachers . . . it is nothing but wishful thinking to imagine that young, immature students will not soon believe it is their right to control the schools."[45]

Abigail Thernstrom, a political scientist at the Manhattan Institute, cites *Tinker* as the beginning of the end of effective school discipline. She also sees it as an unfortunate example of Rousseauian romanticism in the courts. According to Thernstrom, "[Fortas's majority] opinion was a romantic celebration of conflict and permissiveness, even within the schoolhouse walls—as if the future of democratic government and American culture could be placed in jeopardy had the students been told to stage their demonstration elsewhere."[46]

In 1975, a second case that would further diminish the authority of school officials to correct student behavior reached the high court. In *Goss v. Lopez*, the Supreme Court ruled it unconstitutional for schools to suspend students without due process. Justice Byron White, who wrote the majority opinion, strongly favored extending students' rights. Justice Lewis Powell opposed the ruling, fearing that it would ultimately be harmful to students. Thernstrom has aptly characterized the two opinions: "White had raised the specter of schools as institutions with potentially 'untrammeled power.' Suspension—even for just one day—was a 'serious event' that deprived students of their right to an education. Justice Powell believed precisely the opposite; he assumed that suspension created the conditions under which children could learn."[47]

Justice White prevailed, and the judiciary thus joined the progressive educationists and many parents in holding that "students' rights" trump the traditional prerogative of teachers to require compliance with school discipline. The *Goss* ruling helped bring on the era of permissiveness that Justice Black had warned about. From the loftiest of progressive motives, the educational system was robbed of the ability to enforce its codes and rules.

By the mid-1970s, we were on our way to becoming the first society in history to use high principle to weaken the moral authority of teachers. Soon, local officials throughout the county, such as Principal Maltman at Glen Ridge High and Mayor Titel of Lakewood, would be powerless in the face of delinquent students and litigious parents.

WHERE THE REFORMERS GO WRONG

THE PURPOSE of moral education is not to preserve our children's autonomy but to develop the character they will rely on as adults. And as Aristotle clearly showed, children who have been helped to develop good moral habits will find it easier to become autonomous adults. Conversely, children who have been left to their own devices will founder.

Those who oppose directive moral education often call it a form of brainwashing or indoctrination. That is sheer confusion. When you brainwash people, you undermine their autonomy, their rational self-mastery; you diminish their freedom. But when you educate children, teaching them to be competent, self-controlled, and morally responsible in their actions, you *increase* their freedom and enlarge their humanity. The Greeks and Romans understood this very well; so did the great Scholastic and Enlightenment thinkers. Indeed, this is a first principle of every great religion and high civilization. To know what is right and act on it is the highest expression of freedom and personal autonomy.

What Victorians had in mind when they extolled the qualities of a "gentleman" are the virtues we need to inculcate in all our children: honesty, integrity, courage, decency, politeness. These are as important to the well-being of a young male today as they were in nineteenth-century

England. Even today, despite several decades of moral deregulation, most young men understand the term "gentleman" and approve of the ideals it connotes.

To suggest that we place more emphasis on instilling a sense of responsibility and civility into children than on alerting them to their civil and personal rights under law may sound quaint, quixotic, or even reactionary. It is, however, practical and achievable. The fact is that despite appearances to the contrary, most children respond to and respect civility and good manners. If their own manners are wanting, it is because so little is expected (much less demanded) of them.

Far from being oppressive, controlling, or constricting, the manners, instincts, and virtues we recognize in decent, considerate human beings—in the case of males, the manners, instincts, and virtues we associate with being a "gentleman"—are liberating. To educate, humanize, and civilize a boy is to allow him to make the most of himself. As for the community, manners and good morals benefit it far more than even the best of laws.

When parents and teachers fail to instill the gentle qualities in a boy, they fall short in their duty both to him and to society. Some historians and philosophers have skeptically dismissed bourgeois manners and virtues as a means by which an aristocratic elite oppresses the middle and working classes. But that, as political scientist James Q. Wilson points out, is perversely wrong: "Bertrand Russell would . . . sneer that 'the concept of the gentleman was invented by the aristocracy to keep the middle classes in order,' but in truth the concept of the gentleman enabled the middle classes to supplant the aristocracy." [48]

The historian Gertrude Himmelfarb took up this theme in a remarkable book-length historical essay, *The De-Moralization of Society: From Victorian Virtues to Modern Values*. "If, as some historians maintain, Victorians succeeded in 'bourgeoisifying' their ethos," writes Himmelfarb,

> to that extent they also democratized it. In attributing to everyone the same virtues—potentially at least, if not in actuality—they assumed a common human nature and thus a moral . . . equality. Even the "gentlemanly" virtues—honesty, integrity, courage, politeness—were not above the capacity of

the ordinary person. . . . In an aristocratic age, only the exceptional, privileged individual had been seen as a free moral agent, the master of his fate.[49]

The great eighteenth-century conservative political philosopher Edmund Burke argued that in human affairs, a sense of the proprieties is even more important than fidelity to laws: "Manners are of more importance than laws. Upon them, in a great measure, the laws depend. The law touches us but here and there and now and then. Manners are what vex and soothe, corrupt or purify, exalt or debase, barbarize or refine us by a constant, steady uniform insensible operation. Like that of the air we breathe in."[50]

Common sense, convention, tradition, and even modern social science research[51] all converge in support of what I have been calling the Aristotelian tradition of directive character education. Children need standards, they need clear guidelines, they need adults in their lives who are understanding but firmly insistent on responsible behavior. But a resolute adherence to standards has been out of fashion in education circles for more than thirty years.

An Aristotelian education is still a child's best bet. Unfortunately, our era is characterized by the ascendancy of Rousseau and a decided antipathy toward the directive inculcation of the virtues. It is no coincidence that the romantic turn in education has been accompanied by a marked decline in the fortunes and prospects of boys in our country.

TWO BADLY SOCIALIZED BOYS

IN APRIL 1999, the massacre at Columbine High School in Littleton, Colorado, shocked an uncomprehending nation by its cold brutality. It was the seventh school shooting in less than two years. This time, more than ever, the public's need to make sense of such tragedies was palpable. How could it happen? The usual explanations made little sense. Poverty? Eric Harris and Dylan Klebold were not poor. Easy access to weapons? True, but young men, especially in the West, have always had access to guns. Divorce? Both boys' families were intact. A nation of emotionally repressed boys? Boys were much the same back in the 1950s and 1960s, when nobody shot up their schoolmates. And why American boys?

Asking "Why now?" and "Why here?" puts us onto the track of what is missing in the American way of socializing children that was present in the recent past. To find the answers, we need to attend to the views of the progressive-education theorists who advocated abandoning the traditional mission of indoctrinating children in the "old morality." They succeeded in persuading the American educational establishment to adopt instead the romantic moral pedagogy of Rousseau.

Teachers and parents who embraced this view badly underestimated the potential barbarism of children who are not given a directive moral education. That the romantic approach to moral education is harmful is becoming increasingly obvious to the public, but it will take some time for the educational establishment to change. One week after the Colorado shootings, Secretary of Education Richard Riley talked to a group of students at a high school in Annapolis, Maryland. After the secretary rounded up the usual causes and reasons for the atrocity, a student asked him about one he had not mentioned: "Why haven't students been offered ethics classes?" Secretary Riley seemed taken aback by the question.

It is not likely that a single ethics course would have been enough to stop boys such as Harris and Klebold from murdering classmates. On the other hand, a K–12 curriculum infused with moral content would have created a climate that might have made a massacre unthinkable. For such a depraved and immoral act *was* indeed unthinkable in the "simpleminded" days before the schools cast aside their mission of moral edification. An insistence on character development might also have diminished the derisive mistreatment suffered by the perpetrators at the hands of more popular students that apparently was one of the incitements for their gruesome actions.

Teachers, too, would have acted differently. Had K–12 teachers in the Littleton schools seen it as their routine duty to civilize the students in their care, they would never have overlooked the bizarre, antisocial behavior of Klebold and Harris. When the boys appeared in school with T-shirts with the words "Serial Killer" emblazoned on them, their teachers would have sent them home. Nor would the boys have been allowed to wear swastikas or produce grotesquely violent videos. By tolerating these modes of "self-expression," the adults at Columbine High School implicitly sent the message to the students that there's not much wrong with the serial or mass murder of innocent people.

One English teacher at Columbine, Cheryl Lucas, told *Education Week* that both boys had written short stories about death and killing "that were horribly, graphically, violent" and that she had notified school officials. According to Lucas, the officials had taken no action because nothing the boys wrote had violated school policy. Speaking with painful irony, the frustrated teacher explained, "In a free society, you can't take action until they've committed some horrific crime because they are guaranteed freedom of speech."[52] In many high schools, students are confident that their right to free expression will be protected. Counselors and administrators, fearful of challenges by litigious parents who would be backed by the ACLU and other zealous guardians of students' rights, rarely take action.

The love affair of American education with Rousseau's romantic idealization of the child has made it all but inevitable that our public schools fail to do their part in civilizing young "barbarians." Most schools no longer see themselves having a primary role in moral edification. It has become the style not to interfere with the child's self-expression and autonomy. And that is where we find ourselves today.

Many schools have entirely given up the task of character education, setting great numbers of American children adrift without direction. Under the current laissez-faire policy, our schools are harboring a great many inadequately socialized children. But leaving children to discover their own values is a little like putting them in a chemistry lab full of volatile substances and saying, "Discover your own compounds, kids." We should not be surprised when some blow themselves up and destroy those around them.

Add to this the facts that guns are easily available and that violent electronic fantasies are on every TV screen and computer monitor, and the probability of violence becomes extraordinarily high. The harm wrought by psychopathology, media exposure to scenes of violence that glorify the perpetrators and desensitize the viewers to what the victims suffer, and easy access to guns is many times magnified in the morally permissive, laissez-faire environment that most schools today provide.

Of course, parents bear responsibility for their children's moral education. But the schools set the tone and the standard; most parents take their cues from the schools, and those who try for higher standards are undercut when the schools are indifferent. Moral edification has always been a primary mission of the nation's schools. The period since 1970 has been the historical exception.

The schools' almost deliberate abandonment of their moral mission in the last thirty years has done incalculable harm. Today, educators no longer use the commonsense language of morality but speak instead of boys who have "conduct disorders." And we pay insufficient attention to the fact that the increase in conduct disorders (to which the American Psychiatric Association calls attention) has occurred in the decades since the schools abdicated their duty to morally edify the children in their care.[53] That reckless disavowal is still the norm in America's public schools. But it can be reversed.

A WIND OF CHANGE

EVEN BEFORE the spate of school shootings had made it evident that most of today's schools are morally ineffectual, there were voices calling for reform. In the early nineties, a hitherto silent majority of parents, teachers, and community activists began to agitate in favor of old-fashioned moral education. In July 1992, a group called the Character Counts Coalition (organized by the Josephson Institute of Ethics and made up of teachers, youth leaders, politicians, and ethicists) gathered in Aspen, Colorado, for a three-and-a-half-day conference on character education. At the end of the conference, the group put forward the Aspen Declaration on Character Education. Among its principles:

- "The present and future well-being of our society requires an involved, caring citizenry with good moral character."
- "Effective character education is based on core ethical values which form the foundation of democratic society—in particular, respect, responsibility, trustworthiness, caring, justice, fairness, civic virtue and citizenship."
- "Character education is, first and foremost, an obligation of families: it is also an important obligation of faith communities, schools, youth and other human service organizations."[54]

The Character Counts Coalition has attracted a wide and politically diverse following. Its board of advisers includes liberals such as Marian Wright Edelman and conservatives such as William Bennett. Ten U.S. senators from both political parties have joined, along with a number of governors, mayors, and state representatives. The new character education movement is gaining impetus. Undoubtedly, the events in Littleton will bring further support.

For some time now, schools throughout the country have been starting to find their way back to contemporary versions of directive moral education. Teachers, administrators, and parents are once again getting into the business of making it clear to students that they must behave honorably, courteously, and kindly, that they must work hard and strive for excellence. In some schools the whole curriculum is shaped by these imperatives.

Individual schools are showing the way back. Fallon Park Elementary School in Roanoke, Virginia, for example has seen a dramatic change in its students since the principal adopted the Character Counts program in 1998.[55] Every morning the students recite the Pledge of Allegiance. This is followed by a pledge written by the students and teachers: "Each day in our words and actions we will persevere to exhibit respect, caring, fairness, trustworthiness, responsibility and citizenship. These qualities will help us to be successful students who work and play well together." According to the principal, suspensions have declined 60 percent, attendance and grades have improved, and—*mirabile dictu*—misbehavior on school buses has all but disappeared. The school's gym instructor, who has been there for twenty years, has noticed improvement. The kids are practicing good sportsmanship, and even school troublemakers seem to be changing for the better. She recently noticed one such boy encouraging a shy girl to join a game: "It almost brought tears to my eyes . . . this is the best year ever in this school."[56]

Vera White, principal of Jefferson Junior High in Washington, D.C., was stunned some years ago when she realized that children from her school had been part of an angry mob that had attacked police and firefighters with rocks and bottles: "Those are my children. If they didn't care enough to respect the mayor and the fire marshal and everyone else, what good does an education do?" She decided to make character education central to the mission of her school. Students now attend assemblies that focus on positive traits such as respect and responsibility. Ms. White initiated the program in 1992: since then theft and fighting have been rare. Unlike other schools in the area, Jefferson has no bars on its windows and no metal detectors.[57]

F. Washington Jarvis, headmaster at the Roxbury Latin School in Boston and an Episcopal priest, has always emphasized character and discipline. But others are now joining him. Jarvis holds a harsh, non-Rousseauian view of human nature: left untrained, he feels, we are "brutish, selfish, and capable of great cruelty." We must do our utmost to be decent and responsible, and we must demand this of our children and our students. Whenever they behave badly, says the headmaster, "We have to hold up a mirror to the students and say, 'This is who you are. Stop it.' "[58]

Contrast these schools with a typical school such as Littleton's Columbine High. We know that the Littleton killers had attended anger management seminars, had had weekly meetings with a "diversion" officer, had attended a Mothers Against Drunk Driving panel discussion, and had performed compulsory community service. But it seems they had never encountered a Reverend Jarvis or a Principal White.

After Littleton, many a barn door is being shut and padlocked. But a spokesperson for the Littleton School District had asked the right question, "Do you make a high school into an armed prison camp where there are metal detectors that make kids feel imprisoned, or do you count on people's basic goodness and put good rules in place?"[59]

PROGRESSIVE HOSTILITY

ALTHOUGH THE MOVEMENT to reinstate directive moral education and "put good rules in place" is gathering momentum, it is being fiercely resisted in some quarters. Benjamin DeMott, Amherst professor emeritus, wrote a scathing piece for *Harper's Magazine* in 1994 jeering at the revived character education movement. Like Professor Puka, DeMott asks how we can hope to teach ethics in a society where CEOs award themselves large salaries "in the midst of the age of downsizing."[60] Alfie Kohn, a popular education speaker and writer, wrote a long critical piece in the education magazine *Phi Delta Kappan* accusing character education programs of indoctrinating children, making them obedient workers in an unjust society where "the nation's wealth is concentrated in fewer and fewer hands." [61] He claims that reactionary values are already a powerful force in our nation's schools: "Children in American schools are even expected to begin each day by reciting a loyalty oath to the Fatherland, although we call it by a different name." [62] Kohn's comparison—likening the Pledge of Allegiance to a loyalty oath to Hitler's Reich—is a fair example of the mind-set one still finds among some progressives.

Thomas Lasley, dean of the University of Dayton School of Education, another foe of the "old morality," denounces the "values juggernaut" for its hypocrisy:

> Teachers tell students to cooperate, but then they systematically rank students in terms of their class performance. . . . Teachers tell students that respect is essential for social responsibility, but then they call on boys a majority of the time. . . . And finally students are informed that they should be critical thinkers, but then they are evaluated on where they think the same way their teachers do. [63]

SIGNS OF RENEWAL

WOODLAND PARK MIDDLE SCHOOL is a public junior high in a poor area outside of San Diego. It offers a moral education program of a kind romantic critics such as DeMott, Kohn, and Lasley find unacceptably retrograde. Each morning children can attend a fifteen-minute class on "How to Be Successful." It's a course on what Aristotle called the practical virtues. The kids learn the "Eleven Bs," which include: Be responsible. Be on time. Be friendly. Be polite. Be a listener. Be a tough worker. Be a goal setter. And so on. Children are taught all about the work ethic and how to integrate it into their lives.

The program was developed by a California-based group called the Jefferson Center for Character Education. An independent study by California Survey Research measured the impact of the program on twenty-five schools. In the schools that had implemented the program, the number of students who were tardy or sent to the office for minor disciplinary problems had declined by 39 percent. Serious disciplinary problems (fighting, coming to school with weapons) had decreased by 25 percent.[64]

One math teacher, Jerry Harrington, who has been teaching "How to Be Successful" for many years, ran into one of his students a few years ago. Writer Tim Stafford described the encounter in *Christianity Today*.[65] The student, Philip (by then in high school), was bagging groceries, and Mr. Harrington asked him how he had gotten his job. Philip said he had gotten it by applying what he had learned in the class. First, he had set a goal: "I knew I needed to earn $600 in the summer because my mother could not afford to buy my school clothes and school supplies." Adhering closely to the method taught in the course, Philip had then broken his goal down into small parts. Next he had taken what are called "action steps." Step one: He had listed twenty businesses that were within walking or biking distance of his house. Step two: He had gone to each one to apply for a job. At the seventeenth one, the grocery store, he had been hired.

Two years later, Mr. Harrington met Philip's older brother, who told him that Philip was still working. And the older brother told him, "You saved *my* life too." He explained that their mother was an alcoholic who had had a series of boyfriends. Their home life was chaotic. Philip had told his brother about what he had learned in his "How to Be Successful" class. Now both brothers were putting their lives together.

There are millions of American boys who could greatly benefit from courses like Harrington's, and not just poor and neglected boys either. Of course, girls need directive moral education as well. But when we consider that boys are so much more likely to fail at school, to become disengaged, to get into trouble, and generally to lose their way, it is reasonable to conclude that boys need it more.

Jerry Harrington has been teaching for almost thirty years. I spoke with him in the fall of 1999. He told me that, on average, middle school boys are less mature than the girls: "The boys have difficulties at the level of basic organization: being responsible for their backpacks, their homework." Most of the girls understand the idea of personal responsibility and are ready to move on to the idea of being responsible for others. At Harrington's school, it is girls who are active in school events and who hold the leadership positions in student government. The male students are preoccupied with skateboarding, surfing, and in-line skating—

activities with few rules, little structure, no responsibilities. When he asks boys about their long-term goals, a high number of them confidently assert that they plan to become sports stars. But when he inquires about what steps they are taking to realize even that unrealistic goal, he finds that they have a very poor understanding of the relationship of means to ends. Harrington has two daughters and assures me that "girls are very dear to my heart." But, he says, no one seems to be focused on boys: "Every time I turn around, if there is an event or program where someone is going to be lifted up and encouraged, it's for girls." Harrington is unusual in recognizing and talking about boys and their insufficiencies. He is doing what he can to help them, but in too many schools the moral needs of boys are disregarded and unmet.[66]

What real-world help do the DeMotts, Kohns, Lasleys, and Pukas have to offer boys such as Philip and his brother? What do they propose that the schools do about boys with serious character disorders, such as Lyle and Kevin Scherzer and Chris Archer, the Glen Ridge ringleaders, the Lakewood boys, or the Littleton killers? How would Philip and his brother have fared under the latter-day romantic permissive philosophy of these progressive educators?

Lacking guidance and discipline, and ignorant of their moral heritage, many American public school children are ill prepared for real life, confused about how to manage their personal lives, and ethically challenged. Some, indeed, are lethally dangerous. It is by now apparent that such fashionable replacements for directive moral guidance as values clarification, self-esteem programs, anger management, workshops on gender justice, and therapylike exercises designed to put students in touch with their inner nurturers have been shortchanging our schoolchildren all along. Indeed, with the growing realization that the old directive/indoctrinative approach works best in coping with the "perennial invasions of barbarians," schools that openly embrace the mission of moral education are beginning to proliferate.

For the time being, however, the character education movement is no more than incipient. Rousseau still reigns in our schools of education and in philosophies of many parents, teachers, and judges. And as long as a Rousseauian philosophy of ethical romanticism is allowed to shape American education, the nation's children, and especially its boys, will continue to be deprived. In the war against moral standards, it is boys who sustain most of the casualties.

CHAPTER NINE

WAR AND PEACE

THERE HAVE ALWAYS been societies that favored boys over girls. Ours may be the first to deliberately throw the gender switch. If we continue on our present course, boys will, indeed, be tomorrow's second sex.

The new preeminence of girls is gratifying to those who believe that, even now, many girls are silenced and diminished. At long last, it is boys who are learning what it is like to be "the other sex." Recall Peggy Orenstein's approval of a women-centered classroom, whose walls were filled with pictures and celebrations of women, with men conspicuously absent: "Perhaps for the first time, the boys are the ones looking in through the window."[1]

But reversing the positions of the sexes in an unfair system should be no one's idea of justice. A lopsided educational system in which boys (finally!) are on the outside looking in is inherently unjust and socially divisive. The public has given no one a mandate to pursue a policy of privileging girls. Nor is anyone (outside exotic feminist circles) demanding that boys be taught in a feminizing manner. Few parents share Gloria Steinem's belief that boys should be raised like girls.

If organizations and institutions such as the American Association of University Women, the Wellesley Center for Research on Women, the

Harvard Project on Women's Psychology, the McLean Center for Men, the Boys' Project at Tufts University, and the U.S. Department of Education's WEEA Equity Resource Center continue to shape "gender policy" for our schools, the gap that now severely disadvantages boys will become a chasm. And the efforts to "reconstruct" boys—to interest them in dolls, in quilts, in noncompetitive games "where no one is out"—will continue apace.

THE GREAT RELEARNING

RECENTLY, for reasons that have little to do with the educational gender gap, Americans have begun to take a hard look at boys. This is actually auspicious, for the public has a lot to learn about how our educational system has been routinely failing boys, both academically and morally. Indeed, with respect to boys, we may now be entering a period that might be called "The Great Relearning." I borrow the phrase from the novelist Tom Wolfe, who first applied it to lessons learned in the late 1960s by a group of hippies living in the Haight-Ashbury district of San Francisco. What happened to Wolfe's iconoclastic hippies is instructive.

The Haight-Ashbury hippies had collectively decided that hygiene was a middle-class hang-up. So they determined to live without it. For example, baths and showers, while not actually banned, were frowned upon as retrograde. Wolfe was intrigued by these hippies who, he said, "sought nothing less than to sweep aside all codes and restraints of the past and start out at zero."[2] After a while their principled aversion to modern hygiene had consequences that were as unpleasant as they were unforeseen. Wolfe describes them thus: "At the Haight-Ashbury Free Clinic there were doctors who were treating diseases no living doctor had ever encountered before, diseases that had disappeared so long ago they had never even picked up Latin names, diseases such as the mange, the grunge, the itch, the twitch, the thrush, the scroff, the rot."[3] The itching and the manginess eventually began to vex the hippies, leading them individually to seek help from the local free clinics. Step by step, they had to rediscover for themselves the rudiments of modern hygiene. That rueful process of rediscovery is Wolfe's Great Relearning. A Great Relearning is what has to happen whenever reformers go too far—

whenever, in order to start over "from zero," they jettison basic values, well-proven social practices, and plain common sense.

Wolfe's story is both true and amusing. We are, however, familiar with more consequential, less amusing twentieth century experiments with rebuilding humankind from zero: Marxism-Leninism, fascism, Maoism. Each had its share of zealots and social engineers who believed in the plasticity of human nature and their own recipes for improving it. Among the unforeseen consequences of these experiments were mass suffering and genocide on an unprecedented scale. Today, eastern Europeans are in the midst of their own Great Relearning. They have been painfully finding out the extent of the damage wrought by the zealots and of the rebuilding that needs to be done.

America too has had its share of revolutionary developments—not so much political as moral. We have jettisoned a lot of the mores and morals of past generations in the hope that, starting from zero, we would arrive at a society that is more just and free. The new amorality is most dramatically seen in our children. By recklessly denying the importance of giving the young directive moral guidance, parents and educators have cast great numbers of them morally adrift. In defecting from the crucial duties of moral education, we have placed ourselves and our children in jeopardy. In some ways, we are as down and out as those poor hippies who finally found themselves knocking at the door of the free clinic. Now we too face the need for a Great Relearning.

As part of this social and moral deregulation and in the name of an egalitarian ideal, we have denied the plain facts about males and females, laying down the principle that boys and girls are the same and that such differences as we find are the result of social conditioning imposed by a patriarchal male culture intent on subjugating women. We must now relearn what previous generations never doubted: that boys and girls are different in ways that go far beyond the obvious biological differences.

A recent book, *Between Mothers and Sons*, offers a poignant glimpse of several mothers rediscovering the nature of boys.[4] Most of the contributors to this collection of mother-son reflections are self-described feminists, and one might expect the book to be full of advice to mothers on how to cope with their sons' perverse maleness. Instead, it is a compilation of wistful insights into the "soul of boys" as the mothers call into question cherished prejudices they had held about boys that turned out not to square with their own experience as mothers.

Some of the mothers confess to having tried to educate their sons in conformity with feminist precepts, stopping only when it became evident that they were coercing their sons to act against their natures. In these accounts, Mother Nature, not Social Construction, gets the last word. These are stories about how a fashionable ideology is swept away by the powerful love that mothers—including committed feminist mothers—bear for their sons.

Deborah Galyan, a short-story writer and essayist, describes what happened when she sent her son Dylan to a Montessori preschool "run by a goddess-worshiping, multiracial women's collective on Cape Cod":[5]

> [S]omething about it did not honor his boy soul. I think it was the absence of physical competition. Boys who clashed or tussled with each other were separated and counseled by the peacemaker. Sticks were confiscated and turned into tomato stakes in the school garden. . . . It finally came to me . . . I had sent him there to protect him from the very circuitry and compulsions and desires that make him what he is. I had sent him there to protect him from himself.[6]

Galyan then posed painful questions to which she found a liberating answer: "How could I be a good feminist, a good pacifist, and a good mother to a stick-wielding, weapon-generating boy?" And "What exactly is a five-year-old boy?" "A five-year-old boy, I learned from reading summaries of various neurological studies . . . is a beautiful, fierce, testosterone-drenched, cerebrally asymmetrical humanoid carefully engineered to move objects through space, or at very least, to watch others do so."[7]

Janet Burroway, a poet, novelist, and self-described pacifist-liberal, has a son, Tim, who grew up to become a career soldier. She is not sure how exactly he came to move in a direction opposite to her own. She recalls his abiding fascination with plastic planes, toy soldiers, and military history, noting that "his direction was early set."[8] Tim takes her aback in many ways, but she is clearly proud of him: throughout his childhood she was struck by his "chivalric character": "He would, literally, lay down his life for a cause or a friend." And she confesses, "I am forced to be aware of my own contradictions in his presence: a feminist often charmed by his machismo."[9]

Galyan and Burroway discarded some common anti-male prejudices when they discovered that boys have their own distinctive graces and virtues. The love and respect they shared with their sons left them chastened, wiser, and free of the fashionable resentments that many women harbor toward males. All the same, such stories are sobering. They remind us of the strong disapproval with which many women initially approach boys.

Mary Gordon, perhaps the most orthodox feminist in this instructive anthology, is another mother with a disarming son. On one occasion, her David defends his older sister from a bully. "I thought it was really nice of him to stand up for me," said the sister. For a moment, the mother is also moved by David's gallantry. "But after a minute, I didn't want to buy the idea that a woman needs a man to stand up for her." Gordon says that this incident "expressed for me the complexities of being a feminist mother of a son."[10]

Gordon realizes that she cannot be fair to her son unless she overcomes her prejudices: "Would I take my generalized anger against male privilege out on this little child who was dependent upon me for his survival, physical to be sure, but mental as well?" Nevertheless, Gordon remains torn between her principled animosity against "the male" and her maternal love: "We can't afford wholesale male-bashing, nor can we afford to see the male as the permanently unreconstructable gender. Nor can we pretend that things are right as they are. . . . We must love them as they are, often without knowing what it is that's made them that way."[11]

Gordon still firmly believes that males need to be "reconstructed." In saying "We can't afford wholesale male-bashing," she implies that a certain amount of bashing is all right. It does not seem to occur to her that her "generalized anger" is something she should be trying to get rid of "wholesale."

An unacknowledged animus against boys is loose in our society. The women who design events such as Son's Day, who write antiharassment guides, who gather in workshops to determine how to change boys' "gender schema" barely disguise their anger and disapproval. Others, who bear no malice to boys, nevertheless do not credit them with sanity and health, for they regard the average boy as alienated, lonely, emotionally repressed, isolated, at odds with his masculinity, and prone to violence. These "save-the-male" critics of boys start out by giving boys a failing grade. They join the girl partisans in calling for radical change in the way American males are socialized: only by raising boys to be more like girls can we help them become "real boys."

In our schools, therapeutic practices have effectively supplanted the moral education of yesteryear. Ironically, those who pressed for discarding the old directive moral education did so in the name of freedom, for they sincerely believed that moral education "indoctrinated" children and "imposed" a teacher's values on them, something they thought the schools had no right to do. In fact, the "therapism" that took the place of the old morality is far more invasive of the child's privacy and far more insidious in its effects on the child's autonomy than the directive moral education that was once the norm in every school.

It is also unfortunate that so many popular writers and education reformers think ill of American boys. The worst-case sociopathic males—gang rapists, mass murderers—become instant metaphors for everyone's sons. The vast numbers of decent and honorable young men, on the other hand, never inspire disquisitions on the inner nature of the boy next door. The false and corrosive doctrine that equates masculinity with violence has found its way into the mainstream.

We are at the tail end of an extraordinary period of moral deregulation that is leaving many tens of thousands of our boys academically deficient and without adequate guidance. Too many American boys are foundering, unprepared for the demands of family and work. Many have only a vague sense of right and wrong. Many are still being taught by Rousseauian romantics, which is to say that they are badly taught and left to "find their own values."

We have created serious problems for ourselves by abandoning our duty to pass on to our children the moral truths to which they are entitled and failing to give them the guidance they so badly need. We have further allowed socially divisive activists, many of whom take a dim view of men and boys, to wield unwarranted influence in our schools. And because we have allowed ourselves to forget the central purpose of education, we have become overloaded with well-intentioned teachers who undervalue knowledge and learning and overvalue their role as healers, social reformers, and confidence builders.

As part of our Great Relearning, we must again recognize and respect the reality that boys and girls are different, that each sex has its distinctive strengths and graces. We must put an end to all the crisis mongering that pathologizes children: we must be less credulous when sensationalistic "experts" talk of girls as drowning Ophelias or of boys as anxious, isolated Hamlets. Neither sex needs to be "revived" or "rescued"; neither needs to be "regendered." Instead of doing things that do not need doing and should not be done, we must dedicate ourselves to the hard tasks that are both necessary and possible: improving the moral climate in our schools and providing our children with first-rate schooling that equips them for the good life in the new century.

We have created a lot of problems, both for ourselves and for our children. Now we must resolutely set about solving them. I am confident we can do that. American boys, whose very masculinity turns out to be politically incorrect, badly need our support. If you are an optimist, as I am, you believe that good sense and fair play will prevail. If you are a mother of sons, as I am, you know that one of the more agreeable facts of life is that boys will be boys.

NOTES

Preface

1. Sarah Glazer, "Boys' Emotional Needs: Is Growing Up Tougher for Boys Than for Girls?," *Congressional Quarterly Researcher*, June 18, 1999, p. 521.

2. Ibid., p. 523. See also Michael Kimmel, professor of sociology at the State University of New York, Stony Brook, who explains that the Littleton shooters were "not deviants at all" but "over-conformists . . . to traditional notions of masculinity" (*Congressional Quarterly Researcher*, June 18, 1999).

3. American Association of University Women, *The AAUW Report: How Schools Shortchange Girls* (Washington, D.C.: American Association of University Women, 1992).

4. Ms. Foundation for Women, "Synopsis of Research on Girls" (New York: Ms. Foundation, 1995), p. 2.

5. For data on boys' reading deficit and lesser commitment to school, see U.S. Department of Education, *The Condition of Education* (Washington, D.C.: U.S. Department of Education, 1995), pp. 13–14. See also Metropolitan Life Insurance Company, *The American Teacher 1997: Examining Gender Issues in Public Schools* (New York: Metropolitan Life Insurance Company, 1997); and Search Institute, *Starting Out Right: Developmental Assets* (Minneapolis: Search Institute, 1997). For data on college enrollments, see Department of Education, National Center for Education Statistics, "Fall Enrollments in Colleges and Universities," August 1998. See also Tamar Lewin, "U.S. Colleges Begin to Ask: 'Where Have the Men Gone?,' " *New York Times*, December 6, 1998, p. A1; and Ben Gose, "Liberal-Arts Colleges Ask: Where Have the Men Gone?," *Chronicle of Higher Education*, June 6, 1997, p. 23.

6. Carol Gilligan, "The Centrality of Relationship in Human Development: A Puzzle, Some Evidence, and a Theory," in *Development and Vulnerability in Close Relationships*, ed. Gil Noam and Kurt Fischer (Mahwah, N.J.: Erlbaum, 1996), p. 251.

7. Debra Viadero, "Behind the Mask of Masculinity," *Education Week*, May 13, 1998, p. 37.

8. Quotation is from an announcement sent out by the Boys' Project at Tufts, Fall 1999.

9. See, for example, David Hughes, "Boys Catching Up with Girls Thanks to Literacy Hour," *Daily Mail* (London), October 6, 1999. See also Liz Lightfoot, "Boys Are Left Behind by Modern Teaching," *Daily Telegraph*, January 9, 1998; and Charlotte Eagar, "Teaching Boys Better," *Daily Telegraph*, May 24, 1997.

10. Estelle Morris, MP, "Boys Will Be Boys?: Closing the Gender Gap" (London: Labour Party, November 1996), p. 10.

ONE: Where the Boys Are

1. Carol Gilligan, "Prologue," in *Making Connections: The Relational Worlds of Adolescent Girls at Emma Willard School*, ed. Carol Gilligan, Nona Lyons, and Trudy Hanmer (Cambridge, Mass.: Harvard University Press, 1990), p. 4.

2. Anna Quindlen, "Viewing Society's Sins Through the Eyes of a Daughter," *Chicago Tribune*, January 1, 1991, p. 19.

3. Elizabeth Gleick, "Surviving Your Teens," *Time*, February 19, 1996, p. 73.

4. Carolyn See, "For Girls Hardest Lesson of All," *Washington Post Book World*, September 2, 1994, p. D3.

5. Myra and David Sadker, *Failing at Fairness: How America's Schools Cheat Girls* (New York: Scribners, 1994), pp. 77–78.

6. Mary Pipher, *Reviving Ophelia: Saving the Selves of Adolescent Girls* (New York: Putnam, 1994), p. 19.

7. American Psychiatric Association, *Diagnostic and Statistical Manual of Mental Disorders*, 4th ed. (Washington, D.C.: American Psychiatric Association, 1994), p. 347. According to *DSM-IV*, the "lifetime prevalence of Dysthymic Disorder is approximately 6 percent. The point prevalence is approximately 3 percent."

8. Anne C. Petersen et al., "Depression in Adolescence," *American Psychologist* 48, no. 2 (February 1993), p. 155.

9. Daniel Offer and Kimberly A. Schonert-Reichl, "Debunking the Myths of Adolescence: Findings from Recent Research," *Journal of the American Academy of Child and Adolescent Psychiatry* 31, no. 6 (November 1992), pp. 1003–14.

10. Lloyd Johnston, Jerald Bachman, and Patrick O'Malley, *Monitoring the Future: Questionnaire Responses from the Nation's High School Seniors, 1989* (Ann Arbor, Mich.: Survey Research Center, University of Michigan, 1992), p. 32.

11. Pipher, *Reviving Ophelia*, p. 27.

12. *National Injury Mortality Statistics 1979–1996* (Atlanta: Centers for Disease Control and Prevention, 1997). See also http://www.cdc.gov/ncipc/osp/us8179/Suic. Pipher's numbers are in fact slightly off: the CDC reports that the suicide rate among all children aged ten to fourteen years rose by 57 percent, not 75 percent, between 1979 and 1988. The most recent CDC data show that in 1997, 74 girls aged five to fourteen killed themselves; for boys, the number was 233.

13. Elizabeth Debold, Marie Wilson, and Idelisse Malave, *Mother Daughter Revolution: From Betrayal to Power* (Reading, Mass.: Addison-Wesley, 1993), p. 9.

14. Suzanne Daley, "Little Girls Lose Their Self-Esteem on Way to Adolescence, Study Finds," *New York Time*, January 9, 1991, p. B6.

15. Bruce Bower, "Teenage Turning Point," *Science News*, March 23, 1991, p. 184.

16. For other criticisms of the alleged self-esteem crisis, see William Damon, *Greater Expectations: Overcoming the Culture of Indulgence in America's Homes and Schools* (New York: Free Press, 1995), p. 74. See also Kristen C. Kling, et al., "Gender Differences in Self-Esteem: A Meta-Analysis," *Psychological Bulletin* 125, no. 4 (1999), pp. 470–500; Kirk Johnson, "Self-Image Is Suffering from Lack of Esteem," *New York Times*, May 5, 1998, p. F7. See also my *Who Stole Feminism?: How Women*

Have Betrayed Women (New York: Simon & Schuster, 1994; Touchstone, 1995), pp. 136–50.

17. American Association of University Women, *AAUW Report: How Schools Shortchange Girls* (Washington, D.C.: American Association of University Women, 1992), p. 84.

18. Millicent Lawton, "AAUW Builds on History," *Education Week*, September 28, 1994, p. 17.

19. Susan Chira, "Bias Against Girls Is Found Rife in Schools, with Lasting Damages," *New York Times*, February 12, 1992, p. 1.

20. Tamar Lewin, "How Boys Lost Out to Girl Power," *New York Times*, December 12, 1998, sec. 4, p. 1. See also Judith Kleinfeld, "Student Performance: Males Versus Females," *The Public Interest*, Winter 1999, pp. 3–20.

21. American Association of University Women, *AAUW Report: How Schools Shortchange Girls* (Executive Summary), p. 2.

22. Amy Saltzman, "Schooled in Failure?," *U.S. News & World Report*, November 7, 1994, p. 90. Psychologist Judith Kleinfeld had a similar experience when she attempted to locate the Sadker call-out study. Kleinfeld asked, "Is it possible for a study simply to disappear into thin air? Apparently it is: when I telephoned David Sadker, to ask him for a copy of the research, he could not locate one." (In Judith Kleinfeld, "Student Performance: Males Versus Females," p. 14.)

23. See, for example, P. W. Hill, P. Smith-Homes, and K. J. Rowe, *School and Teacher Effectiveness in Victoria: Key Findings from Phase I of the Victoria Quality Schools Project* (Melbourne: Center for Applied Educational Research, 1993). University of Melbourne researchers studied 14,000 students; among their key findings were that (1) "attentiveness has a massive effect on student achievement" (p. 28) and (2) girls are more attentive than boys (pp. 18, 28).

24. Sadker and Sadker, *Failing at Fairness*, p. 279.

25. A Ford Foundation grant made it possible for the *AAUW Report: How Schools Shortchange Girls* to be translated into French, Spanish, and Chinese and made available to UN conference delegates. According to *PR Newswire* (September 1, 1995). "Over a hundred AAUW members are meeting in Beijing and Hauirou at the UN Conference, [to] bring its concerns about access to education for women and girls to the table. . . . *How Schools Shortchange Girls*, a groundbreaking report of gender bias in America's schools, will be addressed during the education reform discussion." See also Anne Bryant, "Education for Girls Should Be Topic A in Beijing," *Houston Chronicle*, August 31, 1995; and Marie Wilson, "Do We Need a Global Agenda for Women?: Opening Up a World of Possibilities for Our Daughters to Conquer," *Chicago Tribune*, August 30, 1995, p. 17.

26. Cindy Krantz, "February Is Self-Esteem Month," *Cincinnati Enquirer*, January 30, 1997, p. B1.

27. See, for example, U.S. Department of Education, *The Condition of Education* (Washington, D.C.: U.S. Department of Education, 1998), pp. 68, 70, 90, 206, 238, 262; Larry Hedges and Amy Nowel, "Sex Differences in Mental Test Scores, Variability, and Numbers of High-Scoring Individuals," *Science*, July 7, 1995, pp. 41–45; Judith Kleinfeld, *The Myth That Schools Shortchange Girls: Social Science in the Service of Deception* (Washington, D.C.: Women's Freedom Network, 1999); Horatio Alger Association, *The State of Our Nation's Youth: 1998–1999* (Alexandria, Va.: Horatio Alger Association, 1999); Metropolitan Life Insurance Company, *The American Teacher, 1997: Examining Gender Issues in Public Schools* (New York: Metropolitan Life Insurance Company, 1997); and Search Institute, *Starting Out Right: Developmental Assets* (Minneapolis: Search Institute, 1997).

28. See Carol Dwyer and Linda Johnson, "Grades, Accomplishments, and Correlates," in *Gender and Fair Assessment*, ed. Warren Willingham and Nancy Cole (Mahwah, N.J.: Erlbaum, 1997), pp. 127–56.

29. Higher Education Research Institute, *The American Freshman: National Norms for Fall 1998* (Los Angeles: Higher Education Research Institute, University of California, Los Angeles, 1998), pp. 36, 54.

30. Higher Education Research Institute, *The American Freshman: Twenty-five-Year Trends* (Los Angeles: Higher Education Research Institute, University of California, Los Angeles, 1991), p. 51. See also Horatio Alger Association, *State of Our Nation's Youth: 1998–1999*, p. 22.

31. Higher Education Research Institute, *The American Freshman: National Norms for Fall 1998*, pp. 39, 57.

32. National Center for Education Statistics, *NAEP 1997 Arts Report Card* (Washington, D.C.: National Center for Education Statistics, 1998).

33. Of students studying abroad, 65 percent are female, 35 percent male; see chart "Study Abroad by U.S. Students, 1996–1997," *Chronicle of Higher Education*, December 11, 1998, p. A71.

34. Fifty-seven percent are female, 43 percent male; see "Peace Corps: General Facts" Web site: http://www.peacecorps.gov.

35. For suspension rates, see U.S. Department of Education, *The Condition of Education 1997* (Washington, D.C.: U.S. Department of Education, 1997), p. 158. For data on repeating grades, see U.S. Department of Education, *The Condition of Education 1995* (Washington, D.C.: U.S. Department of Education, 1995), p. 13. For information on dropouts, U.S. Department of Education, *Digest of Education Statistics 1995* (Washington, D.C.: U.S. Department of Education, 1995), p. 409.

36. For data on special education, see U.S. Department of Education, *The Condition of Education* (Washington, D.C.: U.S. Department of Education, 1994), p. 304. For information on ADHD, see American Psychiatric Association, *Diagnostic and Statistical Manual of Mental Disorders*, vol. 4 (Washington, D.C.: American Psychiatric Association, 1994), p. 82. According to *DSM-IV*, "The disorder is much more frequent in males than in females, with male-to-female ratio ranging from 4:1 to 9:1, depending on the setting."

37. For statistics on alcohol and drugs, see "National Survey Results on Drug Use," in National Institute on Drug Abuse, *Monitoring the Future Study, 1975–1995*, vol. 1, *Secondary School Students* (Rockville, Md.: National Institute on Drug Abuse, 1996), p. 20. See also U.S. Department of Education, *The Condition of Education* (Washington, D.C.: U.S. Department of Education, 1997), p. 300, Table 47–3, "Supplementary Tables." For crime statistics, see U.S. Department of Justice, *Female Offenders in the Juvenile Justice System: Statistics Summary* (Washington, D.C.: U.S. Department of Justice, 1996), p. 3.

38. National Center for Health Statistics, *National Vital Statistics Reports: Deaths: Final Data for 1997* (Hyattsville, Md.: U.S. Department of Health and Human Services, 1999), pp. 28–29.

39. Author's interview with Aaron Watson at Public Education Network Conference, Washington, D.C., November 9, 1997.

40. Letter to the author from Dr. Richard Greig, January 30, 1997.

41. Sarah Glazer, "Boys' Emotional Needs: Is Growing Up Tougher for Boys Than for Girls?," *Congressional Quarterly Researcher*, June 18, 1999, p. 527.

42. See, for example, Laurence Steinberg, *Beyond the Classroom: Why School Reform Has Failed and What Parents Need to Do* (New York: Simon & Schuster, 1996), p. 64.

43. Tamar Lewin, "U.S. Colleges Begin to Ask: 'Where Have the Men Gone?,' " *New York Times*, December 6, 1998, p. A1; see also Brendan I. Koerner, "Where the Boys Aren't," *U.S. News & World Report*, February 8, 1999, p. 46.

44. Lionel Tiger, Barbara Ehrenrich, and Colin Harrison (interviewer), "Who Needs Men?," *Harper's Magazine*, June 1999, pp. 34–46. See also Koerner, "Where the Boys Aren't," p. 46.

45. Marvin Kosters, *Wage Levels and Inequality: Measuring and Interpreting the Trends* (Washington, D.C.: American Enterprise Institute, 1998), p. 38.

46. David Sadker, "Where the Girls Are," *Education Week*, September 4, 1996, p. 49.

47. On the 1998 SAT, girls' average math score was 496, verbal score 502; boys' average math score was 531, verbal score 509 (test takers 674,415 female, 579,235 male) (http://www.collegeboard.org).

48. *College Bound Seniors: 1992 Profile of SAT and Achievement Test Takers* (Princeton, N.J.: Educational Testing Service, 1992), p. iv. See also "Introduction to the 1998 College-Bound Seniors, a Profile of SAT Program Test Takers" (http://www.collegeboard.org/sat/cbsenior/yr1998/nat/intrcb98); and Willingham and Nancy Cole, *Gender and Fair Assessment* (Mahwah, N.J.: Erlbaum, 1997).

49. Public Education Network, "Gender, Race, and Student Achievement" (occasional paper) (Washington, D.C.: Public Education Nework, 1997), p. 15.

50. Office of Educational Research and Improvement, *The Condition of Education 1998* (Washington, D.C.: U.S. Department of Education, 1998), pp. 68–74.

51. In 1973, seventeen-year-old girls were 16 points behind boys in science and 8 points behind in math; by 1996, the gap had narrowed to 8 points for science and 5 points for math. In 1971, boys were 12 points behind girls in reading. By 1996, the gap had increased to 15 points. In 1984 (the first year for which there are records) eleventh-grade boys were 18 points behind the girls in writing; by 1996, the writing gap favoring girls had not changed—18 points. Source: National Center for Education Statistics, *Report in Brief: NAEP 1996 Trends in Academic Progress* (Washington, D.C.: U.S. Department of Education, 1998), pp. 20–21.

52. Larry Hedges and Amy Nowell, "Sex Differences in Mental Test Scores, Variability, and Numbers of High-Scoring Individuals," *Science*, July 7, 1995, pp. 41–45.

53. Ibid., p. 45.

54. Valerie Lee, Xianglei Chen, and Becky Smerdon, *The Influence of School Climate on Gender Differences in the Achievement and Engagement of Young Adolescents* (Washington, D.C.: American Association of University Women Education Foundation, 1996), p. 1.

55. Ibid., p. 32.

56. Ibid., pp. 32, 44.

57. Ibid., p. 34.

58. Gabrielle Lange, "AAUW Responds to the Media: The Gender Bias Debate," *AAUW Outlook*, Spring 1997, p. 14.

59. Metropolitan Life Insurance Company, *The American Teacher 1997: Examining Gender Issues in Public Schools*.

60. Ibid., p. 3.

61. Georgette Ruckers, then a senior at Banneker, Public Education Network Conference, Washington, D.C., Fall 1997.

62. The Search Institute is an educational foundation devoted to advancing the well-being of children and adolescents. See Search Institute, *Starting Out Right: Developmental Assets* (Minneapolis, Minn.: Search Institute, 1997); also Search Institute, *A Fragile Foundation: The State of Developmental Assets Among American Youth* (Minneapolis: Search Institute, 1999).

63. Quoted in Peggy Orenstein, *SchoolGirls: Young Women, Self-Esteem, and the Confidence Gap* (New York: Doubleday, 1994), p. 275.

64. Charles Hymas and Julie Cohen, "The Trouble With Boys," *Sunday Times* (London), June 19, 1994, p. 14.

65. Barclay Mcbain, "The Gender Gap That Threatens to Become a Chasm," *Herald* (Glasglow), September 17, 1996, p. 16.

66. "Tomorrow's Second Sex," *The Economist*, September 28, 1996, p. 23.

67. See, for example, *1999 Catalogue WEEA Equity Resources Center* (Washington, D.C.: U.S. Department of Education). There is no comparable publication for boys.

68. To justify a federal program that focuses exclusively on girls, HHS reminds the public of the findings announced by the AAUW in 1991. "Studies show," says HHS, "that girls tend to lose self-confidence in early adolescence and, as a result, perform less well in school" (from Girl Power! Campaign Information Packet [Washington, D.C.: U.S. Department of Health and Human Services, 1997, "Fact Sheet," p. 2]). But if HHS had looked at Department of Education data, it would have learned that it is boys who perform less well in school. To further reinforce the claim that girls (not boys) are in dire straits and in need of "empowerment," the HHS "fact sheet" notes that ninth-grade girls are "twice as likely to have attempted suicide." Here again HHS adheres to the common but misleading practice of girl advocates of leaving unmentioned the fact that boys actually kill themselves five or six times more frequently than girls do.

69. Lisa Frazier, "Federal Ruling Calls Black Male Initiative Discriminatory," *Washington Post*, January 26, 1996, p. B1.

70. Ibid.

71. Special programs for males have been successfully challenged by women's groups or by the Office of Civil Rights in such places as Detroit, Milwaukee, and Dade County, Florida. For detailed history of the controversy, see Rosemary Salomone, "Single-Sex Schooling: Law, Policy and Research," in *Brookings Papers on Education Policy*, ed. Diane Ravitch (Washington, D.C.: Brookings Institution, 1999), pp. 231–97.

72. "Fairness and Single-Sex Schools," *New York Times*, September 27, 1997, p. 14.

73. Jacques Steinberg, "Chancellor Stands Fast on Girls' School," *New York Times*, September 25, 1997, p. A32.

74. "Why the Large and Growing Gender Gap in African-American Higher Eduation?," *Journal of Blacks in Higher Education*, April 30, 1998, p. 34.

75. Lewin, "U.S. Colleges Begin to Ask: Where Have the Men Gone?"

76. Tamar Lewin, "How Boys Lost Out to Girl Power," *New York Times*, December 12, 1998, sec. 4, p. 3.

77. Lawrence Knutsen, "Survey Shows Girls Setting the Pace in Schools," Associated Press, August 12, 1998 (carried in *The Seattle Times*).

78. Kim Asch, "Girls Overtake Boys in School Performance," *Washington Times*, January 13, 1999, p. A1.

79. Horatio Alger Association, *State of Our Nation's Youth 1998–1999*. The survey conducted by NFO Research, Inc., was based on two small but carefully selected samples of students (a cross section of 2,250 fourteen- to eighteen-year-olds as well as a computer-generated sample of 1,041 students; see p. 4). The researchers are careful to note that this study is not definitive and provides only a "snapshot in time."

80. Ibid., p. 31.

81. Judith Kleinfeld, *The Myth That Schools Shortchange Girls: Social Science in the Service of Deception* (Washington, D.C.: Women's Freedom Network, 1998). A version of this report, "Student Performance: Males Versus Females," appeared in *The Public Interest*, Winter 1999, pp. 3–20.

82. *New York Times*, "Letters," December 21, 1998, p. 28.

83. Lewin, "How Boys Lost Out to Girl Power," sec. 4, p. 3.

84. See AAUW/Greenberg-Lake Full Data Report: *Expectations and Aspirations: Gender Roles and Self-Esteem* (Washington, D.C.: Greenberg-Lake 1990, p. 18, Figure 7.

85. Barbara Sprung, "Addressing Gender Equity in Early Childhood Education," keynote address, 19th Annual Conference of the National Coalition for Sex Equity in Education, Kansas City, Mo., July 12–15, 1998.

86. "Men, Women and the Sex Difference," ABC News Special, February 1, 1995.

two: Reeducating the Nation's Boys

1. A 1998 Roper Starch Worldwide Poll showed that 53 million Americans said "their company of their spouse's company participated in the Day." Approximately one-third of American companies took part in the event; see http://www.ms.foundation.org/press/roper.

2. Memo from Marie Wilson, Ms. Foundation for Women, to groups and individuals working on Son's Day, March 29, 1996.

3. See, for example, Katherine Hanson and Anne McAuliffe, "Gender and Violence: Implications for Peaceful Schools" (http://www.edc.org/womensequity/article/gbv.peace).

4. Elizabeth Gleick, "The Boys on the Bus," *People*, October 30, 1992, p. 125. Quoted in Ruth Shalit, "Romper Room: Sexual Harassment—by Tots," *The New Republic*, March 29, 1993, p. 13.

5. Nan Stein, "Secrets in Public: Sexual Harassment in Public (and Private) Schools," Working Paper No. 256 (Wellesley, Mass.: Wellesley College, Center for Research on Women), rev. 1993, p. 4.

6. "WEEA History," http://www.edc.org/WomensEquity.

7. Katherine Hanson, "WEAA Equity Center Update," memo, February 27, 1998.

8. Katherine Hanson, opening statement in *1999 Catalogue: WEEA Equity Center* (Washington, D.C.: U.S. Department of Education, 1999).

9. Hanson and McAuliffe, "Gender and Violence," p. 2.

10. Ibid., p. 1.

11. Katherine Hanson, "Gendered Violence: Examining Education's Role," Working Paper Series (Newton, Mass.: Center for Equity and Cultural Diversity, 1995), p. 1.

12. Ibid.

13. Hanson and McAuliffe, "Gender and Violence," p. 1.

14. Ibid., p. 2.

15. Ibid., p. 4.

16. Ibid., p. 3.

17. For discussion of methodological problems with Nan Stein's research on school harassment, see my *Who Stole Feminism?: How Women Have Betrayed Women* (New York: Simon & Schuster, 1994; Touchstone, 1995), pp. 181–87.

18. See U.S. Bureau of Justice Statistics, *Violence-Related Injuries Treated in Hospital Emergency Departments* (Washington, D.C.: U.S. Bureau of Justice Statistics, 1999). See also Centers for Disease Control and Prevention, *Injury Visits to Hospital Emergency Departments, United States, 1992–1995* (Hyattsville, Md.: U.S. Department of Health and Human Services, 1998). Of course, not every battered woman goes to an emergency room for treatment, and among those women who go to emergency rooms because of battery, some attribute their injuries to other causes. All the same, there is no evidence to support Hanson's grossly inflated figure. For a sober and reliable assessment of the incidence and severity of domestic violence, see Cathy Young, *Ceasefire: Why Women and Men Must Join Forces to Achieve True Equality* (New York: Free Press, 1999). Noting that the Bureau of Justice study and the CDC study may have underreported the incidence of domestic violence, Young says, "Even if we assume that four out of five such cases are missed, domestic violence would still be ranked far behind falls (27% of injuries) and automobile accidents (13%)" (p. 105).

19. Federal Bureau of Investigation, *Crime in the United States, 1991* (Washington, D.C.: Federal Bureau of Investigation, 1992), pp. 23–24. According to the FBI, "An estimated 106,593 forcible rapes were reported to the law enforcement agencies across the nation during 1991. The 1991 total was 4 percent higher than the 1990 level" (p. 24).

20. Hanson and McAuliffe, "Gender and Violence," p. 3.

21. Ibid.

22. U.S. Department of Education, *1999 Catalog: WEEA Equity Center* (Washington, D.C.: U.S. Department of Education, 1999), inside cover. The WEEA Center offers an online course for Title IX Coordinators.

23. *Research Report: The Wellesley Centers for Women* 1, no. 1 (Fall 1998), p. 3.

24. Merle Froschl et al., grant proposal to Department of Education for *Quit It!* Available through Educational Equity Concepts, New York, N.Y. 1997.

25. Education Equity Concepts and Wellesley College Center for Research on Women, *Quit It!: A Teacher's Guide on Teasing and Bullying for Use with Students in Grades K-3* (New York and Wellesley, Mass.: Educational Equity Concepts and Wellesley College Center for Research on Women, 1998), p. 2.

26. Ibid., p. v.

27. Ibid., p. 87.

28. Ibid., p. 48.

29. Department of Children, Families and Learning, *Girls and Boys Getting Along: Teaching Sexual Harassment Prevention in the Elementary Classroom* (St. Paul, Minn.: Department of Children, Families and Learning, 1997).

30. Ibid., p. 55.

31. "Federal Government Takes Broad View of Peer Sexual Harassment," *School Board News,* September 17, 1996.

32. *Teacher TV,* "Sexual Harassment and Schools," Episode 28 (Washington, D.C.: National Education Association, 1993).

33. Anne Gearan, "Sex Changes Dropped Against 9-Year-Old in Lunch-Line Bump," Associated Press, June 25, 1997.

34. Sharon Lamb, "Sex—When It's Child's Play," *Boston Globe,* April 13, 1997.

35. Author interviews with parents, January and February 1998.

36. Nan Stein and Dominic Cappello, *Gender Violence/Gender Justice: An Interdisciplinary Teaching Guide for Teachers of English, Literature, Social Studies, Psychology, Health, Peer Counseling, and Family and Consumer Sciences* (Wellesley, Mass.: Wellesley College Center for Research on Women, 1999).

37. Ibid., p. vi.

38. Ibid., p. 71.

39. Ibid., p. 69.

40. Ibid., p. 124.

41. Jack O'Sullivan, "A Bad Way to Educate Boys," *Independent* (London), April 3, 1997, p. E8.

42. Nan Stein, "Getting in the Schoolhouse Door: Sexual Assault and Domestic Violence: Organizing in K-12 Schools," keynote address, Sexual Assault and Harassment on Campus Conference, Sponsored by Safe Schools Coalition, Orlando, Florida, October 17, 1997.

43. Metropolitan Life Insurance Company, *The American Teacher 1997: Examining Gender Issues in Public Schools* (New York: Metropolitan Life Insurance Company and Louis Harris & Associates, 1997. Louis Harris & Associates asked students to respond to the statement "I feel that teachers do not listen to what I have to say." Thirty-one percent of boys but only 19 percent of girls said that the statement was "mostly true." See also *AAUW/Greenberg-Lake Full Data Report* (Washington, D.C.: Greenberg-Lake, 1990), p. 18. Reproduced above in Chapter 1, p. 42 (Table 4).

44. The quoted passage is from Minnesota Department of Children, *It's Not Fun/It's Illegal: The Identification and Prevention of Sexual Harassment to Teenagers* (Minneapolis: Minnesota Department of Children, 1995), p. 18. The entire quote is: "In our society, men are usually in control: in control of our country, our businesses, our schools, and have been thought to be in control of the family. . . . You may have noticed that our society treats men and women unequally. Women earn less money, have had fewer career opportunities, have been considered the 'weaker' sex. All of that is begin-

ning to change, but because men have been more powerful in society, it stands to reason that they are usually the harasser."

45. Professor Schlechter's NYU, like most liberal arts colleges, has a real gender gap: its undergraduate enrollment is 60 percent female, 40 percent male. As experts in gender equity, Schlechter and the other conferees are well aware that this gap is growing from year to year. However, taking note of it would reflect on the reasonableness of the standing complaint that American schools are shortchanging girls. That might take the steam out of the NCSEE conference—so it goes unnoted.

46. Research Report: *The Wellesley Centers for Research on Women* 2, no. 1 (Fall 1997), p. 5.

47. In talking about sex differences, it is important to bear in mind that the characterizations do not apply to all girls, not even all "normal" boys or girls. Although there are any number of gentle and shy boys who shrink from violence, it is said that boys are more aggressive than girls because on the whole they are. And although there are many girls who are less nurturing than the average boy, it is said that girls are more nurturing than boys because, on average, they are.

48. Eleanor Emmons Maccoby and Carol Nagy Jacklin, *The Psychology of Sex Differences*, vol. 1 (Palo Alto, Calif.: Stanford University Press, 1974), p. 352.

49. Camille Paglia, *Sex, Art, and American Culture* (New York: Vintage, 1992), p. 53.

50. Camille Paglia, *Sexual Personae: Art and Decadence from Nefertiti to Emily Dickinson* (New Haven, Conn.: Yale University Press, 1990), p. 37.

51. Paglia, *Sex, Art, and American Culture*, p. 24.

52. Paglia, *Sexual Personae*, p. 37.

53. American Association of University Women, *Hostile Hallways: The AAUW Survey on Sexual Harassment in America's Schools* (Washington, D.C.: American Association of University Women, 1993), p. 7.

54. Valerie Lee et al., "The Culture of Sexual Harassment in Secondary Schools," *American Educational Research Journal* 33, no. 2 (Summer 1996), p. 399.

55. Ibid., p. 383.

56. Nina Easton, "The Law of the School Yard," *Los Angeles Times Magazine*, October 2, 1994, p. 16.

57. Hara Estroff Marano, "Big Bad Bully," *Psychology Today*, September 1995, p. 12.

58. Dan Olweus, *Bullying at School* (Oxford: Blackwell, 1993), p. 14. According to Olweus, "there is a trend for boys to be more exposed to bullying than girls" (p. 18). See also, U.S. Department of Education, *Indicators of School Crime and Safety, 1998* (Washington, D.C.: Department of Education, 1998), p. 10. According to this report, "Eight percent of all students in grades 6 through 12 reported they have been victims of bullying at school during the 1992–93 school year."

59. Lisa Sjostrom, *Bullyproof: A Teacher's Guide on Teasing and Bullying for Use with Fourth and Fifth Grade Students*, developed by Nan Stein (Wellesley, Mass., and Washington, D.C.: Wellesley College Center for Research on Women and National Education Association Professional Library, 1996). Sales figure given by Nancy Mullin-Rindler, a research associate at the Wellesley College Center for Research on Women.

60. Ibid., p. 43.

61. Educational Testing Service, *Order in the Classroom: Violence, Discipline, and Student Achievement* (Princeton, N.J.: Educational Testing Service, 1998), p. 21.

62. U.S. Department of Education, *Student's Reports of School Crime: 1989 and 1985* (Washington, D.C.: U.S. Department of Education, 1998), p. 3.

63. National Organization for Women, "Issue Report: Sexual Harassment" (http://www.now.org/issues/harass), April 22, 1998.

THREE: Guys and Dolls

1. *Fox News in Depth*, June 5, 1997.

2. Paul Davis, "Danes Discover Difference Between Boys and Girls: For Years Hasbro Has Known the Difference," *Providence Journal-Bulletin*, September 12, 1995, p. 1E.

3. WEEA Publishing Center, *Gender Equity for Educators, Parents, and Community* (Newton, Mass.: WEEA Publishing Center, 1995), p. 1.

4. Doreen Kimura, "Sex Differences in the Brain," *Scientific American Presents*, Special Issue: "Men: The Scientific Truth About Their Work, Play, Health, and Passions," Summer 1999, vol. 10, no. 2, p. 26.

5. Ibid.

6. CHOICE and Office of Education Research and Improvement, *Creating Sex-Fair Family Day Care: A Guide for Trainers* (Philadelphia, Penn., and Washington, D.C.: CHOICE and Office of Education Research and Improvement, 1991).

7. Ibid., p. 80.

8. Ibid.

9. Ibid., p. 114.

10. Ibid., p. 113.

11. Ibid., p. 87.

12. Ibid., p. 26.

13. Zehba Zhumkhawala, "Dolls, Trucks and Identity: Educators Help Young Children Grow Beyond Gender," *Children's Advocate*, November–December 1997.

14. Ibid.

15. Ibid.

16. Tamar Lewin, "Girls' Schools Gain, Saying Co-ed Isn't Co-equal," *New York Times*, April 11, 1999, Metropolitan sec., p. 1.

17. See Jonathan Mandell, "Rethinking Rumpelstiltskin," Disney online: http://www.Family.go.com. Posted circa May 1998.

18. Myra and David Sadker, *Failing at Fairness: How America's Schools Cheat Girls* (New York: Scribners, 1994), p. 224.

19. Charlotte Zolotow, *William's Doll* (New York: HarperCollins, 1972), p. 5.

20. Ibid., p. 28.

21. Myra and David Sadker, *Failing at Fairness*, p. 224.

22. Ibid., p. 223.

23. "The War on Boys," *National Desk*, PBS, April 9, 1999.

24. Peggy Orenstein, *SchoolGirls: Young Women, Self-Esteem, and the Confidence Gap* (New York: Doubleday, 1994).

25. Ibid., p. 276.

26. Judy Logan, *Teaching Stories* (New York: Kodansha, 1997). Endorsement by Mary Pipher on front cover.

27. Susan Faludi's comments appear on the back cover of *SchoolGirls*.

28. Orenstein, *SchoolGirls*, p. 247.

29. Ibid., p. 248.

30. Ibid., p. 251.

31. Ibid., p. 256.

32. Ibid.

33. Ibid., p. 263.

34. Ibid.

35. Ibid., p. 266.

36. Ibid., p. 267.

37. Ibid., p. 270.

38. Ibid., p. 267.

39. Ibid., p. 274.

40. Laura Pappano, "The Gender Factor," *Boston Globe Magazine*, November 9, 1997, p. 34.

41. "Men, Women and the Sex Difference," ABC News Special, February 1, 1995.

42. Catherine E. Matthews, Wendy Binkley, Amanda Crisp, and Kimberly Gregg, "Challenging Gender Bias in Fifth Grade," *Education Leadership*, December 1997–January 1998, pp. 54–57.

43. Marie Franklin, "The Toll of Gender Roles," *Boston Sunday Globe*, November 3, 1996, p. H9. See also Michael Norman, "From Carol Gilligan's Chair," *New York Times Magazine*, November 9, 1997, p. 50.

44. McLean's William Pollack is the best known of the group; other members include Harvard psychologist Don Kindlon, Tufts University psychologist Barry Brawer, Wellesley College sociologist Joseph Pleck, and State University of New York at Stony Brook sociologist Michael Kimmel.

45. William S. Pollack and Ronald F. Levant, "Coda: A New Psychology of Men: Where Have We Been? Where Are We Going?," in Ronald Levant and William Pollack, eds., *A New Psychology of Men* (New York: HarperCollins, 1995), p. 387.

46. Sandra Lee Bartky, *Femininity and Domination: Studies in the Phenomenology of Oppression* (New York: Routledge, 1990), p. 50.

47. See, for example, B. A. Shaywitz et al., "Sex Differences in the Functional Organization of the Brain for Language," *Nature* 373 (February 16, 1995), pp. 607–8; also Ruben Gur et al., "Sex Differences in Regional Cerebral Glucose Metabolism During a Resting State," *Science* 276 (January 27, 1995), pp. 528–31; and Sandra Witelsen et al., "Women Have Greater Numerical Density of Neurons in Posterior Temporal Cortex," *Neuroscience* 15 (1995), pp. 3418–28. See also Matt Ridley, *The Red Queen: Sex and the Evolution of Human Nature* (New York: Macmillan, 1994); and Michael Gazzaniga, ed., *The Cognitive Neurosciences* (Cambridge, Mass.: MIT Press, 1995).

48. See, for example, Doreen Kimura, "Sex Differences in the Brain"; and Larry Hedges and Amy Nowell, "Sex Differences in Mental Test Scores, Variability, and Numbers of High-Scoring Individuals," *Science* 269 (July 7, 1995), pp. 41–45.

49. See Kimura, "Sex Differences in the Brain," and Hedges and Nowell, "Sex Differences in Mental Test Scores." See also Diane Halpern, *Sex Differences in Cognitive Ability* (Hillsdale, N.J.: Erlbaum, 1992); and Deborah Blum, *Sex on the Brain: The Biological Differences Between Men and Women* (New York: Viking, 1997).

50. Daniel Goleman, *Emotional Intelligence: Why It Can Matter More Than IQ* (New York: Bantam, 1995), p. 131.

51. Ibid.

52. Sheri A. Berenbaum and Melissa Hines, "Early Androgens Are Related to Childhood Sex-Typed Toy Preferences," *Psychological Science* 3, no. 3 (May 1992), pp. 203–6.

53. Ibid., p. 206. See also Kimura, "Sex Differences in the Brain."

54. "Men, Women, and the Sex Difference," ABC News Special, February 1, 1995.

55. Ibid.

56. Ibid.

57. Ibid.

58. Shaywitz et al., "Sex Differences in the Functional Organization of the Brain for Language," pp. 607–8.

59. Steve Connor, "Men and Women: Minds Apart," *Sunday Times* (London), March 2, 1997.

60. Sharon Begley, "Gray Matters," *Newsweek*, March 27, 1995, p. 48.

61. Alice Eagly, "The Science and Politics of Comparing Men and Women," *American Psychologist* 50, no. 3 (March 1995), pp. 145–58.

62. Jim Ritter, "Gender Debate Flares Anew," *Chicago Sun-Times*, March 17, 1996, p. 36.

63. Immanuel Kant, "Of the Distinction of the Beautiful and Sublime in the Inter-relations of the Two Sexes," reprinted in Mary Briody Mahowald, ed., *Philosophy of Woman: An Anthology of Classic to Current Concepts* (Indianapolis: Hackett, 1983), p. 196.

64. Quoted in Stephen Jay Gould, *The Mismeasure of Man* (New York: Norton, 1981), pp. 136–37.

65. Ibid., p. 136.

66. "Points to Ponder," *Reader's Digest*, March 26, 1996, p. 32.

67. See David Buss, *The Evolution of Desire* (New York: Basic Books, 1994), p. 85; and Higher Education Research Council, *The American Freshman: National Norms of Fall 1998* (Los Angeles: Higher Education Research Council, 1998), pp. 48, 66.

68. Celeste Fremon, "Are Schools Failing Our Boys?" (http://www.msnbc.com/News/310934.asp), September 1999.

69. For a review of the literature, see A. D. Pellegrini and Peter K. Smith, "Physical Activity Play: The Nature and Function of a Neglected Aspect of Play," *Child Development* 69, no. 3 (June 1998), pp. 577–98.

70. Eleanor Emmons Maccoby and Carl Nagy Jacklin, *The Psychology of Sex Differences* (Stanford, Calif.: Stanford University Press, 1974), p. 352. See also Janet Lever, "Sex Differences in the Games Children Play," *Social Problems* 23 (1967), pp. 478–87; Deborah Tannen, *You Just Don't Understand: Women and Men in Conversation* (New York: Ballantine, 1990), pp. 43–47.

71. Tannen, *You Just Don't Understand*, p. 43. See also, Leslie Brody, *Gender, Emotion and the Family* (Cambridge, Mass: Harvard University Press, 1999), especially pp. 247–51.

72. Anthony Pellegrini and Jane Perlmutter, "Rough-and-Tumble Play on the Elementary School Playground," *Young Children*, January 1988, pp. 14–17.

73. Ibid., p. 15.

74. Megan Rosenfeld, "Little Boys Blue: Reexamining the Plight of Young Males," *Washington Post*, March 26, 1998, p. 1.

75. Ibid.

76. "The War on Boys," National Desk, PBS, April 9, 1999.

77. Dirk Johnson, "Many Schools Putting an End to Child's Play," *New York Times*, April 7, 1998, p. 1.

78. Ibid.

79. A. D. Pellegrini, Patti Davis Huberty, and Ithel Jones, "The Effects of Recess Timing on Children's Playground and Classroom Behaviors," *American Educational Research Journal* 32, no. 4 (Winter 1995), pp. 845–64. Pellegrini et al. found that "most basically children, but especially boys, exhibited signs of inattention as length of [recess] deprivation increased" (p. 860).

80. Vivian Gussin Paley, *Boys and Girls: Superheroes in the Doll Corner* (Chicago: University of Chicago Press, 1984), p. ix.

81. Ibid., p. 65.

82. Ibid., p. 67.

83. Ibid., p. 41.

84. Ibid., p. 90.

85. Ibid., p. 116.

FOUR: Carol Gilligan and the Incredible Shrinking Girl

1. Gary Taubes, "Fields of Fear," *The Atlantic*, November 1994, p. 107.

2. See, for example, Paul Brodeur, "Annals of Radiation," *The New Yorker*, June 12, 1989.

3. Keith Florig, "Containing the Cost of the EMF Problem," *Science,* July 24, 1992, pp. 468–69, 490, 492.

4. Gina Kolata, "Big Study Sees No Evidence Power Lines Cause Leukemia," *New York Times,* July 3, 1997, p. 1. See also Shankar Vedantam, Knight Ridder News Service, "When Science and Politics Don't Mix," January 19, 1997.

5. Edward Champion, *New England Journal of Medicine,* July 3, 1997, pp. 44–46.

6. William Broad, "Data Tying Cancer to Electric Power Found to Be False," *New York Times,* July 24, 1999, p. 1.

7. Ibid.

8. Some references to Gilligan's "landmark," "ground-breaking" research: Marie Franklin, "The Toll of Gender Roles," *Boston Globe,* November 3, 1996, p. 9; "Time 25," *Time,* June 17, 1996, p. 54; Michael Norman, "From Carol Gilligan's Chair," *New York Times Magazine,* November 9, 1997, p. 50; Carolyn Heilbrun, "How Girls Become Wimps," *New York Times Book Review,* October 4, 1992, p. 13; *Newsweek,* May 11, 1998, p. 56. See also 1997 Heinz Award Announcement (http://www.awards.heinz.org/gilligan).

9. The text is from the 1997 Heinz Award Announcement (http:www.awards.heinz.org/gilligan).

10. See, for example, Zella Luria, "A Methodological Critique," *Signs: Journal of Women in Culture and Society* 11, no. 21 (1986), pp. 316–21; Anne Colby and William Damon, "Listening to a Different Voice: A Review of Gilligan's *In a Different Voice.*" *Merrill-Palmer Quarterly* 29, no. 4 (1983), pp. 473–81; Martha T. Mednick, "On the Politics of Psychological Constructs: Stop the Bandwagon, I Want to Get Off," *American Psychologist* 44, no. 8 (August 1989), p. 1118; and George Sher, "Other Voices, Other Rooms?: Women's Psychology and Moral Theory," in Eva Feder Kittay and Diana T. Meyers, eds., *Women and Moral Theory* (Totowa, N.J.: Rowan and Littlefield, 1987).

11. Francine Prose, "Confident at 11, Confused at 16," *New York Times Magazine,* January 7, 1990, p. 23.

12. Ibid., p. 45.

13. Ibid., p. 23.

14. Ibid., p. 40.

15. Ms. Foundation for Women and Sondra Forsyth, *Girls Seen and Heard* (New York: Tarcher/Putnam, 1998), p. xiii.

16. Ibid., pp. xiv, xv.

17. Ibid., p. xvii.

18. Ms. Foundation, *Synopsis of Research on Girls* (New York: Ms. Foundation, 1995), p. 1.

19. Ibid., p. 5.

20. Carol Gilligan, *In a Different Voice: Psychological Theory and Women's Development* (Cambridge, Mass.: Harvard University Press, 1982).

21. Amy Gross, passage from *Vogue* cited in Gilligan, *In a Different Voice* (Cambridge, Mass.: Harvard University Press, 1993).

22. Lawrence J. Walker, "Sex Differences in the Development of Moral Reasoning: A Critical Review," *Child Development* 55 (1984), p. 681.

23. William Friedman, Amy Robinson, and Britt Friedman, "Sex Differences in Moral Judgments?: A Test of Gilligan's Theory," *Psychology of Women Quarterly* 11 (1987), pp. 37–46.

24. Gilligan, *In a Different Voice,* p. 3.

25. Luria, "A Methodological Critique."

26. Fay J. Crosby, *Juggling: The Unexpected Advantages of Balancing Career and Home for Women and Their Families* (New York: Free Press, 1991), p. 124.

27. Gilligan is celebrated by some (mostly feminist) moral philosophers for her "discovery" of two approaches to morality: the (female) ethic of care and the (male) ethic

of justice. The labeling of these as male and female is her doing, but the distinction is hoary. The tension between care and duty, between the personal and the impersonal, between abstract principle and contextual reality are familiar themes in moral philosophy that transcend gender. All standard theories (John Rawls's hypothetical contractarianism, for example) must assign proper places to care and duty, balancing, for example, considerations of justice with considerations of mercy. See George Sher, "Other Voices, Other Rooms?"; and Marcia Baron, "The Alleged Repugnance of Acting from Duty," *Journal of Philosophy* 81, no. 4 (April 1984), pp. 197–220.

28. Lyn Mikel Brown and Carol Gilligan, *Meeting at the Crossroads: Women's Psychology and Girls' Development* (New York: Ballantine, 1992), p. 15.

29. Carol Gilligan, Nona Lyons, and Trudy Hanmer, eds., *Making Connections: The Relational Worlds of Adolescent Girls at Emma Willard School* (Cambridge, Mass.: Harvard University Press, 1990).

30. Ibid., p. 5.

31. Prose, "Confident at 11, Confused at 16," p. 23.

32. Gilligan et al., *Making Connections*, p. 14.

33. Ibid.

34. Ibid., p. 24.

35. Ibid., pp. 147–61.

36. Ibid., p. 154.

37. Ibid., p. 158.

38. Ibid., p. 147.

39. Gilligan, *In a Different Voice* (1993 edition), p. xvi.

40. Ibid.

41. Ibid.

42. Carol Gilligan, "Remembering Larry," *Journal of Moral Education* 27, no. 2 (1998), p. 134.

43. Brown and Gilligan, *Meeting at the Crossroads*, p. 216.

44. Ibid.

45. Ibid., p. 218.

46. Christopher Lasch, "Gilligan's Island," *The New Republic*, December 7, 1992, pp. 34–39.

47. Brown and Gilligan, *Meeting at the Crossroads*, p. 193.

48. Ibid., p. 194.

49. Ibid., p. 190.

50. Ibid., p. 214.

51. Ibid., p. 196.

52. Ibid., p. 203.

53. Ibid.

54. Ibid., p. 10.

55. Susan Harter et al., "Level of Voice Among Female and Male High School Students: Relational Context, Support, and Gender Orientation," *Developmental Psychology* 34, no. 5 (1998), p. 892.

56. Susan Harter, Patricia Waters, and Nancy Whitesell, "Lack of Voice as a Manifestation of False Self-Behavior Among Adolescents: The School Setting as a Stage upon Which the Drama of Authenticity Is Enacted," *Educational Psychologist* 32, no. 3 (1997), pp. 153–73.

57. Ibid., p. 162.

58. Ibid., p. 153 (abstract).

59. U.S. Department of Education, National Center for Education Statistics, "National Education Longitudinal Study of 1988," Base Year and First Follow-up Survey, tables prepared in 1993, *Digest of Education Statistics 1993* (Washington, D.C.: U.S. Department of Education, 1993), p. 136, Table 140.

60. AAUW/Greenberg-Lake Full Data Report, *Expectations and Aspirations: Gender Roles and Self-Esteem* (Washington, D.C.: American Assoication of University Women, 1990), p. 18.

61. Ibid., p. 13.

62. Metropolitan Life Insurance Company, *The American Teacher 1997: Examining Gender Issues in Public Schools* (New York: Metropolitan Life Insurance Company, 1997), p. 131. A similar question was asked by the 1998–1999 State of Our Nation's Youth Survey, *State of Our Nation's Youth 1998–1999* (Alexandria, Va.: Horatio Alger Association, 1998): 71 percent of girls but only 64 percent of boys said they have an opportunity for open discussion in class.

63. Debra Viadero, "Their Own Voices," *Education Week*, May 13, 1998, p. 37.

64. Gilligan, "Remembering Larry," pp. 134–35.

65. Carol Gilligan, "The Centrality of Relationship in Human Development: A Puzzle, Some Evidence, and a Theory," in Gil Noam and Kurt Fischer, eds., *Development and Vulnerability in Close Relationships* (Mahwah, N.J.: Erlbaum, 1996), p. 251.

FIVE: Gilligan's Island

1. Carol Gilligan, "The Centrality of Relationship in Human Development: A Puzzle, Some Evidence, and a Theory," in *Development and Vulnerability in Close Relationships*, ed. Gil Noam and Kurt Fischer (Mahwah, N.J.: Erlbaum, 1996), p. 252.

2. Ibid., p. 238.

3. Ibid., p. 250.

4. Quoted in Marie Franklin, "The Toll of Gender Roles," *Boston Globe*, November 3, 1996, p. 9.

5. Carol Gilligan, *In a Different Voice: Psychological Theory and Women's Development* (Cambridge, Mass.: Harvard University Press, 1982), pp. 7–11.

6. Nancy Chodorow, *The Reproduction of Mothering: Psychoanalysis and the Sociology of Gender* (Berkeley: University of California Press, 1978), p. 9.

7. Ibid., p. 7.

8. Ibid., p. 180.

9. Ibid., p. 181.

10. Ibid., p. 214.

11. Gilligan, *In a Different Voice*, p. 8.

12. Ibid.

13. Chodorow, *The Reproduction of Mothering*, p. 219.

14. Michael Norman, "From Carol Gilligan's Chair," *New York Times Magazine*, November 9, 1997, p. 50.

15. Gilligan, "The Centrality of Relationship in Human Development," p. 251.

16. Ibid.

17. Norman, "From Carol Gilligan's Chair," p. 50.

18. Ibid.

19. Gilligan, "The Centrality of Relationship in Human Development," p. 258.

20. Ibid., p. 251.

21. Norman, "From Carol Gilligan's Chair," p. 50.

22. Gilligan, "The Centrality of Relationship in Human Development," p. 238; Franklin, "The Toll of Gender Roles," p. 9.

23. See Chapter 3 for a discussion of how biological differences between males and females may account for differences in reading abilities.

24. http://www.census.gov/population/socdemo.

25. Daniel Patrick Moynihan, *The Negro Family: The Case for National Action* (Washington, D.C.: U.S. Department of Labor, 1965). Quoted in National Fatherhood Initiative, *Father Facts* (Gaithersburg, Md.: National Fatherhood Initiative, 1998), p. 57.

26. David Blankenhorn, *Fatherless America: Confronting Our Most Urgent Social Problem* (New York: Basic Books, 1995), p. 31.

27. Elaine Ciulla Kamarck and William Galston, *Putting Children First: A Progressive Family Policy for the 1990s* (Washington, D.C.: Progressive Policy Institute, 1990), p. 14.

28. Cynthia Harper and Sara McLanahan, "Father Absence and Youth Incarceration," presented at annual meeting of the American Sociological Association, San Francisco, August 1998.

29. Blankenhorn, *Fatherless America*.

30. Debra Viadero, "Their Own Voice," *Education Week*, May 13, 1998, p. 38.

31. Information sheet from Harvard Graduate School of Education, "Women's Psychology, Boys' Development and the Culture of Manhood," September 1995.

32. Information sheet from the Program for Educational Change Agents, Tufts University, Medford, Massachusetts, 1998–99.

33. Viadero, "Their Own Voice," p. 37.

34. Norman, "From Carol Gilligan's Chair," p. 50.

35. Gilligan, "The Centrality of Relationship in Human Development," p. 251.

36. Stephen Ambrose, *Citizen Soldiers* (New York: Simon & Schuster, 1997), p. 473.

37. Ibid.

38. Ibid., pp. 471–72.

39. The most popular book calling for the rescue of boys from the constraints of a harmful masculinity is William Pollack, *Real Boys: Rescuing Our Sons from the Myths of Boyhood* (New York: Random House, 1998).

six: Save the Males

1. McLean Hospital press release (http://www.mcleanhospital.org/PublicAffairs/boys1998), June 4, 1998.

2. Ibid. (In the study, as in the McLean press release, the word "healthy," when applied to boys, is invariably encased in ironic scare quotes.)

3. William Pollack, *Real Boys: Rescuing Our Sons from the Myths of Boyhood* (New York: Random House, 1998).

4. http://www.williampollack.com/talks, July 12, 1999.

5. William Pollack, "Listening to Boys' Voices," May 22, 1998, p. 28. (Available through McLean Hospital Public Affairs Office, Belmont, Massachusetts.)

6. McLean Hospital press release, p. 2.

7. Pollack, "Listening to Boys' Voices," p. 24.

8. Ibid., p. 10.

9. Ibid.

10. Ibid., p. 9.

11. Ibid., p. 17.

12. Ibid., p. 18.

13. American Psychiatric Association, *Diagnostic and Statistical Manual of Mental Disorders*, 4th ed. (Washington, D.C.: American Psychiatric Association, 1994), pp. 111–12. For an excellent critique of Pollack's work on boys, see Gwen Broude, "Boys Will Be Boys," *Public Interest* 136 (Summer 1999), pp. 3–17. It was Broude's article that brought the *DSM-IV* data on separation anxiety to my attention.

14. McLean Hospital press release, p. 2.

15. Pollack, "Listening to Boys' Voices," p. 11.

16. Russell D. Clark and Elaine Hatfield, "Gender Differences in Receptivity to Sexual Offers," *Journal of Psychology and Human Sexuality* 2 (1989), pp. 39–55.

17. "Harvard and Yale Restrict Use of Their Names," Associated Press, October 13, 1998. See also http://www.nytimes.com/library/national/science.

18. Megan Rosenfeld, "Reexamining the Plight of Young Males," *Washington Post*, March 26, 1998, p. A1.

19. Barbara Kantrowitz and Claudia Kalb, "Boys Will Be Boys," *Newsweek*, May 11, 1998, p. 57. See also http://www.nytimes.com/library/national/science.

20. "The Difference Between Boys and Girls: Why Boys Hide Their Emotions," ABC, June 5, 1998.

21. Tom Duffy, "Behind the Silence," *People*, September 21, 1998, p. 175.

22. *Saturday Today*, March 28, 1998.

23. FBI Uniform Crime Report (http://www.fbi.gov/ucr/Cius_97/97crime). See also U.S. Department of Justice, *Juvenile Offenders and Victims: A National Report* (Washington, D.C.: U.S. Department of Justice, 1995).

24. Some passages in *Real Boys* show that Pollack has a genuine understanding of the needs of boys. There is, for example, an excellent discussion of the ways our schools neglect boys and favor girls. He notes that our "coeducational schools . . . have evolved into institutions that are better at satisfying the needs of girls than those of boys . . . not providing the kind of classroom activities that will help most boys to thrive." Unfortunately, such passages are rare. Most of his book is about a male culture that is harming boys, as it harms girls. The demoralization of girls is the paradigm. Even as he is pointing out that our schools are unfairly neglecting boys, Pollack treats girls as the default victims of our culture, adding only that "adolescent boys, *just like adolescent girls*, are suffering from a crisis in self-esteem" (emphasis in original) (p. 239).

25. Pollack, *Real Boys*, p. 6.

26. See, for example, Anne C. Petersen et al., "Depression in Adolescence," *American Psychologist* 48, no. 2 (February 1993), p. 155; and Daniel Offer and Kimberly A. Schonert-Reichl, "Debunking the Myths of Adolescence: Findings from Recent Research," *Journal of American Adolescent Psychiatry* 31, no. 6 (November 1992), pp. 1003–14. See also entry on "Separation Anxiety Disorder," in *Diagnostic and Statistical Manual of Mental Disorders*, 4th ed., p. 112.

27. Susan Faludi, *Stiffed: The Betrayal of the American Male* (New York: Morrow, 1999).

28. Ibid., p. 358.

29. Ibid., p. 9.

30. Ibid., p. 39.

31. David Myers and Ed Diener, "Who Is Happy?," *Psychological Science* 6, no. 1 (January 1995), p. 14. For data from the National Opinion Research Center, see http://www.icpsr.umich.edu/gss99.

32. Faludi, *Stiffed*, p. 27.

33. Ibid., p. 6. Regier is one of the researchers cited in Faludi's supporting footnote (p. 612, footnote 5).

34. *DSM-IV*, the official desk reference of the American Psychiatric Assoication, reports that the prevalence of clinical depression among men is 2 to 3 percent.

35. Jim Windolf, "A Nation of Nuts," *Wall Street Journal*, October 22, 1997.

36. Pat Sebranek and Dave Kemper, *Write Source 2000 Teacher's Guide* (Burlington, Wis.: The Write Source/D.C. Health, 1995), p. 70. In a 1999 interview, one of the writers, Dave Kemper, told me that in future editions most of the "feeling" questions and self-esteem exercises will be eliminated.

37. Jack Levin and Arnold Arluke, "An Exploratory Analysis of Sex Differences in Gossip," *Sex Roles* 12 (1985), pp. 281–85.

38. Diane McGuinness and John Symonds, "Sex Differences in Choice Behavior: The Object-Person Dimension," *Perception* 6, no. 6 (1977), pp. 691–94.

39. See, for example, Leslie Brody and Judith Hall, "Gender and Emotion," in *Handbook of Emotions*, ed. Michael Lewis and Jeannette Haviland (New York: Guilford, 1993), p. 452.

40. Jane Bybee, "Repress Yourself," *Psychology Today*, September-October 1997, p. 12. See also Jane Bybee, "Is Repression Adaptive?: Relationships to Socioemotional Adjustment, Academic Performance, and Self-Image," *American Journal of Orthopsychiatry* 6, no. 1 (January 1997), pp. 59–69.

41. Emily Nussbaum, "Good Grief: The Case for Repression," *Lingua Franca*, October 1997, p. 49.

42. George Bonanno, "When Avoiding Unpleasant Emotions Might Not Be Such a Bad Thing: Verbal-Autonomic Response Dissociation and Midlife Conjugal Bereavement," *Journal of Personality and Social Psychology* 69, no. 5 (1995), pp. 975–89.

43. Hanna Kaminer and Peretz Lavie, "Sleep and Dreams in Well-Adjusted and Less Adjusted Holocaust Survivors," in *Handbook of Bereavement: Theory, Research and Intervention,* ed. Margaret S. Stroebe, W. Stroebe, and R. Hanson (Cambridge: Cambridge University Press, 1993), p. 345.

44. Ibid.

45. Pollack, *Real Boys,* p. 50

46. Fay Weldon, "Where Women Are Women and So Are Men," *Harper's Magazine,* May 1998, p. 66.

47. At the very end of one of his last books, *Civilization and Its Discontents,* Freud sternly cautioned his followers to resist the temptation to talk of whole groups as suffering neurosis brought about by "the culture." Whatever its drawbacks as a diagnostic and therapeutic technique, Freudian psychology should not be faulted for the way Pipher, Gilligan, and Pollack seek to pathologize our children. Freud acknowledged that in important respects the development of civilization shows similarities to the development of individuals. And he noted the temptation to say "that under the influence of cultural urges, some civilizations, or some epochs of civilization—possibly the whole of mankind—have become 'neurotic.' " But he warned that "it is dangerous, not only with men but with concepts [such as neurosis], to tear them from the sphere in which they originate and have been evolved." Freud even predicted that "one day someone will venture to embark upon a pathology of cultural communities" using psychoanalytic concepts. Though he had invented psychoanalysis, he deplored the day it would be used in that way.

48. Nussbaum, "Good Grief," p. 49.

49. Quoted in Sharon Begley, "You're O.K., I'm Terrific: 'Self-Esteem' Backfires," *Newsweek,* July 13, 1998, p. 69. See also Roy F. Baumeister, Laura Smart, and Joseph Boden, "Relation of Threatened Egotism to Violence and Aggression: The Dark Side of High Self-Esteem," *Psychological Review* 103, no. 1 (1996), pp. 5–33; and Kirk Johnson, "Self-Image Is Suffering from Lack of Esteem," *New York Times,* May 5, 1998.

50. John P. Hewitt, *The Myth of Self-Esteem: Finding Happiness and Solving Problems in America* (New York: St. Martin's Press, 1998), p. 51.

51. Ibid., p. 85.

seven: Why Johnny Can't, Like, Read and Write

1. Story told by Dr. Carl Boyd, president and CEO of the Art of Positive Teaching, an educational foundation in Kansas City (keynote address, National Coalition for Sex Equity Experts, July 1998). For an interesting (albeit controversial) discussion of the effects of teachers' expectations on students, see Robert Rosenthal and Lenore Jackson, *Pygmalion in the Classroom: Teacher Expectations and Pupils' Intellectual Development* (New York: Irvington, 1992) (originally published 1968).

2. Steven Zemelman, Harvey Daniels, and Arthur Hyde, *Best Practice: New Standards for Teaching and Learning in America's Schools* (Portsmouth, N.H.: Heineman, 1998), p. 51.

3. Alfie Kohn, *What to Look for in a Classroom* (San Francisco: Jossey-Bass, 1998), p. 51.

4. E. D. Hirsch, Jr., *The Schools We Need: And Why We Don't Have Them* (New York: Doubleday, 1996), p. 9.

5. U.S. Department of Education, *Pursuing Excellence: A Study of U.S. Twelfth-Grade Mathematics and Science Achievement in International Context* (Washington, D.C.: U.S. Government Printing Office, 1998). See also Harold Stevenson, *A TIMSS Primer* (Washington, D.C.: Thomas B. Fordham Foundation, 1998) (for full data report, see http://www.csteep.bc.edu/timss).

6. Liz Lightfoot, "Boys Left Behind by Modern Teaching," *Daily Telegraph*, January 5, 1998. Estelle Morris, MP, expressed similar sentiments in a 1996 Labour Party consultation paper, "Boys Will Be Boys?: Closing the Gender Gap." Morris: "Boys' underachievement not only represents a massive waste of talent and ability. It is also personally disastrous and socially destructive. If we do not act quickly we will reap a harvest of young men who are unemployable and face decades of social division."

7. Lester Thurow, "Players and Spectators," *Washington Post Book World*, April 18, 1999, p. 5.

8. Larry Hedges and Amy Nowell, "Sex Differences in Mental Test Scores, Variability, and Numbers of High-Scoring Individuals," *Science* 269 (July 7, 1995), p. 45.

9. Robert Bray et al., *Can Boys Do Better?* (Bristol: Secondary Heads Association, 1997).

10. Ibid., p. 17.

11. Barclay Mcbain, "The Gender Gap That Threatens to Become a Chasm," *Herald* (Glasgow), September 17, 1996, p. 16.

12. "Top Marks to the Lads," *Daily Telegraph*, January 17, 1998.

13. Ibid.

14. Ibid.

15. Bray et al., *Can Boys Do Better?*, p. 1.

16. Annette MacDonald, Lesley Saunders, and Pauline Benefield, *Boys' Achievement, Progress, Motivation and Participation* (Slough, Berkshire, England: National Foundation for Educational Research, 1999), p. 18.

17. Ibid., p. 13.

18. Liz Lightfoot, "Boys Need a Ripping Yarn to Keep Up Interest," *Daily Telegraph*, April 24, 1999.

19. John O'Leary, "Boys Close Literary Gender Gap," *Times* (London), October 7, 1999.

20. David Hughes, "Boys Catching Up with Girls Thanks to Literary Hour," *Daily Mail*, October 6, 1999, p. 20.

21. Ibid.

22. John Clare, "Primary Schools Failing to Teach Reading Properly," *Daily Telegraph*, July 6, 1999, p. 12.

23. U.S. Department of Education, *The Condition of Education* (Washington, D.C.: U.S. Department of Education, 1995), p. 13.

24. National Center for Education Statistics, *NAEP [National Assessment of Educational Progress] 1998 Reading Report Card for the Nation and the States* (Washington, D.C.: U.S. Department of Education, 1999), p. 42.

25. U.S. Department of Education, *NAEP 1994 Reading Report Card for the Nation and the States* (Washington, D.C.: U.S. Department of Education, 1996), p. 138.

26. Higher Education Research Institute, *The American Freshman: National Norms for Fall 1998* (Los Angeles: Higher Education Research Institute, 1998), pp. 39, 57.

27. Friedrich Froebel, *The Student's Froebel*, ed. W. H. Herford (Boston: Heath, 1904), pp. 5–6. (The quotation is cited in Hirsch, *The Schools We Need.* See especially Hirsch's Chapter 4, "Critique of Thought World," for a thorough and astute analysis of the influence of romanticism on American education, pp. 69–126.)

28. Zemelman et al., *Best Practice*, p. 9.

29. Ibid., book summary on back cover. See Hirsch's Chapter 5, "Reality's Revenge," *The Schools We Need,* for his critique of *Best Practice* (pp. 127–76).

30. Ibid., p. 4.

31. Ibid., p. 5.

32. H. O. Rugg and Ann Shumaker, *The Child-Centered School* (Yonkers-on-Hudson, N.Y.: World Book, 1928).

33. Diane Ravitch, *The Troubled Crusade: American Education 1945–1980* (New York: Basic Books, 1983), p. 50.

34. Lynn Olson, "Lessons of a Century," *Education Week,* April 21, 1998.

35. Mary Field Belenky et al., *Women's Ways of Knowing* (New York: Basic Books, 1986). Quotations are from a summary of the book in the *American Association of University Women Report: How Schools Shortchange Girls* (Washington, D.C.: American Association of University Women Educational Foundation, 1992), p. 72.

36. Zemelman et al., *Best Practice,* p. 6.

37. Lightfoot, "Boys Left Behind by Modern Teaching."

38. Bonnie Macmillan, *Why Schoolchildren Can't Read* (London: Institute of Economic Affairs, 1997), p. 124.

39. Ibid., p. 125.

40. Janet Daley, "Progressive Education in Britain," *Ex Femina* (Washington, D.C.: Independent Women's Forum, October 1998), p. 13.

41. June Kronholz, "At Many U.S. Schools, the Valedictorian Is Now a Tricky Issue," *Wall Street Journal,* May 17, 1999, p. 1.

42. Ann O'Hanlon, "Ruckus Over the Honor Roll," *Washington Post,* April 8, 1997, p. D1.

43. Ibid.

44. Hirsch, *The Schools We Need,* p. 245.

45. Charles Hymas, "Boys Get Their Own Classes to Catch Up," *Times* (London), July 19, 1994, p. 1.

46. Ibid.

47. John Danforth, "Single-Sex Education vs. Woman at VMI," *Washington Times,* January 17, 1996, p. A15.

48. New York City N.O.W., http://www.now.org.

49. Deborah Brake, "Single-Sex Education After VMI" posted on Internet at edequity@tristam.edc.org, April 20, 1998.

50. Judith Shapiro, "What Women Can Teach Men," *Baltimore Sun,* November 28, 1994, p. 11A.

51. Megan Rosenfeld, "All-Male Classes Raise Grades and Hackles," *Washington Post,* March 26, 1998, p. A16.

52. Author's interview with Walter Sallee.

53. Damon Bradley, "On Not Letting Georgette Do It: The Case for Single-Sex Boys' Education," *The Vincent/Curtis Educational Register* (Boston: Vincent/Curtis, 1996), p. 5. Diane Hulse, director of the Collegiate Middle School, an all-boys academy in New York City, did a small study comparing the attitudes of 186 boys at Collegiate to 239 children at a comparable coed school. She found that the Collegiate boys were less vulnerable to pressure, felt they had greater control over their academic performance, and had more egalitarian attitudes toward women. See Diane Hulse, *Brad and Cory: A Study of Middle School Boys* (Hunting Valley, Ohio: University School Press, 1997).

54. *United States v. Virginia,* 116.S Ct 2264, June 26, 1996.

55. *New York Times,* October 9, 1997, p. A22.

56. Fact sheet: "Single Gender Academics Pilot Program" (http://www.cde.ca.gov), May 7, 1999.

57. Richard Lee Colvin, "Can Same-Sex Classes Aid Desperate Communities?," *Los Angeles Times,* January 10, 1996, p. 1.

58. See, for example, Rosemary Salomone, "Single-Sex Schooling: Law, Policy, and Research," in *Brookings Papers on Education Policy,* ed. Diane Ravitch (Washington, D.C.: Brookings Institution, 1999), p. 264; and "Schools for Girls," *Wall Street Journal,* March 13, 1998, p. A16.

59. Nick Anderson, "One-Sex Schoools Don't Escape Bias, Study Says," *Los Angeles Times,* March 12, 1998, metro A1.

60. John O'Leary, "A-Level Analysis Finds Boys Do Better in Single-Sex Schools," *Times* (London), July 14, 1997.

61. See, for example, American Association of University Women, *Separated by Sex: A Critical Look at Single-Sex Education for Girls* (Washington, D.C.: American Association of University Women, 1998), p. 70.

eight: The Moral Life of Boys

1. Josephson Institute of Ethics, *1998 Report Card on the Ethics of American Youth* (Marina Del Ray, Calif.: Josephson Institute of Ethics, 1999).

2. American Psychiatric Association, *Diagnostic and Statistical Manual of Mental Disorders,* 4th ed. (Washington, D.C.: American Psychiatric Association, 1994), p. 85.

3. Ibid., p. 88.

4. Office of Juvenile Justice and Delinquency Prevention, *Female Offenders in the Juvenile Justice System: Statistics Summary* (Pittsburgh, Pa.: Office of Juvenile Justice and Delinquency Prevention, 1996), p. 3.

5. Alfons Crijnen, Thomas Achenbach, and Frank Verhulst, "Comparisons of Problems Reported by Parents of Children in 12 Cultures: Total Problems, Externalizing, and Internalizing," *Journal of the American Academy of Child and Adolescent Psychiatry* 36, no. 9 (September 1997), pp. 1269–77.

6. Anna Mundow, "The Child Predators," *Irish Times,* January 27, 1997, p. 8.

7. Janet Daley, "Young Men *Always* Behave Badly," *Daily Telegraph,* July 20, 1998.

8. Quoted in Bernard Lefkowitz, *Our Guys: The Glen Ridge Rape and the Secret Life of the Perfect Suburb* (Berkeley and Los Angeles: University of California Press, 1997), back cover.

9. Judy Mann, *The Difference: Growing Up Female in America* (New York: Warner, 1994), p. 246.

10. Susan Faludi, *Stiffed: The Betrayal of the American Male* (New York: Morrow, 1999), p. 47.

11. Mann, *The Difference,* p. 243.

12. Lefkowitz, *Our Guys,* pp. 1–2.

13. Ibid., pp. 4–5.

14. Ibid., p. 7.

15. Ibid., p. 424.

16. Ibid., p. 80.

17. Ibid., p. 73.

18. Ibid., p. 82.

19. Jane Gross, "Where 'Boys Will Be Boys,' and Adults Are Befuddled," *New York Times,* March 29, 1993, p. A1.

20. Joan Didion, "Trouble in Lakewood," *The New Yorker,* July 26, 1993, p. 50. See also William Damon, *Greater Expectations: Overcoming the Culture of Indulgence in America's Homes and Schools* (New York: Free Press, 1995), pp. 42–45.

21. Gross, "Where 'Boys Will Be Boys,' and Adults Are Befuddled."

22. "Ethical Choices: Individual Voices," Thirteen/WNET (New York, 1997).

23. Abigail Thernstrom, "Where Did All the Order Go?: School Discipline and the Law," in *Brookings Papers on Education Policy 1999,* ed. Diane Ravitch (Washington, D.C.: Brookings Institution), pp. 299–325.

24. Aristotle, *Ethics*, tr. J.A.K. Thomson (London: Penguin, 1976), p. 109.

25. Ibid., pp. 91, 92.

26. Jean-Jacques Rousseau, "Émile," in *The Philosophical Foundations of Education*, ed. Steven Cahn (New York: Harper & Row, 1970), p. 163; selection taken from *The Émile of Jean Jacques Rousseau: Selections*, ed. William Boyd (New York: Teachers College, Columbia University, 1962), pp. 11–128.

27. William Boyd, ed., *The Émile of Jean Jacques Rousseau* (New York: Teachers College Press, 1970), p. 41.

28. Rousseau, "Émile," ed. Cahn, p. 158.

29. Ibid., p. 162.

30. Ibid., p. 174.

31. He is said to have fathered five illegitimate children by an uneducated servant, Thérèse Le Vasseur. All the children were sent to foundling homes, which in those days was the equivalent of a death sentence. See Ronald Grimsley, "Jean-Jacques Rousseau," in *Encyclopedia of Philosophy*, vol. 7 (New York: Macmillan, 1967), p. 218.

32. Rousseau, "Émile," p. 160.

33. Ibid., p. 163.

34. Saint Augustine, *The Confessions of St. Augustine*, tr. John K. Ryan (New York: Doubleday, 1960).

35. Nancy F. and Theodore R. Sizer, eds., *Moral Education: Five Lectures* (Cambridge, Mass.: Harvard University Press, 1970).

36. Ibid., pp. 3–7.

37. Ibid., p. 5.

38. Ibid., pp. 8–9.

39. Sidney Simon and Howard Kirschenbaum, eds., *Readings in Values Clarification* (Minneapolis: Winston Press, 1973), p. 18.

40. See, for example, Lawrence Kohlberg, "The Cognitive-Developmental Approach," *Phi Delta Kappan*, June 1975, pp. 670–75.

41. Lawrence Kohlberg, "Moral Education Reappraised," *The Humanist*, November–December 1978, pp. 14–15. Kohlberg, renouncing his earlier position, wrote, "Some years of active involvement with the practice of moral education . . . has led me to realize that my notion . . . was mistaken. . . . The educator must be a socializer, teaching value content and behavior and not [merely] a process-facilitator of development. . . . I no longer hold these negative views of indoctrinative moral education and I believe the concepts guiding moral education must be partly 'indoctrinative.' This is true, by necessity, in a world in which children engage in stealing, cheating and aggression."

42. Pat Sebranek, Dave Kemper, and Randall VanderMey, *Write Source 2000 Sourcebook: Student Workshops, Activities, and Strategies* (Wilmington, Mass.: Houghton Mifflin, 1995), p. 217.

43. John Stuart Mill, *On Liberty* (Chicago: Regnery, 1955), pp. 14, 84.

44. *Tinker v. Des Moines School District*, 393 U.S. 503, February 24, 1969.

45. Ibid., Justice Black, dissenting.

46. Thernstrom, "Where Did All the Order Go?," p. 304.

47. Ibid., p. 306.

48. James Q. Wilson, "Incivility and Crime: The Role of Moral Habituation," in *The Content of America's Character*, ed. Don Eberly (New York: Madison, 1995), p. 67.

49. Gertrude Himmelfarb, *The De-Moralization of Society: From Victorian Virtues to Modern Values* (New York: Random House, 1994), pp. 50–51.

50. Quoted in ibid., p. 52.

51. See, for example, Laurence Steinberg, *Beyond the Classroom: Why School Reform Has Failed and What Parents Need to Do* (New York: Simon & Schuster, 1996).

52. Jessica Portner, "Everybody Wants to Know Why," *Education Week*, April 28,

1999, p. 16; see also Kathleen Kennedy Manzo, "Shootings Spur Move to Police Students' Work," *Education Week*, May 26, 1999, p. 14.

53. American Psychiatric Association, *Diagnostic and Statistical Manual of Mental Disorders*, 4th ed., p. 88.

54. "Character Education Manifesto," available from the Josephson Institute of Ethics, Marina Del Ray, California, or from Kevin Ryan, Director, Boston University Center for the Advancement of Ethics and Character.

55. Donald Baker, "Bringing Character into the Classroom," *Washington Post*, February 4, 1999, metro, p. 1.

56. Ibid.

57. Colleen O'Connor, "Making Character Count," *Dallas Morning News*, March 10, 1995, p. 1C.

58. Wray Herbert and Missy Daniel, "The Moral Child," *U.S. News & World Report*, June 3, 1996, p. 52.

59. Portner, "Everybody Wants to Know Why," p. 17.

60. Benjamin DeMott, "Morality Plays," *Harper's Magazine*, December 1994, p. 67.

61. Alfie Kohn, "How Not to Teach Values: A Critical Look at Character Education," *Phi Delta Kappan*, February 1997, p. 431.

62. Ibid., p. 433.

63. Thomas J. Lasley II, "The Missing Ingredient in Character Education," *Phi Delta Kappan*, April 1997, p. 654.

64. Richard Satnick, *The Thomas Jefferson Center Values Education Project* (Los Angeles: California Survey Research, 1991).

65. Tim Stafford, "Helping Johnny Be Good," *Christianity Today*, September 11, 1995, p. 34.

66. For an excellent practical guide to the moral development of boys, see Michael Gurian, *A Fine Young Man* (New York: Tarcher/Putnam, 1998).

NINE: War and Peace

1. Peggy Orenstein, *SchoolGirls: Young Women, Self-Esteem, and the Confidence Gap* (New York: Doubleday, 1994), p. 248.

2. Tom Wolfe, "The Great Relearning," *Orange County Register*, January 24, 1988, p. JO1.

3. Ibid.

4. Patricia Stevens, ed., *Between Mothers and Sons: Women Writers Talk About Having Sons and Raising Men* (New York: Scribners, 1999).

5. Deborah Galyan, "Watching *Star Trek* with Dylan," in *Between Mothers and Sons*, ed. Stevens, p. 50.

6. Ibid., pp. 50–51.

7. Ibid., pp. 51–52.

8. Janet Burroway, "Soldier Son," in *Between Mothers and Sons*, ed. Stevens, p. 37.

9. Ibid., p. 40.

10. Mary Gordon, "Mother and Son," in *Between Mothers and Sons*, ed. Stevens, p. 163.

11. Ibid., p. 164.

INDEX

ABOUT THE AUTHOR

CHRISTINA HOFF SOMMERS is the W. H. Brady Fellow at the American Enterprise Institute in Washington, D.C. She has a Ph.D. in philosophy from Brandeis University and was formerly professor of philosophy at Clark University in Worcester, Massachusetts. Sommers has written for numerous publications, including *The Wall Street Journal, The New York Times, The Washington Post, The New Republic,* and many others. She is the author of *Who Stole Feminism? How Women Have Betrayed Women.* She is married with two sons and lives in Chevy Chase, Maryland.